Guiseley Terriers:
A Small Part in The Great War

Guiseley Terriers:
A Small Part in The Great War

A HISTORY OF THE
1/6TH BATTALION, DUKE OF WELLINGTON'S
(WEST RIDING) REGIMENT

Stephen Barber

Pen & Sword
MILITARY

First published in Great Britain in 2018 by
PEN & SWORD MILITARY
an imprint of
Pen and Sword Books Ltd
47 Church Street
Barnsley
South Yorkshire S70 2AS

ISBN 978 1 52670 352 1

Printed and bound in England by
TJ International Ltd, Padstow, Cornwall

Typeset in Times New Roman
by CHIC GRAPHICS

Pen & Sword Books Ltd incorporates the imprints of
Pen & Sword Archaeology, Atlas, Aviation, Battleground, Discovery, Family
History, History, Maritime, Military, Naval, Politics, Railways, Select, Social
History, Transport, True Crime, Claymore Press, Frontline Books, Leo Cooper,
Praetorian Press, Remember When, Seaforth Publishing and Wharncliffe.

For a complete list of Pen and Sword titles please contact
Pen and Sword Books Limited
47 Church Street, Barnsley, South Yorkshire, S70 2AS, England
E-mail: enquiries@pen-and-sword.co.uk
Website: www.pen-and-sword.co.uk

Contents

**Extract from Kelly's Directory, 'Military Personnel, 1912,
West Riding of Yorkshire'**

Bingley Territorial Force
West Riding Regiment 6th Battalion H Company – Hill Side Road
Captain Norman C. Prince commanding – Colour Serjeant Stephen Sweet, drill instructor.

Guiseley Territorial Force
West Riding Regiment (Duke of Wellington's 6th Battalion C Company
Drill Hall and armoury – Victoria Road
Captain Wilfred Claughton, commanding – Serjeant Thomas Joseph Sherridan, drill instructor.

Haworth Territorial Force
Duke of Wellington's (West Riding Regiment) 6th Battalion G Company
Drill Hall – Minnie Street
Captain Wilfred H. Hudleston – Serjeant George Finding, drill instructor.

Keighley Territorial Force
The Drill Hall and armoury of D and E Companies of the 6th Territorial Force Battalion
Duke of Wellington's (West Riding Regiment) – Lawkholme Lane.
Head Quarters – 62 Dalton Lane
D Company Captain M. Wright, commanding – E company Captain Raymond V.
Marriner commanding
Major W.M. Gabriel, medical officer – Colour Serjeant Andrew Harry Franklin, drill
instructor.

Settle Territorial Force
6th Battalion Duke of Wellington's (West Riding Regiment) F Company
Drill Hall – Castleberg Lane
Lieutenant K. Nicholson commanding – Serjeant William Naden drill instructor.

Skipton Territorial Force
The Drill Hall and armoury, Otley Street. 6th Battalion Duke of Wellington's (West
Riding Regiment) A, B and H.Q. Companies.

* * *

Approximate structure of the British Army during the Great War (Infantry)

Unit	Number of Men	Commanded by
Section	15–20	Corporal or Lance Corporal
Platoon	60–70	Lieutenant or 2nd Lieutenant
Company	200–250	Major or Captain
Battalion	1,000–1,200	Lieutenant Colonel
Brigade	3,000–4,000	Brigadier General
Division	16,000–18,000	Major General
Corps	48,000–50,000	Lieutenant General
Army	150,000–200,000	General

An infantry regiment had a number of battalions, but these did not always serve together,
and were often split among other brigades.

Foreword

Visitors to Saint Oswald's Church in Guiseley, near Leeds, will most certainly notice the thirteenth century bell tower, the Jacobean pulpit and the altar rail where Patrick Bronte and Maria Branwell, parents of the literary daughters, were married in 1812. They may not immediately notice two stained glass windows in the south wall which show images of two warrior saints: Saint Martin slicing his cloak to give to a beggar and Saint George slaying the dragon. These windows were commissioned by the family of Lieutenant Malcolm Colin McGregor Law, in remembrance of him and the men who served in the 6th Battalion, Duke of Wellington's Regiment, 49th and 62nd Divisions, who fell in the Great War. For several decades after the end of the war, people from Guiseley would have looked upon these windows and the roll of honour carved in the lychgate and known most of the men who served and died in the regiment. This is the story of those men and covers the time from 4 August 1914 to 16 June 1919.

The stained-glass windows in the south wall of St Oswald's Church, Guiseley.

Guiseley was the location of C Company of the 1/6th Battalion of the Duke of Wellington's (West Riding) Regiment (1/6th DWR). This unit was part of the Territorial Force (TF). As a Guiseley man, I have to make special mention of those who served in this unit as the battalion's story unfolds. I have pieced together the day-by-day movements and actions of the 1/6th DWR during the First World War, using the war diary of the 1/6th DWR as a guide. This was a written record of a unit's actions overseas, movements and casualties, usually completed by the adjutant (an officer who assists the commanding officer). The men of the TF held civilian jobs and did their soldiering on a part-time basis, like the modern Army Reserves. Their motives for joining the ranks would have been as varied as the men themselves, some would have served for the extra money, some to gain favour with an employer or just to have a good time with their friends whilst getting paid. Whatever their motives, their story is one of bravery and hardship almost beyond comprehension.

In Guiseley the names of the men of the town who died in the Great War are read out on Remembrance Sunday by the Rector of Saint Oswald's; poppy wreaths are laid, the Last Post is played and a two-minute silence is observed. The First World War changed the hopes and dreams of millions of people forever. Records show that 1,118,264 British and Empire soldiers, sailors and airmen died, of whom 162,000 have no known grave. Around 40,000 of these men are buried in unnamed graves, marked 'Known unto God' but it can be estimated that the remainder, almost 122,000 men, disappeared forever. Their mortal remains still lie under the battlefields of the Great War or were lost at sea.

As the years pass, the memory of the Great War is fading; those who fought and survived have passed away and former battlefields have reverted to more peaceful settings. Today it is almost impossible for us to understand the comradeship of the trenches, the anxiety of those at home fearing the telegram reporting death or wounds, the scale of pain and suffering endured by casualties, the incredible courage and self-sacrifice shown by ordinary men in battle living with the reality of instant death. As an example, Ferme-Olivier Military Cemetery, 7 miles north-west of Ypres, contains the graves of 408 men who died in the Great War and in plot 2, row E can be found a collective grave containing the remains of thirty-seven men from the 3rd Battalion, The Monmouthshire Regiment who, on 29 December 1915, were on parade behind the lines when they were all killed by a single large calibre German shell, fired from a naval gun.

In this book, I refer to the conflict as the Great War, a title which the men who fought would have recognised. I have used the original names of areas the men and women who served would have recognised. Ypres is now known as Ieper and Nieuport known as Neiuwpoort. In a similar vein, distances are measured in miles (1.60km) and yards (0.91m).

Great effort has been made to identify, request and receive permission from copyright holders of images for their use. Some requests have gone unanswered but acknowledgement of images has been accredited where known. Unless otherwise indicated, all images are in the public domain or have been taken by the author. Any

C (Guiseley) Company of the 6th (TF) Duke of Wellington's (West Riding) Regiment at Guiseley returning from summer camp 1913. Aireborough Historical Society

Same view from a lower angle in 2016.

Revelation 14:13
'They may rest from their labours and their works do follow them.'

Haworth Drill Hall on Minnie Street, now private dwellings.

'Defence not defiance', the carving on the gable end of the
building. This was the motto of the Rifle Volunteer Corps, taken
from the poem of the same name by Martin Farquhar Tupper.

Keighley Drill Hall
on Lawkholme
Lane, still used as a
Reserve Force and
cadet centre.

Skipton Drill Hall
and armoury on
Otley Street, now
offices.

Guiseley Drill Hall and armoury on Victoria Road, now private flats.

Left: The somewhat weathered inscription 'Volunteers Drill Hall' with a date stone of 1892 on the Skipton Drill Hall.

Ilkley Drill Hall, once used by the 4th West Riding Howitzer Brigade, on the A65 Leeds Road.

ILKLEY CIVIC SOCIETY

DRILL HALL
Built 1911 for
Territorials 4th West Riding
Howitzer Brigade

WWII Home Guard HQ

Business Centre 1991

Cap badge and collar badge of the Duke of Wellington's (West Riding) Regiment.

The cap badge of the Duke of Wellington's (West Riding) Regiment was the type in use from 1898, except for the period 1958-1969 when the Yorkshire Brigade badge was worn by the men of the regiment. The predecessor regiment was raised in 1702 as the Earl of Huntingdon's Regiment of Foot and in 1747 it was ranked as the 33rd Regiment of Foot and was formerly known by that number from 1751. In 1782, it was re-designated the 33rd (The 1st Yorkshire West Riding) Regiment of Foot. In 1853, following the Duke of Wellington's death the previous year, Queen Victoria granted the regiment the secondary title, 'The Duke of Wellington's', to commemorate the duke's association with the regiment, he having been a major of the 33rd in 1793 and Colonel of the Regiment 1806-1816. The name now became the 33rd (The Duke of Wellington's) Regiment of Foot. It was almost certainly at this time that the crest associated with the Wellesley family was adopted, out of a ducal coronet, a demi-lion rampant holding a 'forked pennon (or flag), flowing to the sinister' (to the left of the bearer as held).

As part of the Cardwell/Childers reforms, in 1881 the Regiment merged with the 76th Regiment of Foot, a unit also associated with Wellington, who had served as a subaltern in it in 1787. The 76th was also known as the Hindoostan Regiment, after the battle honour and elephant badge granted for its action at the storming of Bangalore in 1791. It was formerly named the 76th (Hindoostan) Regiment of Foot in 1803 but that title was dropped in 1812. The merged regiment became for a short period the Halifax Regiment (Duke of Wellington's) before, in the same year, becoming The Duke of Wellington's (West Riding) Regiment. The badge of the merged unit carried forward the Wellesley crest from the 33rd and the elephant motif of the 76th, which eventually became the collar badge.

The family coat of arms of the Duke of Wellington (above) and the cap badge of the Yorkshire Regiment (below).

With the change of headdress in 1898, a new cap badge was designed, retaining the crest but with the addition of a scroll bearing the duke's motto, *Virtutis Fortuna Comes* ('Fortune Favours the Brave', or alternatively, 'Fortune is the Companion of Bravery'), plus a second scroll bearing the regimental title 'The West Riding'. In 1920 the name was changed to the Duke of Wellington's Regiment (West Riding), with no change to the basic badge design. In 1958, the regiment became part of the Yorkshire Brigade and

adopted a cap badge depicting a crowned white rose above a scroll inscribed 'Yorkshire'. When the Yorkshire Brigade was broken up in 1968-1969, the regiment once again regained its independence and adopted the previous design of cap badge.

In 2006 the Yorkshire Regiment was formed by merging the regiment with The Green Howards and The Prince of Wales's Own Regiment of Yorkshire, with the DWR becoming its 3rd Battalion (Duke of Wellington's). On 20 July 2013, the 3rd Battalion of the Yorkshire Regiment was disbanded, with the personnel dispersed to the two remaining battalions of the regiment. The Yorkshire Regiment has as a principal element of its badge, the demi-lion and pennant from the Wellesley crest.

The 6th West Yorkshire Militia cap badge.

The 6th West Yorkshire Militia shoulder title and belt buckle.

* * *

Acknowledgements

I would like to thank Matt Jones, Irene Moore and Tara Moran from Pen & Sword for their invaluable help, advice and guidance, which was very much appreciated; Andy McGoldrick for the photographs of West Yorkshire Militia items; David Cochrane of The Duke of Wellington's (West Riding) Regimental Museum at Bankfield, Halifax, for the pre-war annual camp photographs; Jane and Mark Hudson for the photographs of Acting Serjeant Richard Hudson; Carlo Harrison of the Aireborough Historical Society for numerous photographs; Andy Wade of the 'Men of Worth' project; Michael and Betty Hutchinson for the images of Private Leonard Parker; Chris Foster from the '*Craven's Part in the Great War*' project (cpgw.org.uk) for the numerous photos of the fallen; David Whithorn of the '*Bus to Bradford*' Bradford Pals' project for the images of Private Charles Young; Reverend David Pickett of St Oswald's Church in Guiseley for the photographs of the church windows and headstones; Alex Daniels, my battlefield travelling companion; and my wife, Susan, for all your encouragement and inspiration.

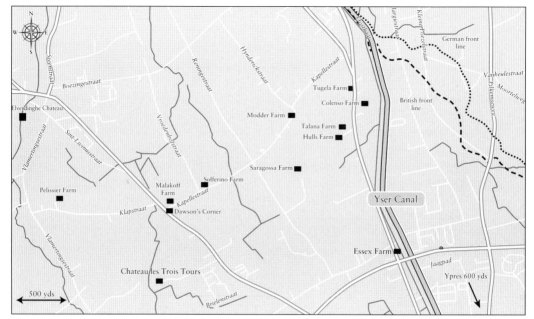

Ypres Farms overview.

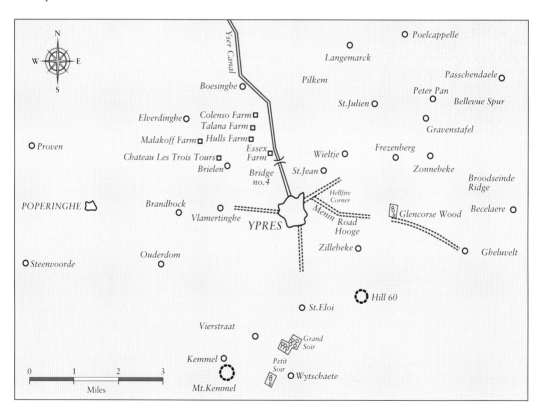

Ypres overview.

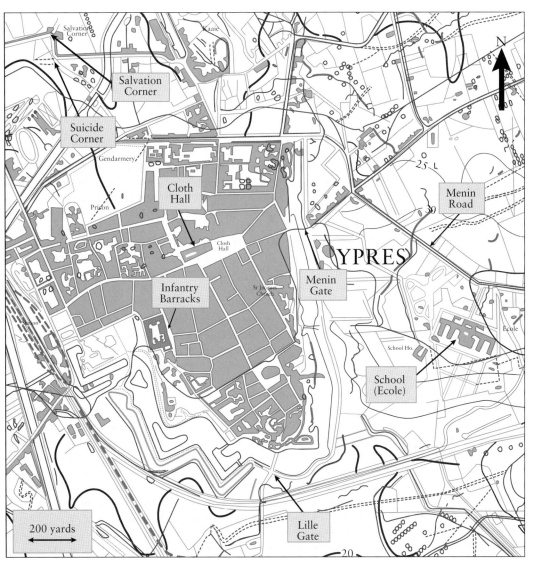

Ypres Town Map.

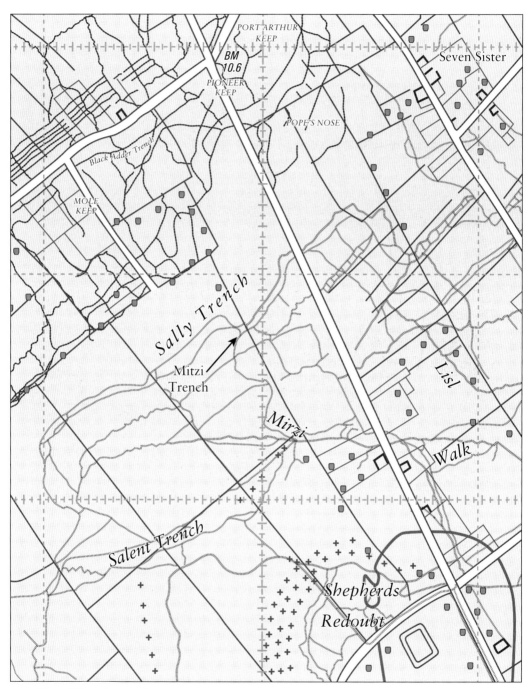

Neuve Chapelle overview.

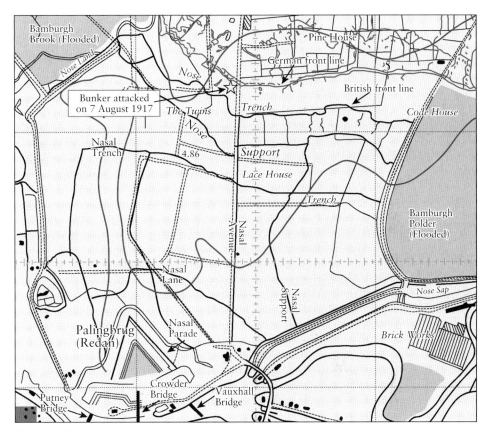

Nose and Nasal trench.

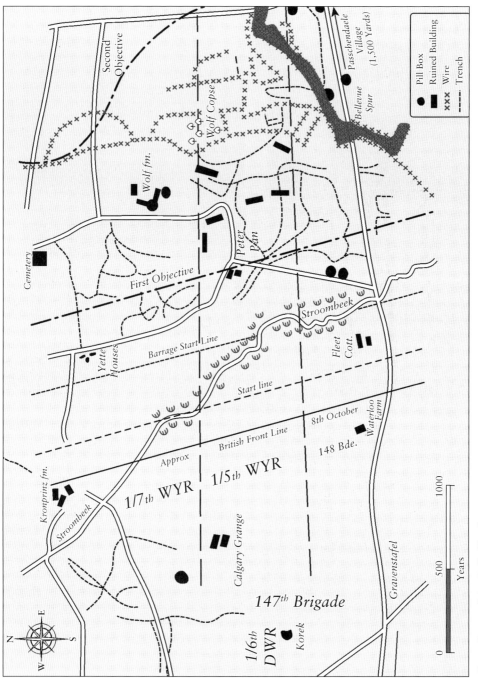

Legend:
- ● Pill Box
- ■ Ruined Building
- ××× Wire
- —·— Trench

Second Objective

Passchendaele Village (1,500 Yards)

Bellevue Spur

Wolf Copse

Wolf fm.

Cemetery

Peter Pan

First Objective

Stroombeek

Yette Houses

Barrage Start Line

Fleet Cott.

Start line

Waterloo Farm

8th October

British Front Line

148 Bde.

Kronprinz fm.

Approx

1/7th WYR   1/5th WYR

Stroombeek

Calgary Grange

Korek

147th Brigade

1/6th DWR

Gravenstafel

0   500   1000
Years

Peter Pan and the Belle Vue Spur.

xviii

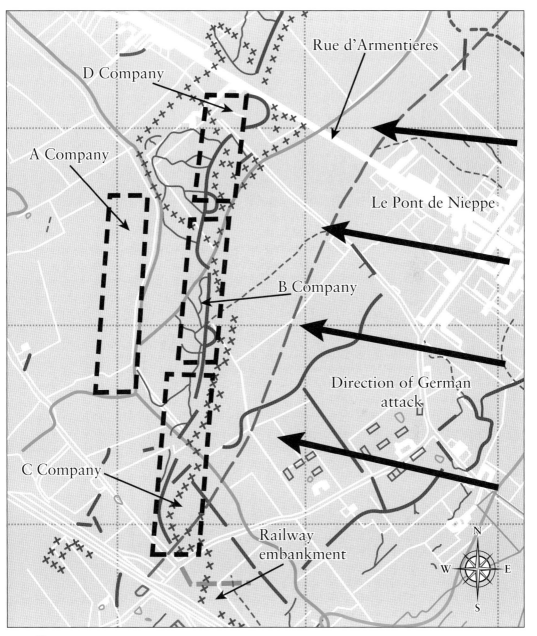

D Company

Rue d'Armentières

A Company

Le Pont de Nieppe

B Company

Direction of German
attack

C Company

Railway
embankment

N
W E
S

Nieppe overview.

Origins

The 6th West Yorkshire Militia was created by Act of Parliament on 15 July 1853 with the headquarters temporarily established at Leeds. Before this date, going back to at least 1760, the towns and cities of the West Riding formed their own militias of local men who were recruited by ballot, as opposed to being volunteers, and in times of national emergency, such as the Napoleonic Wars, the militia could be brought to a state of readiness. Civil disorder could also mean deployment, as occurred in May 1808 when the Halifax Militia was deployed to Rochdale and Manchester to quell rioting weavers.

In 1859, in addition to militia units, the formation of the Volunteer Rifle Corps (VRC) was proposed. The VRC would be established using the Volunteer Act 1804 which had been used to form local defence forces during the Napoleonic War. The men would be enrolled on oath to the Queen and in the main would comprise men who were unable to join the militia or saw no full-time role in the regular army such as gentlemen, professional men, merchants, tradesmen and other 'respectable' members of the community.

Increased tension with a resurgent France under the leadership of Napoleon III, nephew of Napoleon I, was causing concern in the corridors of power in Westminster. Louis-Napoleon Bonaparte (as he was then known) was elected French president in 1848 but was denied a second term in power by the French constitution, so in 1851 he organised a *coup d'état* and took the throne as Emperor Napoleon III. Despite being allied with the United Kingdom in the Crimean War of 1853-1856, Napoleon III aimed to reassert French influence in Europe and beyond.

On the evening of 14 January 1858 Napoleon III and the Empress Eugénie visited the Rue le Peletier opera house in Paris and, as the royal carriage pulled up outside the building, three bombs were thrown, killing eight members of the escort and bystanders and injuring over a hundred more. The emperor and empress were unharmed and, as a show of defiance, continued with their visit to the opera. The leader of the would-be assassins was an Italian national called Felice Orsini who was himself injured in the attack and quickly arrested. A co-conspirator, a French surgeon named Simon Bernard, had claimed asylum in the United Kingdom which, despite French requests, refused to extradite him. Tensions between the two countries increased when it was discovered that the bombs had been made in the United Kingdom where Orsini had been living. He had not made a secret of his dislike of Napoleon III as he had conducted a country-wide speaking tour in England denouncing French interference in Italian affairs. In 1858 Orsini went to the guillotine and French anti-British fervour continued.

In 1859 war broke out between France and the Austrian Empire and the fear that Great Britain would become involved in a European war seemed likely. Following the Crimean War, it was clear that with half the army distributed across the empire on garrison duty, the forces available to defend Great Britain from invasion were spread invitingly thin. The threat of French invasion resulted in discussions in Westminster about the formation of a home defence arrangement separate from the militia. France was seen as a serious threat, similar to that which the former Soviet Union presented during the decades of the Cold War. As a self-funding organisation, the VRC was an attractive proposition for the government of the day.

PUNCH, OR THE LONDON CHARIVARI.—November 12, 1859.

Mr. Bull. "INVASION, INDEED! THAT'S A GAME TWO CAN PLAY AT!—WHY, TO HEAR THESE POODLES TALK, ONE WOULD THINK MY BULL-DOG WAS DEAD!"

Cartoon from 12 November 1859 edition of Punch.

CIRCULAR

Promulgated by Order of the Secretary of State for War for the Guidance of Volunteer Rifle Corps.

War Office, 1st September 1859.

COURSE OF RIFLE TRAINING for the VOLUNTEER RIFLE CORPS, supposed to train by Squads of 20 or 24 at a time, where two Instructors are available, or half these Numbers where there is only one.

PRELIMINARY DRILLS.

The Minimum Number of Drills, and Time to be employed in each, before Target Practice is on any account to commence.

Days.	Cleaning Arms.		Theoretical Principles.		Aiming Drill.		Position Drill per Musketry Regulations.	Snapping Caps, 10 Caps to be expended.	Blank Firing, 10 Rounds to be expended.	Judging Distance Drill.	Total Hours.
	Lessons per Musketry Regulations.	Time.	Lessons per Musketry Regulations.	Time.	Distance.	Time.					
		Hour.		Hour.	Yards.	Hour.	Hour.	Hour.	Hour.	Hour.	Hours.
1st	1st	¼	—	—	100	¼	¼	¼	—	¼	2¼
2nd	—	—	1 and 2	¼	200	¼	¼	¼	—	¼	2¼
3rd	3rd	¼	—	—	300	¼	¼	¼	—	¼	2¼
4th	—	—	3 and 4	¼	400	¼	¼	¼	—	¼	2¼
5th	4th	¼	—	—	500	¼	¼	¼	¼	¼	2¼
6th	—	—	5 and 6	¼	600	¼	¼	¼	—	¼	2¼

TARGET PRACTICE.

Days.	Number of Rounds to be fired in												REMARKS.
	3rd Class.				2nd Class.				1st Class.				
	Yds. 150	Yds. 200	Yds. 250	Yds. 300	Yds. 400	Yds. 500	Yds. 550	Yds. 600	Yds. 650	Yds. 700	Yds. 800	Yds. 900	
7th	5	5	—	—	—	—	—	—	—	—	—	—	1st Period.
8th	—	—	5	5	—	—	—	—	—	—	—	—	
9th	5	5	—	—	5	5	—	—	—	—	—	—	2nd Period—3rd Class to fire from 150 to 300 yards; 2nd Class from 400 to 600 yards.
10th	—	—	5	5	—	—	5	5	—	—	—	—	
11th	5	5	—	—	5	5	—	—	5	5	—	—	3rd Period—3rd and 2nd Class to fire as before; 1st Class from 650 to 900 yards.
12th	—	—	5	5	—	—	5	5	—	—	5	5	

P.S.—Should it be desirable to execute the Platoon and Skirmishing Practices, two more days will be required for the purpose, viz., 13th day, File-firing at 300 yards, standing, 10 rounds; Volley-firing at 400 yards, kneeling, 10 rounds. 14th day, Skirmishing, Advancing, and Retiring (each man judging his own distance), between 400 and 200 yards, 10 rounds.

LONDON : Printed by GEORGE E. EYRE and WILLIAM SPOTTISWOODE, Printers to the Queen's most Excellent Majesty. For Her Majesty's Stationery Office.

In December 1859 a meeting of influential inhabitants of the parish of Guiseley was held which at that time encompassed Carlton, Rawdon, Yeadon and Horsforth. The meeting was held at Horsforth and amongst those present were: Matthew William Thompson (later Sir Matthew William Thompson, Baronet of Park Gate House, Guiseley, twice Mayor of Bradford 1862 and 1872, director and chairman of the Midland Railway Company, Liberal MP for Bradford 1867-

Extract from the VRC handbook 1859.

1872); the Rev W.H.B. Stocker of Horsforth; the Rev T.B. Ferris, Rector of Guiseley; Henry Granville Baker Esq of Ling Bob, Horsforth; Dr William M. Pinder of Lee House, Horsforth; Mr F. Knowles, Mr J. Whittaker; Mr D. Gill; Mr S. Morfitt and Mr B. Fall.

By January 1860, enough recruits had been obtained and sufficient funds secured from benefactors to enable an application to be forwarded to the Lord Lieutenant of the West Riding, the 6th Earl Fitzwilliam, to form a VRC for the parish of Guiseley. The VRC was initially autonomous and did not receive any government funding for uniforms, equipment or weapons but instead was reliant on the generosity of donations and subscriptions. The largest donation given on its formation was £50 (£4,250 today) by Matthew W. Thompson which most probably secured his captaincy. Other donations were given by Mr W.R. Crompton Stansfield of Esholt Hall £25, Mr R. Milligan of Acacia, Rawdon £25, the Rev T.B. Ferris, Rector of Guiseley (later to become chaplain to the 25th VRC) £10 and numerous other benefactors, totalling over £200 (£17,000). The 25th VRC was formed in the parish of Guiseley by authority of the Lord Lieutenant in 1860 and was commanded by Captain Matthew William Thompson.

Sir Matthew William Thompson (Aireborough Historical Society)

Headstone in St Oswald's graveyard and memorial plaque in St Oswald's Church

Recruits were to be drawn from the parish of Guiseley and the original location of the drill room used for parades was at Henshaw in Yeadon, near to the Woolpack Inn which was the setting for the annual prize giving dinner for several years. In the event of invasion, the roll of the VRC was not to fight a pitched battle with an invading army, but instead they were to attack the enemy's flank and cause disruption behind the lines as the invaders advanced across the country. Rifle shooting became the lead discipline and considerable sums of prize money could be won by the most accurate shot.

One of the original members of the 25th VRC was James Hardwick of Guiseley who died in 1927 aged 87. In his early life he worked as a hand-loom weaver at his parents' house at Greenbottom and later worked for thirty years at Nunroyd Mill. A newspaper article at the time of his death in 1927 recalled many of Mr Hardwick's reminiscences. He stated the 25th Guiseley VRC wore a grey uniform with red piping with an 'Austrian knot' cuff design as well as 'picturesque' hats. The cap badge of the VRC was generally that of a French-style curled bugle horn surmounted with a royal crown with the number of the corps set within the curl of the horn. He recalled that the Guiseley unit won many prizes for shooting in both local and nationwide competitions. In 1869, Serjeant Whitaker won The West Riding Enfield Cup, The Reverend R. Brooks Challenge Cup was won by Lieutenant Knowles and The Ebor Challenge Cup was won by Corporal Whalley. At this time, the unit was using the Pattern 1853 Enfield rifle which was a muzzle loading .577 calibre rifle and the standard British military weapon of that period.

Pattern 1853 Enfield Rifled Musket (Public domain – Smithsonian)

By 1862 the VRC numbered 134,000 riflemen, 24,000 artillery gunners, mainly on coastal batteries, 2,900 engineers and a small contingent of mounted troops.

The VRC differed from the militia in many ways. The militia was an alternative to a standing army where men would volunteer to undertake several weeks basic training at an army depot, after which they would return to civilian life, but had to attend regular training and a two-week summer camp. The man had to agree to serve for a fixed period for which they received military pay for their time and an annual financial retainer. They also had to agree

NCO's belt badge from the 25th Guiseley VRC. It would be positioned on the front of the shoulder belt. (West Yorkshire Rifle Volunteers)

VRC Serjeant's tunic of the period showing the 'Austrian knot' cuff design. Above that is a diamond shaped annual efficiency badge and each of the four stars represent five years efficiency. (Victorian Wars Forum)

to serve overseas if required. This arrangement suited men whose employment allowed frequent absences, such as labourers or agricultural workers. The VRC volunteer was initially unpaid and was only to serve in the United Kingdom. They could give fourteen days' notice of resignation (unless under active service) and had to pay for their own uniforms, firearms and ammunition which had to be approved by the War Office to ensure uniformity.

A Royal Commission set up in 1862 made several recommendations which became law in 1863 with the passing of the Volunteer Act. This enabled several individual VRC units to combine into administrative battalions, although a number of smaller units had already done this. The Act also granted central government financial support which enabled the appointment of permanent staff such as an adjutant and permanent drill serjeant instructors for the individual units. It also empowered local authorities to establish shooting ranges and restrict public access to the same. The 25th Guiseley VRC used a newly created range on Baildon Moor and the 15th North Craven unit used a range at Attermire Scar.

The Volunteer Act 1863 also gave the provision of a twenty shillings per man grant to replace worn out uniform and equipment. The 2nd Administrative Battalion of the VRC was originally formed of five companies from the townships of Burley-in-Wharfedale, Guiseley, Ingleton, Settle and Skipton, with the 35th Keighley and 42nd Haworth VRC joining in 1866. A silver three-handled challenge cup was provided by the officers of the 2nd Administrative Battalion for the best shooting team on which was inscribed:

'Presented by the officers of the 2nd Administrative Battalion, West Riding of Yorkshire Rifle Volunteers to be competed for annually by the several companies forming the regiment.'

The 23rd Burley-in-Wharfedale VRC was fortunate in having a former Crimea War veteran and serving police constable as their Serjeant Drill Instructor. George Reekie was born in Cupar, Fife and served for twelve years in the Scots Fusilier Guards, taking part in the Battles of Alma, Balaclava, Inkerman and Sebastopol. He was discharged

The remains of the Baildon range butts near the 18th hole of the present-day golf course.

An engraving from the Illustrated London News *of October 1863, showing members of the Middlesex Rifle Corps. This shows the typical uniform the volunteers would have worn.*

The 2ⁿᵈ Administrative Battalion Challenge Cup. (Reproduced with permission of Andy McGoldrick)

from the army in March 1857 and settled in Doncaster where he married and the following year he joined the West Riding Constabulary. He was posted to Otley where his beat area was Guiseley and on the formation of the VRC he received permission from the chief constable to instruct the new unit on a part-time basis. With the creation of full-time drill instructors, he resigned from the police in May 1862 and became the instructor of the unit, which included a house on Peel Place in the village.

In October 1862 a shooting competition took place at Attermire Range near Settle with two teams of ten men each from Guiseley and Settle competing. The men shot five rounds each at ranges of 200, 500 and 700 yards at stationary targets using the pattern 1853 Enfield rifle. Captain Matthew W. Thompson led the Guiseley team and Captain Walter Morrison MP successfully led the Settle team to victory, winning the competition 234 points to Guiseley's 205.

Attermire Scar shooting range above Settle.

A maker's mark of Woods target, 1860, T. Richards & Co, Bishopsgate, London on one of the metal target plates.

Metal target plates in the butts area at Attermire Scar.

Captain Walter Morrison later went on to become a lieutenant colonel of the 2nd Administrative Battalion and its commanding officer. He was born in London in 1836, the son of James Morrison, Liberal MP for Ipswich. James Morrison was a self-made man whose fortune lay in haberdashery and banking. He also owned numerous properties throughout the UK including the Malham Tarn Estate and the elegant Georgian mansion Tarn House. On his father's death, Walter inherited around £2 million (around £170 million today) and the Malham Tarn Estate. He was MP for Plymouth (1861-1874) and Skipton (1886-1892, 1895-1900), Sherriff of the West Riding (1883), Chairman of the Craven Bank (1905), a Justice of the Peace and Honorary Colonel of the 3rd Volunteer Battalion of the West Riding Regiment. He

Walter Morrison (CPGW)

was a staunch supporter of the church and education in Malhamdale and in 1897 he funded the building of the chapel at Giggleswick School, of which he was vice-chairman of the governors. He also funded the book *Craven's part in the Great War* which was presented free of charge to all the soldiers and families of the deceased who enlisted in the Skipton Parliamentary Division during the Great War. He was a founder member and captain of the Settle VRC.

Walter Morrison's grave at St Michael the Archangel Church, Kirkby Malham.

In May 1871 the 2nd Administrative Battalion attended the annual camp at Barc near Morecambe. The Guiseley and Burley Companies formed the advance party which arrived two days before the main body to establish the camp. The rest of the battalion was transported by a special train which departed from Keighley, calling at Skipton, Settle and Ingleton to collect men. This was the first time the battalion had been under canvas and on arrival at Morecambe station they were met by the Guiseley and Burley contingent. The 600 men of the battalion then formed up in four ranks and, with rifles shouldered and bayonets fixed, marched a mile to the campsite accompanied by two bands. Three drill parades were held each day at 7am, 10.20am and 3pm with each session lasting about two hours. Plenty of recreation time was allowed and after the last parade the men were allowed to visit the local hostelries in the area. A report from the *Leeds Mercury* newspaper reported on life at the camp:

Many of them took to the opportunity of going into town, several thirsty sons of mars adjourning to the beer shops whilst others of a more gallant and amorous nature betook themselves to the fine promenade at the end of the pier where there was a gay assemblage of ladies. Those of a terpsichorean turn of mind were secured and twirled gaily round in a mazy dance to the strains of an excellent band. As ten o'clock, the limit of their pass, approached, those of them who had a clearly defined conception of military discipline marched back to their camp but there were a few who, under the influence perhaps of an exaggerated thirst and exaggerated its requirements, a mistake which rendered their ideas of time indefinite and inclined them to regard discipline as unnecessarily severe. But there was no breach of the peace or good order and by degrees the stragglers returned to their quarters. The lights were put out but for hours afterwards the camp was alive with animated conversation followed by hearty laughter which was kept up with much spirit all over the camp. The novelty of the situation no doubt affording ample scope for ludicrous and amusing comment.

Whilst at the camp, the battalion marched 3 miles to Lancaster church to attend a service.

Throughout the 1860s and early 1870s the 25th Guiseley VRC enjoyed considerable support in both attendance and finances, but around about 1873 interest seems to have declined. As a result, the 25th VRC was disbanded in September 1876 and the Commanding Officer, Captain Henry Harrison Milligan of Benton Park House, the Chaplain, Reverend Thomas B. Ferris and Honorary Surgeon, Dr William M. Pinder all resigned their commissions.

In 1880, the 2nd Administrative Battalion was re-titled the 9th Yorkshire (West Riding) VRC with the individual numbered units becoming companies of a single battalion. In February 1883, following the Childers reforms of the British Army (Hugh Childers was the then Liberal Secretary of State for War), the 4th (Halifax), 6th (Huddersfield) and 9th (Skipton) Battalions of the West Riding VRC became the 1st, 2nd and 3rd (Volunteer) Battalion of the Duke of Wellington's (West Riding) Regiment and the 6th West Yorkshire Militia became the 3rd (Militia) Battalion of the Duke of Wellington's (West Riding) Regiment, bringing the volunteer formations into line with the regular army.

The former VRC now had to conform to the dress and uniform regulations of the parent regiment and as such lost the independence they previously enjoyed. The Duke of Wellington's Regiment wore scarlet tunics and trousers with white lapels on the jacket but the former VRC units were permitted to keep the 'Austrian knot' cuff decoration, much to the delight of the regular battalions as they did not want to be mistaken for the part-time amateurs. The former 25th VRC had been reformed and now became C2 Company of the 3rd (Volunteer) Battalion DWR. (The 24th Burley-in-Wharfedale VRC became C1 Company) and moved to a drill hut located on Springfield Place, Guiseley.

In June 1884 the 3rd (Volunteer) Battalion DWR had their annual camp at Bare near Morecambe and around 680 men attended. The battalion was under the command of Lieutenant Colonel Garnett-Orme who announced that strict military discipline would be maintained in camp and any breach of regulations would subject the offender to punishment. The 'holiday camp' attitude, which had prevailed in previous years, was over. No man would be allowed to leave camp until after the afternoon parade and when walking out the dress code was tunic, forage cap and waist belt without bayonet. Men were not allowed to leave camp unless they were properly dressed and on no account were they to be seen smoking in the street. Reveille was 6am, parade for recruits and guard mounting was 7am, breakfast 8am, fall-in 10.30am, dinner bugle 1pm, fall-in 2pm, tea 5pm, guard mounting 7pm, retreat (everybody back in camp) 8pm, Last Post and perfect silence in camp for 11pm. The ration allowance for each man was: 1½ lb of bread, 1lb of meat, 1lb of potatoes, 2oz of butter, 2 pints of tea, coffee or cocoa and 1 pint of beer or ginger beer.

The annual camp in 1890 took place in May of that year at Strensall and the volunteers had the opportunity of training with the regular army and militia. A large-scale exercise was held on Strensall Common and surrounding areas, which involved units from the 1st West Riding Regiment, 2nd East Yorkshire Regiment, 1st Durham Light Infantry, 4th (Militia) Durham Light Infantry and the 24th Field Battery Royal Artillery acting as the attacking force. The defending units were 1st and 2nd (Volunteer) Battalions West Yorkshire Regiment, 3rd (Volunteer) Battalion West Riding Regiment plus two guns from the 24th Field Battery Royal Artillery. The total number of men involved in the exercise was just over 2,000, with each man receiving twenty rounds of blank ammunition and the artillery ten blank rounds for each gun. The chief umpire was Major General Stevenson, GOC North-East District and after a lively mock battle, which included the attacking force seizing the bridge over the River Foss near Strensall village, the attackers finally pushed home their advantage near Lords Moor Lane which, in the opinion of the umpire, resulted in the defeat of the defenders.

On Saturday, 23 May 1896, three battalions from the West Yorkshire Volunteer Infantry Brigade attended the annual camp on the racecourse at Scarborough. The units comprised the 2nd (Huddersfield) and 3rd (Skipton) Battalions of the (Volunteer) West Riding Regiment and the 2nd (Bradford) Battalion of the (Volunteer) West Yorkshire Regiment. The camp was held on the racecourse at Irton Moor, about a mile west of the suburb of Falsgrave (now the site of GCHQ Irton Moor). Advance parties of men from the three battalions had arrived earlier in the week and erected 400 bell tents and several marquees. The various battalions began to arrive at Scarborough train station on Saturday evening and, accompanied by their respective regimental bands, marched the 2 miles to the campsite. On arrival each man received a meat pie and a pint of ale or ginger beer. The camp routine would have seemed familiar to veterans of the regiment. Reveille was sounded at 5.30am, breakfast at 8.30am, dinner at 1pm, evening meal 5.30pm, guard mounting at 9pm and lights out at 10.45pm. After church parade on Sunday, the men were allowed to go into Scarborough for recreation. A Royal Navy

Private Charles Frederick Thompson from the Burley-in-Wharfedale company of the 3rd (V) West Riding Regiment pictured at Scarborough.

Private Charles Frederick Thompson in RAF uniform in 1918. (Courtesy of Micheal and Betty Hutchinson)

warship was anchored in the bay and some of the men took pleasure boat trips around the bay.

In February 1900, along with their regular army comrades, men from the 3rd (Militia) West Riding Regiment and the 3rd (Volunteer) West Riding Regiment served in South Africa during the Second Boer War. On 1 January 1900 notice was received to the effect that 30 officers and 340 other ranks of the 3rd (Militia) West Riding Regiment would be embodied on 17 January and were to proceed from Halifax to Cork in Ireland to relieve a regular battalion that had been sent to South Africa. The 3rd (Militia) Battalion was under the command of Lieutenant Colonel A.K. Wyllie and were joined in Cork by 4 officers and 131 men from the 1st, 2nd and 3rd (Volunteer) Battalions of the West Riding Regiment. On 27 February 1900, the unit sailed from Queenstown (now known as Cobh) in Ireland aboard the SS *Goorkha* of the Union Steamship Line. Amongst the officers and men were Lieutenant Sydney Fox Marriner (later to become the adjutant of the 1/6th DWR) and Colour Serjeant John Churchman (later to become captain and quartermaster of the 1/6th DWR).

In total 27 officers and 488 other ranks from the West Riding militia and volunteers sailed on the SS *Goorkha* along with 24 officers and 483 men of the 4th (Militia) Bedfordshire Regiment.

For those men that remained in the UK, the annual camp in June 1900 was held at Aldershot. The weather caused problems; first a torrential thunderstorm nearly washed the camp away and then a heatwave with cloudless skies and hot sun followed for the rest of the week. Several volunteer battalions from the Northern and Southern Armies

January 1900, the thirty-six men of the Keighley contingent, 3rd (Volunteer) West Riding Regiment marching along North Street for service in the Boer War. (DWR Museum)

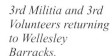

3rd Militia and 3rd Volunteers returning to Wellesley Barracks.

were also present at the camp, which made the number of men almost 20,000. A large-scale exercise, or 'sham fight' as they were known, had to be cut short as a man from the 4th Inniskilling Fusiliers collapsed and died of heatstroke. In total four men died due to the hot weather that week and later inquests found that insufficient food and water had been provided and the field service caps gave insufficient protection from the sun. Private Whalley from the 1st (Volunteer) DWR (Halifax) also died in the Connaught Hospital from typhus.

On 23 May 1903 the members of the 3rd (Volunteer) West Riding Regiment received access to a new rifle range on Hawksworth Moor above Menston. The opening ceremony was performed by the Lord Mayor of Leeds, Mr John Ward, in the presence of a large and enthusiastic crowd of well-wishers. The range and butts had been constructed for the Leeds Shooting Club on land provided by Mr F.H. Fawkes of Farnley Hall. It was constructed to military specification and was equipped with the latest style of target frames known as 'Jeffries' targets. These were a windmill-type apparatus which when rotated exposed the targets.

The now disused butts of the Hawksworth Range with the later style of target cradles. The range finally closed in 1987.

The view towards the rear of the Butts. The ridge line of Otley Chevin and Guiseley Moor can be seen in the distance.

In the presence of a cinematographer, the Lord Mayor had the honour of firing the first shot at a target and, to the loud cheers of the assembled crowd, it was signalled to be a bullseye. There were sixteen separate targets and the men could shoot from distances up to 800 yards.

The first summer annual camp of the 6th DWR as a Territorial Force unit was held at Redcar near Middlesbrough in 1908. In 1909 the camp was at Marske near Saltburn and in 1910 at Peel on the Isle of Man.

In August 1911 the camp was held at the Palace Road Camp, Ripon. The 2nd and 3rd West Riding Territorial Brigades attended and the YMCA erected refreshment and recreation tents. Special services were held in Ripon Cathedral for each brigade. In 1912 the camp was at Flamborough on the East Yorkshire coast, 1913 at Aberystwyth in Wales and Marske again in 1914.

On Saturday, 17 September 1912, the Guiseley Company moved into new accommodation on Victoria Road. A purpose-built drill hall had been constructed which comprised of a basement miniature rifle range, ground floor lecture room and first floor quartermasters, Serjeants and officers' rooms. The building was funded by the West Riding County Territorial Association. There was no formal opening ceremony but the company of 120 men celebrated the occasion with an evening social gathering at which the officers, Captain Wilfred Claughton and Lieutenant Ashley, attended with their wives.

Pre-war photograph of men from Skipton serving in the 6th DWR. (DWR museum)

Right: C Company cadets at Marske, July 1914. Standing L to R: L/Cpl Robert Boothman, L/Cpl Tom Moorhouse, Cpl Wilfred James. Sitting L to R: unknown, Pte Barratt, Pte Archie Lee. (DWR museum)

The machine gun section of the 6th DWR at Marske July 1914. (DWR museum)

The battalion camp at Marske, July 1914. (DWR museum)

Annual camp at Ripon 1911. (DWR museum)

The postcard was sent by Private John Holt Lister to his brother Frank. In 1911 John was 18, an art student, and Frank was 20 and working as an assistant art master. They were living at home with their parents, Clara and Frank senior, a consulting engineer who in 1899 built and patented his own car. John Holt Lister accompanied the battalion when it was sent to the Western Front in April 1915. He was commissioned on 18 December 1916 and managed to remain in the 1/6th DWR. He survived the war and was finally discharged as a lieutenant.

Postcard from Ripon 1911. The men of the 6th DWR parade before Major-General T.S. Baldock. In the centre is Colonel North and Regimental Serjeant Major (later Captain) Churchman is standing on the left. (DWR museum)

Rear image of the same postcard.

Bempton Lane, Flamborough. Annual camp 1912. (DWR museum)

Bridlington Road, Flamborough. Annual camp 1912. (DWR museum)

Organisation of a British infantry battalion c.1905. (Modern Warfare – Ubique)

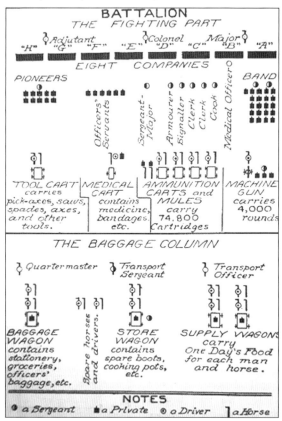

Chapter 1

Embodiment and Deployment

The 6th Duke of Wellington's (West Riding) Regiment (DWR) was formed on 1 April 1908 as part of the Haldane reforms of the British Army. Richard Haldane was the Secretary of State for War from December 1905 to June 1912, and proposed that militias, yeomanry units (men who had access to a horse) and volunteer forces (VF), whose primary role was home defence in a state of emergency, would be combined to create the Territorial Force (TF). Prior to 1908, the Guiseley unit was known as K Company of the 3rd (Volunteer Battalion), The Duke of Wellington's (West Riding) Regiment. The now demolished drill hall used by this unit was located on Springfield Place, Guiseley. This building was used by the Guiseley Territorial Force until 1912 when a new drill hall was built on Victoria Road.

The new TF units of 1908 became a numbered battalion of the local regular army regiment. As well as weekly training sessions, they attended an annual summer training and weekend camps. They were part-time soldiers like the modern Army Reserve and received regular army pay for their time. The men were legally bound to attend the training camps and could find themselves in front of the local magistrate if they defaulted without a good reason.

Their terms of service did not require the men to serve overseas, but they could volunteer as, virtually to a man, they did in 1914. A number of TF men, for whatever reason, did not volunteer and others were required to remain in the United Kingdom, for home service.

On 15 August 1914 orders were issued to separate the home service men from those who had undertaken to serve overseas. This was with the intention of forming reserves made up of the home service men. On 31 August 1914 authority was given to establish a second line division for each of the first line units where more than sixty per cent of the men had volunteered. These divisions were formed from late 1914 onwards, although the permissible strength of a second line unit was initially only half of the normal establishment. This was raised to full establishment early in 1915, after which many of the men were sent overseas, with some playing important parts in the fighting.

When the Military Service Act (conscription) was introduced in 1916, all men were deemed to have agreed to overseas service and thus all second line units became available to be sent abroad. It was at this time that the foreign service battalion was given the prefix number 1 to become the 1/6th DWR, and the home service battalion became known as the 2/6th DWR. Later in the war, the 2/6th DWR was mobilised for foreign service and a home service training battalion was created which became the 3/6th DWR. The men volunteering for overseas service were entitled to wear the Imperial Service Badge above the right breast tunic pocket. The badge, which was made of cupro-nickel, was declared obsolete in October 1920 when the Territorial Force was renamed the Territorial Army.

Imperial service badge.

The 1/6th DWR were part of the West Riding Division, later titled 49th (West Riding) Division. The home service battalion was titled 2/6th DWR and became part of the 2nd West Riding Division, later titled 62nd (2nd West Riding) Division. Many men from Bingley, Haworth, Guiseley, Keighley, Settle, Skipton and the other towns from which the 6th DWR recruited, served in the 2/6th DWR which suffered heavy losses on 3 May 1917 during the attack on the Hindenburg Line at Bullecourt in France.

In August 1914 the West Riding (Territorial) Division (later renamed 49th Division) comprised the following units:

1st West Riding Infantry Brigade (later renamed 146 Brigade) – 1/5th, 1/6th, 1/7th and 1/8th Battalions of the West Yorkshire Regiment.
2nd West Riding Infantry Brigade (later renamed 147 Brigade) – 1/4th, 1/5th, 1/6th and 1/7th Battalions of the Duke of Wellington's (West Riding) Regiment.
3rd West Riding Infantry Brigade (later renamed 148 Brigade) – 1/4th and 1/5th Battalions of the King's Own Yorkshire Light Infantry and the 1/4th and 1/5th Battalions of the York and Lancaster Regiment.
Within 147 Brigade the 1/4th DWR had drill halls in Halifax, Brighouse, Cleckheaton, Elland and Sowerby Bridge.
The 1/5th DWR originated from the Huddersfield area and the 1/7th DWR were based around the Milnsbridge area.

The division was commanded by Major General T.S. Baldock CB and Brigadier General E.F. Brereton DSO commanded the 2nd West Riding Infantry Brigade.

On 26 July 1914 the men of the 2nd West Riding Infantry Brigade attended a two-week summer training camp at Marske, located between Redcar and Saltburn in North Yorkshire. This was the annual training for the brigade units which included the 1/6th DWR comprising seven companies from the following towns: A and B – Skipton, C – Guiseley, D and E – Keighley, F – Settle, G – Haworth and H – Bingley.

Shoulder badge o[f] the 49th (West Riding Division)

Even before the men departed for the camp, tensions had been running high in Europe since the 28 June assassination of Archduke Franz Ferdinand, heir presumptive of the Austro-Hungarian Empire, in Sarajevo, Serbia. A complex series of treaties and alliances existed between Serbia, Russia and France as well as Germany and Austria-Hungary. On 28 July Austria-Hungary declared war on Serbia and on 29 July, there was a general mobilisation of the Russian army which produced an ultimatum from Germany for the Russians to stand down. The following day the mobilisation of the German and French armies was ordered by their respective governments but the Germans had secretly been concentrating troops on the French/Belgian border for several days. On 1 August, Germany declared war on Russia and secretly signed an alliance treaty with the Ottoman Empire. The next day, 2 August, the German army crossed the border into Luxembourg without a declaration of war. On Monday 3 August Germany declared war on France and the Belgian government refused permission for German forces to pass through its territory. On the same day, the 'terriers' camp was broken up and the companies returned to their local drill halls.

On Tuesday 4 August the government of the United Kingdom sent an ultimatum to Germany not to invade Belgium. On the same day, German troops crossed the Belgian border to attack the city of Liège and, just before midnight on 4 August 1914, the Government of the United Kingdom declared war on Germany. The various companies of the 6th DWR received their embodiment orders and the men from Guiseley mustered and marched from the drill hall on Victoria Road to Guiseley station where they boarded a train and travelled to Skipton to join the rest of the battalion.

1914 – Posing outside the Drill Hall on Victoria Road, Guiseley are a group of men about to be trained for service abroad. Lieutenant Malcolm C.M. Law (in uniform) seated in the centre. (Aireborough Historical Society)

On the evening of Tuesday, 4 August 1914, Captain Chaffer and Lieutenant Law departed from Guiseley station with sixty-two men. Crowds assembled from the drill

The Drill Hall, 101years later, now converted into flats.

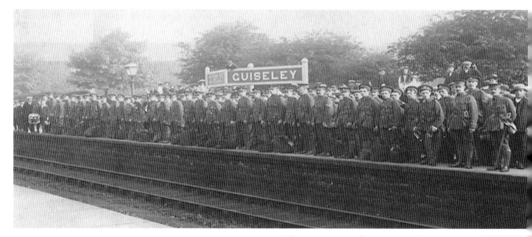

Embodiment – C Company on Platform 1, Guiseley Train Station, August 1914. (Aireborough Historical Society)

Same location in 2016.

hall on Victoria Road to the station to cheer them on their way. The *Wharfedale and Airedale Observer* reported:

> *Long before the hour of the march to the railway station crowds began to gather in Victoria Road, at the tram terminus and along Station Road and by nine o'clock these thoroughfares were packed by a seething mass of the inhabitants, anxious and desirous of giving the Territorials an enthusiastic send-off.*

Canon Francis Howson, Rector of St Oswald's Church in Guiseley placed a roll of honour in the church porch and the church bell was rung for two minutes each day at 12.45pm to remind the inhabitants of the town to pray for the men. Mr Hollingsworth, headmaster of St Oswald's school on The Green, assembled photographs of former pupils to create a patriotic gallery of those who were serving their country.

The 1/6th DWR became part of 147 (West Riding) Brigade of the 49th Division and on 5 August the battalion moved to the small village of Healing in Lincolnshire, between Immingham and Grimsby, to commence training and coastal defence. After about a month they moved 4 miles inland to the village of Riby where they were billeted in a tented camp. Riby was a brigade camp so also present were the other units

Some of the men of F (Settle) Company that called themselves the 'Lucky 13', were serving with the 1/6th Duke of Wellington's (West Riding Regiment). Rear left to right – Walter Yates, Fred Close, Robert Clark, John M. Morphet (killed), Arthur Parker, Thomas Brayshaw, William H. Brassington (killed), William Hirst. Front row, left to right – Charlie Parker, John R. Jackman (killed), John Cardus, Charles Peachy (killed), John S. Hepworth (killed). Taken at Riby Park, Lincolnshire, October 1914. (The Brayshaw Library, Giggleswick School)

that formed the brigade, namely the 1/4th, 1/5th and 1/7th Battalions of the DWR, as well as a battery of artillery from the 4th (West Riding) Howitzer Brigade, Royal Field Artillery. The 10th (Otley) Battery had their HQ at the drill hall in Nelson Street, Otley, opposite the bus station where the Post Office now stands. The 11th (Ilkley) Battery was based in what is now a business centre on Leeds Road and the 4th (Burley-in-Wharfedale) ammunition column was located on Peel Place in a building, since demolished, which was later known as Victoria Hall and is now the site of the scout and guide hut.

Walter Yates enlisted as a private in September 1914 and was posted to France in April 1915. He was commissioned in August 1916; before the war he was the assistant master at Settle school. He eventually became an acting captain and went on to win the Military Cross. The citation reads:

> *For good leadership and devotion to duty whilst in command of the right company. The right flank was completely in the air and the enemy made strong and continuous attacks but the gallantry and example of this officer inspired the company to stick to their position even when the battalion some distance to the right had vacated the line.*

After the war, he moved to Benoni, near Johannesburg in South Africa.

Walter Yates, Fred Close, William H. Brassington, John R. Jackman

Fred Close was born in the United States in 1889 but his family returned to Settle when he was two. Before the war he worked as a clerk at John Delaney's quarry and, whilst serving in the regiment, he was promoted to serjeant and awarded the Meritorious Service Medal. He was discharged in July 1919 and resumed his job at the quarry. He lived at Halstead Cottages in Giggleswick and died in August 1955, aged 70.

William Henry Brassington of Ribble View, Settle, joined the 1/6th DWR at the outbreak of war. He was promoted to serjeant and in November 1915 he was awarded the Military Medal. In August 1916, he was sent for officer training and in December 1916 he was commissioned as an officer in the Machine Gun Corps (Heavy) later to become the Tank Corps. He was killed on 25 August 1918 near Bapaume. His captain wrote:

Early this morning he started off, one of the bravest men anyone could find; he had done magnificent work with his tank, and had knocked out many enemy machine gun nests. He was a fine representative of our Citizen Army, and his country has lost a real hero..

His commanding officer wrote:

He died in fighting the enemy and guiding his tank to its objective near Bapaume. The tank was struck right in front by a large calibre shell, and Lieutenant Brassington and the driver were instantly killed. His death is a great loss to the battalion, for there were few officers who knew more about a tank than he,

He is buried in Achiet-le-Grand Communal Cemetery Extension.

John Robinson Jackman from Hughenden, Long Preston, joined the 1/6th DWR at the outbreak of war. He was educated at Sedburgh School and before the war he was in the wool business with his father. In September 1915, he was wounded in the eye by glass from a trench periscope which had been hit by a bullet. In December 1915 he was commissioned as an officer and in November 1917 transferred to the Royal Flying Corps which was to become the Royal Air Force in April 1918. He was trained as an air observer in No.98 Squadron but on 17 June 1918 he was reported missing after a sortie. A letter sent to his parents reads:

Six of us were returning after a successful bombing expedition, when we were attacked by twenty to thirty enemy machines. A fight ensued, in which two of our machines were brought down within the enemies' lines. Lieut. Jackman was flying in one of the two.

He is also buried at Achiet-le-Grand Communal Cemetery Extension.

John Thomas Cardus was born in Settle in 1886 and before the war worked as a warper at Langcliffe Mill in the town and enlisted in the 1/6th DWR on 8 September 1914 when the battalion was at Healing. He was wounded by a bullet in the right side and hip on 14 April 1918 and evacuated initially to the 99th Field Ambulance, then to No.64 Casualty Clearing Station (CCS). He wounds were serious enough to warrant a transfer to the 55th (Canadian) General Hospital at Boulogne before being evacuated to the UK and receiving treatment at the Royal Victoria Hospital in Folkstone. He was eventually discharged on 31 March 1919 and in 1920 he received a £35 (£1,658 today) gratuity from the pension tribunal board. He eventually moved to Rainhall Road, Barnoldswick.

William Henry Hirst enlisted on 8 September 1914 and was later promoted to serjeant. On 1 December 1917 he was medically discharged through sickness and awarded the Silver War Badge. This was issued to service personnel from the United Kingdom and Empire forces who had been honourably discharged due to wounds or sickness from military service during the Great War. The badge, also known as the Discharge Badge, the Wound Badge or Services Rendered Badge, was first issued in September 1916, along with an official certificate of entitlement. It was about the size of a modern 50p coin, and was to be worn on the right breast of civilian clothes. In the early years of the war, a practice had developed whereby women took it upon themselves to confront and publicly embarrass military-

The Silver War Badge (Europeana 1914-1918 project)

age men not in uniform by presenting them with white feathers as a suggestion of cowardice. Substantial numbers of men who had been discharged with wounds or sickness found themselves on the receiving end of such harassment, so the badge was worn to discourage such activity.

Charles Parker, William H. Hirst, John T. Cardus, Arthur Parker

Charles Parker was commissioned as a second lieutenant in June 1917, posted to the 3rd DWR and was later awarded the Military Cross. Before the war he lived at The Green, Settle and was employed as a clerk to the local Board of Guardians. His father James was a local government officer acting as the relieving officer (issuing poor relief funds) and his three sisters, Mary, Grace and Hilda were all school teachers. His older brother Clifton worked as a tea dealer.

Arthur Parker was a solicitor's clerk and lived at The Green, Settle. He was promoted to colour serjeant and survived the war and was discharged in June 1919. The fate of some of the other men featured in the photograph is mentioned further in the book.

On 1 September 1914, Private Stanley Procter (19) of Victoria Road, Earby died of pneumonia at Grimsby hospital. Before the war he worked as a weaver at B & W Hartley in Earby. He was a pre-war 'terrier' having joined up in October 1912 at Skipton and is buried at Wheatlands Cemetery, Earby.

In October 1914, the battalion moved again to Doncaster, where shooting and trench routines were practised. The men were billeted in schools around the town, with the officers accommodated in hotels and private houses. In December 1914 the 1/6th DWR was reorganised. The two Skipton companies (A and B) became A Company, Bingley (G) and Haworth (H) became B Company, Guiseley (C) and Settle (F) become C Company and the two Keighley companies (D and E) became D Company. Whilst the unit was at Doncaster, Captain and Adjutant Godfrey Henry Ermen, from Gargrave was taken ill and sent home to recuperate. He died on 4 May 1915 at Milton House, Gargrave and was buried with full military honours in St Andrew's Church in the village. He was the general manager of the English Sewing Company of Belle Vue Mills, Skipton which manufactured Dewhurst's cotton products. He was the son of German immigrant parents and had previously served in the 6th Manchester Regiment and saw active service in the Second Boer War.

Private S. Procter's headstone. (CPGW)

At Doncaster the battalion was joined by Bandmaster George Ramplin who, at 74 years of age, was the oldest member of the regiment. He had an illustrious career in the military, starting at the age of 15 when he joined the band of the 20th Hussars before transferring to the 13th Hussars where he rose to the rank of trumpet-major. He transferred again to the 19th Hussars with whom he served in the Egyptian Campaign of 1882. After his retirement from the army, he became bandmaster of the City of Leeds Police Band and when they were disbanded three years later, he took up a position as bandmaster of the 22nd Bombay Infantry in India, a position which he held for three years. He returned to Leeds and became bandmaster of the Leeds Artillery where he

Headstone in St Andrew's churchyard. Captain Godfrey Henry Ermen. (CPGW)

remained for fourteen years. In 1910 he finally retired, but in 1912 the call of the khaki resulted in his appointment as bandmaster to the 1/6th DWR.

Four brothers from Skipton who enlisted shortly after the outbreak of war also served with the 1/6th DWR at Doncaster. William (24), John (26), Thomas (33) and Arthur (19) were the sons of Edward and Annie Ireland of King's Street, Skipton.

John worked as a labourer at a brewery and originally joined the Skipton Company of the 3rd (Volunteer) West Riding Regiment in 1906 and transferred to the TF in 1908. He survived the war and was discharged in March 1919.

9

The Ireland brothers. (British Newspaper Archive)

Bandmaster George Ramplin. (British Newspaper Archive)

1915. The signal platoon of the 1/6th DWR. Lieutenant Anthony Slingsby is standing to the left. In the rear rank, second man from the right is Private Sam Bancroft of Silsden, who later transferred to the Royal Engineers, 49th Divisional Signal Company. He was originally a member of the Keighley Company and landed in France with the battalion in 1915. He died of wounds on 11 October 1918 at No.23 Casualty Clearing Station at Agnez-lès-Duisans. He was the former scout master of the 1st Silsden Scout Troop and left a widow, Nora. (CPGW)

Thomas was employed as a plate-layer (laying and maintaining train tracks) for the Midland Railway Company and on arrival in France he transferred to the Royal Engineers. He survived and was discharged in March 1919. William was an over-looker at a cotton mill. He was promoted to serjeant and in August 1917 he was killed by a German shell at Nieuport. Arthur was employed as a bobbin-carrier at a cotton mill at the outbreak of war. He survived and was discharged in February 1919. Whilst the brothers were in training at Doncaster, they received the sad news that their mother Annie had died and were all granted compassionate leave to attend the funeral.

The officers of the 1/6th Duke of Wellington's (West Riding) Regiment. (CPGW)

On 9 March 1915, Private Thomas Higson Percy, 21 of Tems Street, Giggleswick, died at the Bradford Royal Infirmary under anaesthetic during an operation for a hernia, caused by being accidently thrown over the handlebars of a bicycle at Doncaster on 26 January. He was a pre-war 'terrier' having originally signed up in 1910 and is buried in St John the Evangelist Graveyard at Langcliffe near Settle.

Private T.H. Percy's headstone. (CPGW)

11

Chapter 2

Deployment to the Western Front – Fleurbaix

Between 12 and 15 April 1915, the 1/6th DWR was posted to the Western Front as part of the British Expeditionary Force (BEF). They arrived via Southampton and Folkestone and on 26 April, after a period of familiarisation which involved shadowing men of the London Regiment in the front line, the battalion moved to the front and relieved the Kensington Battalion of that regiment at Fleurbaix in the Pas de Calais region of France. The strength of the battalion was 29 officers and 1,004 other ranks, with one officer and ten other ranks attached, plus Serjeant Roux of the French 357 Infanterie Régiment as interpreter. It was at this time that the West Riding Division was renamed the 49th Division, and the West Riding Brigade renamed 147 Brigade.

On 22 April 1915 the Germans used chlorine gas to attack the French army near the village Gravenstafel north-east of Ypres. Approximately 171 tons of gas was released from cylinders which drifted across no man's land in a greenish-yellow cloud towards the allied line held by French Territorial and Moroccan colonial troops. None of these men had any protection from the toxic chemicals and understandably fled in panic from the trenches. Nearly 6,000 casualties were recorded, but the Germans failed to exploit the gas attack and the line was held with the help of 2 and 3 Canadian Brigades.

Rudimentary protection against a chlorine gas attack was quickly provided which consisted of cotton wool wrapped in gauze which was soaked in sodium hyposulphite liquid, known by the men as 'hypo'. Old ammunition boxes containing 'hypo' were placed at intervals along the trench to soak the gauze. These were uncomfortable to wear, difficult to keep in position and practically useless against anything but a weak concentration of chlorine. The P helmet was quickly developed which consisted of a cloth hood, impregnated with sodium phenate and a vision window made from an early form of plastic called mica. This was very fragile and the smallest crack would render the helmet useless. They had to be inspected at least three times a day and there was a high wastage rate due to damage. Later versions were treated with phenate hexamine and were known as PH helmets which had two glass eye pieces in place of the mica window. These provided enhanced protection, but after a short period of use the vision apertures misted up and prolonged use resulted in a build-up of exhaled CO_2. Later versions had a rubber tube installed through which the wearer could exhale.

On 27 April 1915 the battalion suffered the first combat fatality of the war. Private

A Vickers machine gun team wearing PH helmets.

P helmet with mica vision window.

James Walsh, (18) from Keighley was on a working party when he was killed by a rifle bullet and on 29 April, Private's Fred Pickles (23) from Keighley and Thomas Critcheson from Methley were both killed by a shell whilst in the reserve billets area and Private James William (Willie) Scott was wounded by a bullet. The two dead men had to be buried where the shell landed due to Private Pickles being so badly mutilated. The following day, 30 April, was quiet with no casualties.

<u>CASUALTIES:</u> In April the battalion had 3 men killed and 2 wounded.

A Grenadier Guards unit during a PH helmet inspection. (Big Push magazine)

May 1915

On 2 May 1915 the battalion was relieved by the 1/4th DWR and moved to billets on the Rue de Quesne at Fleurbaix. Private James William (Willie) Scott from Century Place, Embsay who had been wounded on 29 April, died at No.2 Casualty Clearing Station (CCS) at Merville. Before the war, he was employed at the Skipton Rock Company. He had been on sentry duty when he was hit in the neck by a bullet which lodged against his spinal column causing instant paralysis. He is buried at Merville Communal Cemetery.

Private James W. Scott. (CPGW)

The CCS was part of the casualty evacuation chain further back from the front line than the Regimental Aid Posts (RAP) and Advanced Dressing Stations (ADS). It was staffed by men of the Royal Army Medical Corps (RAMC), with attached Royal Engineers (RE) and men of the Army Service Corps (ASC). The role of the CCS was to treat a man sufficiently for his return to duty or to prepare him for evacuation to a base

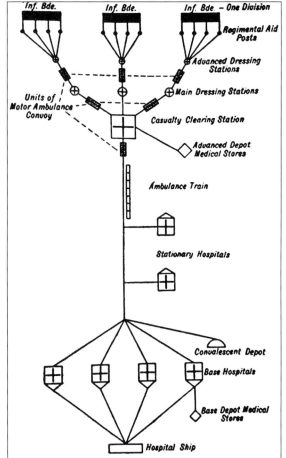

Diagram illustrating the medical evacuation system of the BEF.

hospital. It was not a place for a long-term stay. CCSs were generally located near railway lines to facilitate movement of casualties from the battlefield and on to the base hospitals. Although they were quite large, CCSs were mobile and moved quite frequently, especially in the wake of the great German offensives in the spring of 1918 and the allied advances later that year. The locations of wartime CCSs can often be identified today from the cluster of military cemeteries that surround them.

On 3 and 4 May a working party of 200 men was employed digging bombproof shelters. On 5 May, the battalion relieved the 1/4th DWR in the front line trenches during which one man was wounded. On 6 May Private Alan Linfoot (21) of 18 Prospect Street, Rawdon was accidently shot in the thigh and died of his injuries. Another soldier, Private Pickles, was cleaning his loaded rifle when he pulled the trigger. Private Linfoot was a pre-war 'terrier' who joined the TF in September 1911 at Guiseley. Before the war he worked on Yeadon High Street as a leather presser. One other man was also wounded after being shot in the face.

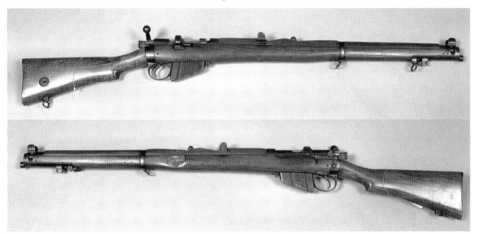

Short Magazine Lee-Enfield Mk I (also known as SMLE) .303 calibre, maximum sighted range, 3,000 yards, 10 round box magazine. (Armémuseum, Stockholm)

On 7 May, Private Thomas Foster (27) from Foulridge near Colne was wounded in the head and died almost immediately. He had previously served in the 3rd (Volunteer) Battalion of the West Riding Regiment before transferring to the 1/6th DWR in 1908. Before the war, he worked on the railway and left a wife and four children. The sad news of his death came in a letter from another local 'terrier' to his wife at Skipton.

At 4.30am on 9 May a heavy German artillery barrage landed at Dead Dog Farm dug-outs which lasted for most of the day but only caused one casualty. Private John Ireland, one of four brothers serving in the battalion, was hit on the side of the head by shrapnel and evacuated to the UK. He recovered from his wound and by the

Private Thomas Foster (CPGW)

end of the month he was fit enough to return to the battalion. Later that day the battalion was relieved by the 1/4th DWR and moved to brigade reserve at Croix Blanche, 2 miles to the rear. During the relief, Private Harry Thomas (36) from Barnoldswick was shot in the head and killed. Eight other men were also wounded by rifle and shell fire. Harry Thomas was born in Manchester but lived in Barnoldswick and worked as a weaver at Thomas Nutter & Co at Wellhouse Mill. He was a pre-war 'terrier' who joined the TF at Skipton in 1913, having had previous service in the 2nd (Volunteer) Battalion of the East Lancashire Regiment.

At this stage of the war, British soldiers still wore their cloth service cap which provided no ballistic protection whatsoever. The distinctive 'Brodie' steel helmet did not become general issue until the beginning of 1916 and hand grenades, or bombs as they were known, consisted of the type 1 grenade. This was a metal cylinder with a detachable 12-inch long cane handle and a contact detonator which exploded when it hit a hard surface. The device was armed by pulling a pin at the top and after it was thrown, linen streamers attached to the handle unfurled to ensure it landed nose first. This grenade was very unpopular with the troops as it was liable to explode prematurely if it came into contact with an object whilst being thrown – highly likely in a trench environment.

Type 1 hand grenade. (York Museums Trust)

As a safer option, the troops made their own hand-thrown explosives, consisting of empty jam tins filled with explosive and 'dockyard confetti' (i.e. empty bullet cases, barbed wire snippings, nails, nuts and bolts) for shrapnel and a simple burning fuse. A 'trench industry' production line made the devices,which proved quite effective. The Mills bomb was developed and patented by William Mills and initially manufactured at the Mills factory in Birmingham. Between April 1915 and late 1918, over 75 million had been produced. According to Mills' original design notes, the outer casing grooves were to aid the thrower's grip in wet or muddy conditions, not to assist fragmentation. The Mk.1 Type 5 Mills bomb became general issue during May 1915, with the Type 23 rifle grenade following shortly after.

On 10 May the battalion occupied the brigade reserve trenches and dug-outs and on 11 and 12 May, they moved about a mile to the rear into billets on the Rue de Quesne

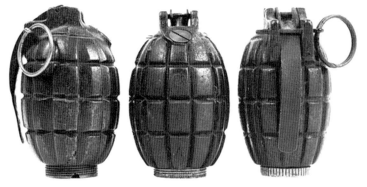

Mk.1 type 5 Mills Bomb later known as the hand grenade.

at Fleurbaix. On 13 May the battalion relieved the 1/4th DWR in the front line trenches during which three men were wounded by rifle fire, one of which was reported as self-inflicted. On 14 May at 12.11am orders were received for a test SOS (response to enemy attack) and an artillery bombardment commenced on the German lines for thirty minutes, followed by rapid rifle fire.

Private Harold Little (24) from Keighley was killed after being shot in the head and five other men were wounded. Harold Little was born in Skipton but lived and worked in Keighley as a self-employed coal merchant. He was a pre-war 'terrier' who joined the TF at Keighley in 1912. He left a wife and two children and was the brother of Private Stanley Little (22), also from Keighley, who was serving in the 2/6th DWR when he was killed on 23 March 1917.

The same routine was carried out the following day at midnight, 5am and 9am. The rapid rifle fire lasted for three minutes, a five minutes pause, then two minutes rapid fire. The next day, 16 May, three men were wounded by shrapnel. The following day was wet and the trenches quickly became very muddy. The battalion was relieved by the 1/4th DWR and returned to billets at Rue de Quesne, during which one man was wounded. The battalion spent 18 and 19 May in billets, but Private Arthur Wilson (23), from Earby near Barnoldswick, was killed by a shell explosion whilst returning to the reserve billets after working on a communications trench. Born in Silsden, he lived and worked in Earby as a cotton weaver for the Coates Manufacturing Co at Victoria Shed and enlisted in October 1914. He was a Sunday school teacher at the Methodist church in the town and a member of the church choir.

Private Arthur Wilson (CPGW)

On 20 May one man was wounded whilst in the trenches on a working party and the next day the battalion relieved the 1/4th DWR in the trenches. Two men were wounded, one self-inflicted and another man was injured by his own bayonet whilst jumping from the parapet to escape German shell fire. During the next two days, 21 and 22 May, several men were diagnosed with German measles (rubella). Diseases like this were a serious concern due to the speed which it spreads in close confinement and, although rarely fatal, epidemic proportions amongst the men could impact on the unit's fighting ability.

On 23 May HQ dug-out at Dead Dog Farm was shelled, but no injuries were caused although one man suffered two compound fractures of the legs after a shell, fired at a German aircraft, fell

Captain Charles H. Petty. (CPGW)

through the roof of his dug-out. Lieutenant (later Captain) Charles Henry Petty from Crosshills near Keighley was wounded in the abdomen by a bullet which ricocheted off a spade. He survived the war but died of his wounds on 2 June 1921 aged 28. He was the son of Francis William and Edith Petty of Lingstead Hall, Glusburn. After the war, he entered the family business in Bradford with his yarn merchant father. He is buried in the north-east corner of St Andrew's church graveyard, Kildwick.

On 24 May several German shells landed along the Convent Wall trenches but no casualties were caused. Located in this section of the line were the ruins of a Carthusian abbey whose perimeter formed part of the

The headstone of Captain Charles H. Petty.

Convent Wall trench system. During the war, seventy allied soldiers were buried in the grounds of the abbey and at the end of the war the remains were exhumed and reburied at the Rue-David Commonwealth War Graves Commission (CWGC) Cemetery at Fleurbaix.

On 25 May the British artillery bombarded the German lines. The barrage was fired at midnight, 1am, 3am and 8am and one man was wounded by a ricochet bullet. At 5.30pm, the battalion was relieved by the 1/4th DWR. A and B Companies went into billets, C went to Croix Blanche and D went to Croix Marechal as support. The following three days were spent in billets and at 5.30pm on 29 May, the battalion relieved the 1/4th DWR in the front line. Lance Corporal Seth Lake from Keighley was killed after being shot in the head during the relief. Before the war, he was employed as a labourer and he joined the TF in June 1914 having previously served in the 3rd (Volunteer) Battalion of the West Riding Regiment. He left a wife and three children.

On 30 May Lieutenant Hedley Knowles (22) from Skipton was killed and two soldiers injured by the premature explosion of a type 23 rifle grenade at the bombing training school at Fleurbaix. The type 23 rifle grenade came with a screw-on rod which, when attached, was placed down the barrel of the rifle. The grenade itself was held in situ by a holder on the muzzle of the rifle. Whilst in the holder, the pin was pulled, but the fly-off lever was held in position. The butt of the rifle was placed on the ground and the grenade was launched by firing a special blank cartridge. Accuracy with this weapon system was gained by experience as there was no specific aiming sight. The grenade had a flight range of about 137 yards and the fuse took five seconds to detonate. The effective 'kill' radius was 30 yards but could be extended to 100 yards on hard ground. If required, the type 23 could be thrown like a conventional grenade. Before the war, Hedley Knowles had worked as an articled clerk for his father Marmaduke Redmayne Knowles, who was the clerk to the Skipton Rural District Council.

Lieutenant Hedley Knowles (CPGW)

Three other soldiers were wounded in the face and eyes by broken glass from trench periscopes, used to observe the front from the relative safety of the trench. On 31 May notification was received that the 49th Division had been transferred to the Indian Corps, under the command of General Sir James Willcocks.

Type 23 rifle grenade.

CASUALTIES: In May the battalion had 12 men killed and 58 wounded

June 1915
There was sporadic German shelling on 1 June 1915 and one man was wounded by rifle fire. On 2 June, thirty-two German shells fell to the rear of battalion HQ and Private William Chisman from Bradford was shot in the head and died of his injuries at No.10 Stationary Hospital at St Omer on 8 June. Two other men were wounded by rifle fire.

In the British Army of the 1980s there was a superstition that could trace its origins back to the trenches of the Great War. When a group of soldiers paused for a cigarette break (as nearly everybody smoked!), there was a great reluctance to be the third man to light his cigarette from the match, as to do so would bring bad luck. This was known as 'the third light'. At night, when a soldier struck a match to light a cigarette, the flame would be seen by a German sniper, the second man to take a light would give the sniper an aiming point and when the flame moved to the third man, the shot would be fired.

At 6pm the battalion was relieved by the 1/4th DWR and went into billets at Rue de Quesne. Working parties were provided on 3 June when one man was wounded by

19

shrapnel and another was shot in the back whilst returning to the billet. On 4 June when a working party was provided to dig a communication trench, two men were wounded by rifle fire. At 4pm a shrapnel shell exploded above a working party causing serious injuries to six men.

Shrapnel shells were used extensively by both sides. They were fired like conventional artillery, but were fitted with a time fuse which was adjusted to detonate whilst the shell was still in flight. It was usually timed to explode when the projectile was 15 to 20 feet above ground level and once detonated, the projectiles in the shell, usually lead balls, were fired out of the iron shell case by an explosive charge, spraying the ground below.

On 5 June Private Peter Spencer (21) from Bingley died from a bullet wound to the chest and Private Frederick W. Cartman (26) from Skipton, died from wounds he received on 31 May. Private Cartman had been operating a trench water pump when he was shot by a sniper. He was from a well-known family of Skipton sportsmen and for several seasons he was a member of the Skipton Council Cricket Team. His cousin, Private Thomas Boothman Cartman (22) from Brook View, Skipton died of wounds on 12 July 1916 whilst serving

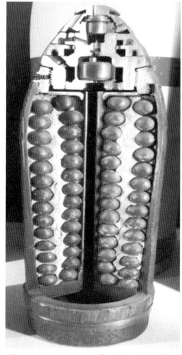

Cutaway section of a British 18lb shrapnel shell.

in the 10th (Service) DWR. His other cousin, Private Charles Branston (20) from Brook Street, Skipton was killed in action on 12 October 1916 whilst serving with the 2nd DWR.

On 6 June a church service was held and later that day the battalion relieved the 1/4th DWR in the front line. The following day was described as quiet with no shelling, but Private John Midgley (25) from Ingrow, Keighley was shot in the neck and killed.

Two extra mobile field kitchens also arrived, making one available per company. The field kitchens were horse drawn and positioned to the rear of the line along with the battalion transport contingent. Hot food was prepared and carried to the front line in containers, but enemy activity often prevented this. As an alternative, the men used the Tommy Cooker. This was the trade name given to what was a small portable tin of solid fuel on which pans or tins were placed. The fuel was solidified alcohol which was smokeless, an important factor given the accuracy of German snipers, and although notoriously slow, they were often used to heat tins of Maconochie stew.

On 10 June 1915 Private Sam Hargreaves (21), from Skipton, was shot in the head and killed and one other man was wounded in the head by shrapnel. Sam Hargreaves was one of three brothers who died during the war. He was a pre-war 'terrier', having joined up in 1912, and before the war he was employed by Hartley Bros. of Union Street, Skipton as a weaver. He was the brother of Private John Robert Hargreaves

(26), who was serving in the Grenadier Guards when he died of pneumonia at Caterham Hospital on 26 April 1915. His other brother, George Hargreaves (21) was serving in the Tank Corps when he was killed in action on 29 September 1918.

On 12 June 1915 the battalion was relieved by the 1/4th DWR and returned to billets at Rue de Quesne, Fleurbaix. A Company was billeted at Croix Blanche. On 13 June a church parade was held and between 2pm and 3pm the Germans shelled the area near the billets but no casualties were caused. On 14 June the German artillery was active between 9.30pm and 11pm but again without casualties, but the following day 174 high explosive shells landed during the day. Amazingly only one man was slightly wounded on the nose by shrapnel. On 16 June, B Company relieved A Company at Croix Blanche.

Private Frederick W. Cartman.

The 17th was described as a quiet day, the only excitement being a German aircraft which was seen flying over the billeting area. There was, however, time for a game of cricket. A Company played C on a pitch which was shell cratered and close to the reserve trenches. C Company won by an impressive 97 runs to 22. Lance Corporal John (Jack) Middleton Morphett of Settle, one of the 'lucky thirteen', scored twelve runs and took six wickets. Jack was an accomplished cricketer having been part of the Settle team which won the Ribblesdale cricket league in 1914. Before the war he worked as a school attendance officer for the county council but was originally from Sedbergh, where he trained as a solicitor's clerk. Unfortunately, just short of two months later he was killed by a German bullet. Lance Corporal (later promoted to colour serjeant)

Private Sam Hargreaves. (Both CPGW)

Arthur Parker, an old team mate from Settle Cricket Club and one of the 'lucky thirteen', also played. Second Lieutenant Nicholas Geldard from Cappleside, Rathmell near Settle (later promoted to captain and winner of the Distinguished Service Order (DSO) and Military Cross (MC)) managed a modest three runs. He was educated at Giggleswick School, Winchester College and Cambridge University where he took a degree in engineering. Between 1911 and 1913, he worked in South Africa for John Fowler & Co. Steam Plough Works of Leeds and later in the war, he was promoted to the rank of major and was attached to the Tank Corps. After the war, he became the assistant manager of John Fowler & Co. in Leeds. He died on 27 July 1965 at Middleton Hospital near Ilkley, aged 76.

Another member of the C Company XI was Corporal Hugh Marsden Claughton, grandson of the former Guiseley boot factory owner, Hugh Claughton and nephew of Major Wilfred Claughton, former officer commanding the Guiseley Company. Hugh Marsden Claughton was a former Yorkshire Cricket Club player who made his county debut on 22 June 1914 against Leicestershire at Bradford Park Avenue. In the match at Fleurbaix, he scored twenty runs and took five wickets. On 24 November 1916 he was commissioned as a second lieutenant in the Machine Gun Corps (Heavy), which on 27 July 1917 became the became the Tank Corps. He was posted to the 7th Battalion and later promoted to the rank of captain. He survived the war and spent several years as a professional cricketer. He saw out his later years in the Harrogate area and died in 1990, aged 88.

Hugh's brother, Harry Claughton, also played in the match. Harry was a former pupil of Ilkley Grammar School and before the war he was the manager of the family boot factory in Guiseley. He transferred to the Army Pay Corps (APC) and was promoted to lance serjeant. He survived the war and was discharged in January 1919. The third brother Sidney Claughton enlisted in the Royal Garrison Artillery (RGA) in December 1915 but remained on the army reserve list until March 1917 when he was mobilised. He was discharged in January 1919.

On 25 June 1915, the *West Yorkshire Pioneer* newspaper printed the following account of the cricket match:

The following is a report sent by a Lance Corporal in the Settle Territorials, who is at the front:

A cricket match of considerable interest was played between teams of 'A' and 'C' Companies of the 6th Duke of Wellington's Regiment on Thursday evening, 17th instant. The ground situated between two burnt down farm houses, not far behind the firing line, was in a rough condition, dotted here and there with shell holes, and during the progress of the game, shells were bursting not far away on both right and left. The game was keenly followed by men of the companies concerned, with aeroplanes hovering over and around an old game in a new setting. The lads from Settle and Guiseley proved far too strong for the Skiptonians, as will be seen from the scores etc., below, Morphet and Claughton both bowled in fine style, and the men of 'A' Company put a very feeble show.

'C' Company
Lance-Corpl. J.M. Morphet b Burgess – 12
Pte. H. Claughton c E. Smith b Drummond – 2
Pte. H.M. Claughton c Petty b J. Smith – 20
Pte. Patterson b Lambert – 22
Pte. Chas. Parker c Lieut. Supple b Lambert – 7
Lieut. Whitaker lbw b Lambert – 3
Lieut. N. Geldard b Lambert – 3
Pte. F. Close lbw b Lieut. Supple – 0
Pte. J. Cardus not out – 11
Lance-Corpl. Denison b Lambert – 1
Pte. C. Peachy b Lambert – 0
Lance-Corpl. Arthur Parker b Lambert – 0
Extras – 16
Total – 97

'A' Company
Pte. Burgess c Peachy b Morphet – 4
Pte. Rimmer c Lieut. Whitaker b H.M. Claughton – 0
Pte. Drummond c Denison b Morphet – 0
Lance-Corpl. Ireland c Patterson b Morphet – 1
Pte. Petty c and b H.M. Claughton – 8
Pte. Kaye b H.M. Claughton – 0
Pte. J. Smith b H.M. Claughton – 5
Pte. Walton c A. Parker (wicket keeper) b Morphet – 0
Lieut. E.J.C. Supple c Lieut. Geldard b Claughton – 0
Pte. N. Smith b Morphet – 3
Pte. E. Smith b Morphet – 0
Lance-Corpl. Lambert not out – 0
Extras – 1
Total – 22

On 18 June the battalion relieved the 1/4th DWR in the front line without incident. The following day was quiet with no casualties, but on 20 June, the Germans shelled the area of the HQ dug-outs. Luckily, a shell which landed close to the dug-out was a dud, but others were not as two men were wounded in the head and neck by shrapnel. On 21 June one man was slightly wounded on the shoulder. The remainder of the day passed relatively quietly and there were no further casualties.

Hugh Marsden Claughton pictured as an officer in the Machine Gun Corps (Heavy), later known as The Tank Corps. (Susan CMH, Ancestry.com)

On 22 June 1915 Second Lieutenant (later Captain) Barclay Godfrey Buxton joined the battalion. He was the son of the Reverend Barclay F. Buxton, a Methodist missionary in Japan and the great-grandson of Sir Thomas Buxton, 1st Baronet, slavery abolitionist and social reformer, who was the great nephew of Elizabeth Fry, the Quaker prison reformer and member of the chocolate-making dynasty. His elder brother, Second Lieutenant George Barclay Buxton, The Norfolk Regiment, was attached to the Royal Flying Corps, when he was killed in action on 28 July 1917.

Second Lieutenant Barclay Godfrey Buxton was later to become the officer commanding D Company and was very much respected by the men under his command. Before the war, he spent a year at Trinity College, Cambridge studying maths and was a member of the Cambridge Christian Union. Having a Quaker background, he took solace from the Bible which has numerous warrior saints who fought on the side of righteousness; he took the view that if wrong was to be righted, a Christian should be one of those doing it.

At the outbreak of war, he joined the Royal Army Medical Corps at Bury St Edmonds as a private and was posted to the 1st East Anglian Field Ambulance Unit and treated returning wounded soldiers at King's College, Cambridge. A friend's father who was the land agent to Lord Hothfield of Skipton Castle, wrote a letter to his son stating that junior officers were required for the 1/6th DWR and, late in 1914, the newly commissioned Second Lieutenant Buxton joined the regiment. The family name of Barclay stems from the Quaker family who founded Barclays Bank. Captain Barclay Godfrey Buxton MC was seriously wounded in 1918 by shrapnel damage to both legs and invalided back to the UK. After the war, his injuries restricted missionary work abroad, so he founded a missionary training college at Upper Norwood in south-east London. He died in 1986, aged 90.

On 23 June three shells landed near the HQ dug-out but fortunately no injuries were caused although one man was wounded by rifle fire. The following day passed quietly and on 25 June, the battalion was relieved from the Fleurbaix front by the 5th Black Watch and the East Lancashire Regiment. They moved to reserve billets at Doulieu, where the remainder of the month was spent cleaning kit and equipment.

Second Lieutenant (later Captain) Barclay Godfrey Buxton MC. (CPGW)

CASUALTIES: In June the battalion had 4 men killed and 28 wounded.

Chapter 3

Ypres

July 1915

On 1 July 1915 the battalion moved to Sint Jan-ter-Biezen in Belgium, 10 miles west of the town of Ypres. The battalion was now part of VI Corps of the Second Army commanded by General Herbert Plumer who had formerly been the General Officer Commanding (GOC) the Northern Command of which the West Riding Division was a part. Most of the pre-deployment training in the UK had been carried out under his command, so it was rumoured he had more than a passing interest in the 49th Division.

The men were accommodated in a tented camp and began a routine of inspections, parades and church services. On 7 July 1915 the commanding officer (CO), adjutant and four company commanders travelled by London motor bus to the village of Elverdinghe and then on to Brielen, just west of Ypres. They were to act as an advance party as the battalion was due to take over the front line north of Ypres around the Yser canal. On 8 July the battalion moved from Sint Jan-ter-Biezen to Brielen into another tented camp, where they remained for the next four days. Also on 8 July, at divisional HQ at the Chateau les Trois Tours, just west of Brielen, Major General T.S. Baldock was wounded by shrapnel and Major General E.M. Percival took command of the 49th Division.

On 13 July 1915 orders were given to relieve the 1/7th DWR which was holding the line north of Ypres on the banks of the Yser canal. The canal runs northwards from Ypres towards Nieuport where it joins the English Channel on the Belgian coast. Bridges across the canal in this sector were well within the sights of the German machine guns and were constantly destroyed by shell fire. As the 1/6th DWR began the relief, the Germans began firing phosgene gas shells and launched an attack on a short section of the line that was repelled but two men from the battalion were wounded by gas inhalation. The relief was postponed until the following day when the men of the 1/6th DWR replaced their comrades from the 1/7th DWR, one platoon at a time.

The area on both sides of the canal was described as sheer desolation. Wet weather had turned the whole area into a quagmire, the front line in places was more than 2ft deep in thick mud with portions completely isolated from neighbouring posts. The only access to these posts was across country which could be extremely hazardous during daylight hours. Stretches of communication trenches were waist deep in muddy water – and this was in the summer months. Conditions were to get worse as autumn and winter approached, although winter frosts gave a temporary relief from the mud. In various locations, the German line was no more than 15 yards from the British and they made use of their higher position to pump water from their trenches which then flowed downhill towards the British line. If a man was wounded early in the day, he would have to wait until after dark to be safely evacuated to the aid post, which itself was not without added risk as the German machine guns routinely swept the canal crossings throughout the night. During a relief, it was not uncommon for a man to become stuck fast in the mud and have to be rescued by his comrades, sometimes leaving his boots in the mud and continuing in stockinged feet. No regular division had stayed in the line for more than six weeks, but the men of the 49th Division were to hold the line here for six months.

On 15 July Lieutenant Anthony Edward King Slingsby (26), from Carla Beck, Carleton, Skipton, was shot in the head and killed whilst laying a telephone cable opposite a German trench. He was the officer commanding the signal platoon and before the war had been a district commissioner for the Boy Scouts. When he obtained his commission in the 6th DWR, many of the older boys in his scout troop also joined the TF and became the core of the battalion's signal platoon. He was one of five brothers, only two of whom survived the war.

One of his brothers, Captain Arthur Morris Slingsby attended Wellington College near Sandhurst before being commissioned in the Indian Army in 1908. He was killed on 8 March 1916 in Mesopotamia (Iraq) whilst serving with the 56th Punjabi Rifles and is commemorated on the Basra Memorial. His other brother, Lieutenant Stephen Henry Slingsby RN, was killed on 31 May 1916 whilst serving on HMS *Defence*. The ship sank with the loss of the entire complement of 903 men during the Battle of Jutland. Lieutenant Charles Slingsby, cousin of Anthony, was accidently killed on 7 August 1915 whilst training with the Argyll and Sutherland Highlanders in Edinburgh. Another cousin, Captain Henry Lawrence Slingsby, adjutant of the 10th Duke of Cornwall's Light Infantry, died of wounds on 11 August 1917.

Lieutenant Anthony Slingsby.

The parents of Lieutenant Anthony Slingsby received the news of his death in a letter sent by one of his men who was formerly the groom to his father, Mr J.A. Slingsby JP. Enquires were made by Mr Slingsby with his son's bankers but later the same day official news arrived which confirmed the bad news. Lieutenant Slingsby had been offered a staff appointment in the relative safety of the rear area but he declined as it would mean leaving 'his boys'. He had studied at Oxford University where he was his college's Captain of the Boats and President of the College Committee. He is buried in Bard Cottage Cemetery near Ypres.

A newly appointed officer was encouraged to open a bank account, usually with the firm of Cox & Co. The company acted as any normal bank, but most officers had their accounts with them since they understood the army way of life. The firm did not just issue pay and manage officers' bank accounts. Its insurance department could arrange to insure the officer's kit, the income tax department could deal with his tax returns and the standing order department would ensure that his tailor was paid regularly. Cox's also sent a cashier with a supply of money to every hospital ship as it arrived to enable wounded officers to cash cheques. There had also been instances of the bank locating captured officers and informing relatives of their whereabouts. A missing officer's cheque was often the first intimation of his being a prisoner of war as all cheques cashed by officer prisoners in Germany passed through the hands of Cox & Co.

On 30 July a memorial service was held in Skipton Parish Church in memory of Lieutenant Slingsby. The Skipton 'bulldog' scout troop, of which he was a past scout master, was present along with scout troops from Carleton, Skipton Grammar School, Skipton Parish Church, 1st and 2nd Silsden, Barnoldswick and Kildwick numbering about 200 boys. Black hatbands were placed round the boy's headdress and scoutmasters wore black armbands. The parade formed up in the club room of the bulldog troop and marched to the church via Coach Street and Water Street. The service was taken by Archdeacon Cook who read the 30th Psalm. (*I will extol thee, O Lord; for thou hast lifted me up, and hast not made my foes to rejoice over me.*)

Also on 15 July, Private Horace Marshall (24) from Middlesmoor, near Pateley Bridge, was killed. Before the war he had been working on a farm at Hetton, near Skipton. On the same day, his friend, Private Rhodes Spence (20) from Silsden was caught in a shell explosion and suffered a fractured pelvis and femur. He died of his injuries on 17 July in No.10 CCS at Abeele. Before the war he was employed as a weaver at Messrs. John Knox, Airedale Shed, Silsden and enlisted in December 1914. He is buried at Lijssenthoek Military Cemetery.

Private Rhodes Spence. (All CPGW)

Private Horace Marshall.

Two other men were wounded by bullet and shrapnel. The trenches were waterlogged and thick with mud and German trench mortars kept up a constant bombardment of the British lines. Mortars (Minenwerfer or mine-thrower) and grenade throwers (Granatenwerfer) were widely used by both sides but the Germans were quicker off the mark in their use. They were portable, required fewer men and less training to operate than conventional artillery and could be fired from the relative safety of the trench. Also, their high trajectory meant they could be positioned close to the enemy and still be effective.

The 2-inch Medium Trench Mortar, nicknamed the 'Toffee Apple' or 'Plum Pudding' mortar, was a British smooth bore muzzle-loading medium trench mortar in use in the First World War from mid-1915 to mid-1917. The designation '2-inch' refers to the mortar barrel, into which only the 22in bomb shaft, but not the bomb itself, was inserted; the spherical bomb itself was 9in (230mm) in diameter and weighed 42lb (19kg).

Granatenwerfer (grenade thrower).

The 2-inch medium trench mortar.

2017, an unexploded projectile from a Granatenwerfer on the old front line at Neuve Chapelle.

Stock pile of 2-inch 'Toffee Apple' mortar bombs (Wikipedia)

The German line in places was only 20 yards from the British trenches, so great care had to be taken as it was well within throwing distance of German stick grenades. On 16 July trench mortars and grenades were causing problems and four men were wounded. The next day was wet, causing the trenches to flood and two men were wounded by shell fire. On 18 July, a sentry from C Company shot and killed a German who was seen close to the British trench parapet. The body was recovered and documents on it showed he belonged to the 240th Infantry Regiment. German trench mortars were causing casualties amongst the forward lines so the same day an artillery barrage was requested to target a particularly troublesome enemy sap which contained a trench mortar. The barrage lasted about half an hour, after which it was considerably quieter, but the casualties continued. Private William Lister (27) from Barnoldswick was shot in the head and killed. He is buried in Artillery Wood Cemetery, 4 miles north of Ypres. He was a member of the Barnoldswick football team and the brother-in-law of Private John Robert Parker (19) from Barnoldswick, who was serving in the 1/6th DWR when he was killed in action on 11 April 1918.

Also on 18 July, Private Stephen Bishop (37) and Private John Wiggan, both from Skipton, were killed and six other men wounded by a German grenade that landed in the trench.

Later that day, the battalion was relieved by the 1/7th DWR and withdrew to dug-outs on both sides of the Yser canal. On 20 July two men went to England for seven days leave and Private Arthur Smith (21) from Keighley was killed and four other men were wounded by shrapnel.

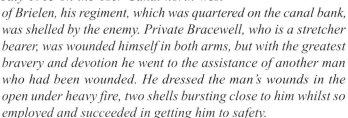

One of the battalion stretcher bearers, Private Fred Bracewell from Barnoldswick, was awarded a Distinguished Conduct Medal (DCM) for his bravery in treating the wounded men. His citation reads:

Private John Wiggan.

For conspicuous gallantry on the 20th July 1915 on the Yser Canal north-west of Brielen, his regiment, which was quartered on the canal bank, was shelled by the enemy. Private Bracewell, who is a stretcher bearer, was wounded himself in both arms, but with the greatest bravery and devotion he went to the assistance of another man who had been wounded. He dressed the man's wounds in the open under heavy fire, two shells bursting close to him whilst so employed and succeeded in getting him to safety.

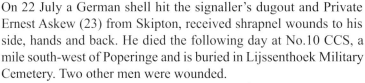

Private Stephen Bishop

On 22 July a German shell hit the signaller's dugout and Private Ernest Askew (23) from Skipton, received shrapnel wounds to his side, hands and back. He died the following day at No.10 CCS, a mile south-west of Poperinge and is buried in Lijssenthoek Military Cemetery. Two other men were wounded.

Private William Lister.

On 23 July the battalion relieved the 1/7th DWR in the front line trenches, during which Private John Halsted from Burnley suffered shrapnel wounds to his arms, legs and abdomen. He died of his injuries the following day and was buried in Ferme-Olivier Cemetery near Elverdinge. Five other men were also wounded. On a lighter note, one man went to England for seven days' leave.

On 24 July the bombing section set up a catapult system to launch grenades into the German lines and Private Albert Bailey (19) from Keighley, Lance Corporal Gilbert Horner from Trafford Grove, Harehills, Leeds and Private Percy Wade from Keighley were all killed by sniper bullets to the head. The men were buried in Colne Valley

Private Ernest Askew. (All CPGW)

Cemetery. Seven other men were also wounded by bullets and shrapnel. On 27 July five men were wounded by shell fire.

On 28 July the battalion was relieved by the 1/7th DWR and retired to the canal bank dug-outs. The Germans bombarded the dug-outs, wounding three men. However, two fortunate men, the pioneer serjeant major and the signals serjeant, left for seven days' leave in England. On 29 July, the area of the canal dug-outs was heavily shelled again by the German artillery and three other men were wounded by shell and rifle fire. Two officers, three NCOs and a private proceeded to England for seven days leave.

On 30 July Private William Henry Bolton (23) from Esp Lane, Barnoldswick received shrapnel wounds to his legs and died of his injuries. Five other men were also wounded by shrapnel. Private Bolton was a distinguished amateur boxer in his home town which earned him the nickname of 'Basher Bolton' and, as was often the case, his mother received the news of his death in a letter from one of her son's comrades. He is buried in Ferme-Olivier Cemetery.

On 31 July Private Herbert Dove was wounded in the left knee by shrapnel. Later that day the battalion was withdrawn to divisional reserve where hot baths were provided.

CASUALTIES: In July the battalion had 12 men killed and 58 wounded.

Private William H. Bolton. (CPGW)

August 1915

On 1 August 1915 the battalion was under canvas in the divisional reserve area. Seven officers and 300 men were provided for fatigue duty and on 2 August, the battalion relieved the 1/7th DWR on the Yser canal front. The quick relief was due to an outbreak of food poisoning amongst the men of the 1/7th which was so severe that about 100 men were hospitalised. One NCO and two men went to England for seven days leave and one man was wounded in the head by a rifle bullet. The following day was a dull, quiet day but one man was wounded in the back by rifle fire whilst on a ration carrying party and Private Herbert Dove (29) from Steeton died of a gangrene infection from the shrapnel wounds to his left knee received on 31 July. He died

Private Herbert Dove.

at the 2nd Canadian Stationary Hospital at Le Touquet and is buried at Le Touquet-Paris Plage Communal Cemetery near Étaples. He enlisted on 7 August 1914 at Skipton and was married with a young child.

Wind and rain arrived on 4 August and the German trenches were unusually quiet but three men were still wounded by bullet and shell fire.

On 5 August Private Norman Smith (26) from Greenfield Street, Skipton was killed by a German grenade and one other man hit by shrapnel in the head. Private Smith enlisted in October 1914 and before the war he had been a journeyman tailor employed by Mr G. Leathley, of Otley Street, Skipton. He is buried in Colne Valley Cemetery in Belgium.

One other man was hit in the head by

Private Norman Smith. (CPGW)

2381 PRIVATE
H. DOVE
DUKE OF WELLINGTON'S REGT.
3RD AUGUST 1915

Private Dove's headstone. (Both CPGW)

31

a bullet whilst on a ration carrying party. A banner was also seen over the German lines which read *'Warsaw has been conquered'*. This was meant to be seen by the British and refers to the Russian army's withdrawal from Warsaw which enabled the Germans to capture it without a fight. Heavy rain fell on 6 August and there was a lively artillery duel in the afternoon which caused about 20 yards of trench to collapse. Two men were wounded by the blast and one other man wounded in the thigh by a ricochet bullet. On 7 August the battalion was relieved by the 1/7th DWR and moved to the divisional reserve area where they remained for two days. On 10 August, two men were wounded in the thigh and shoulder by bullets whilst on working parties.

On the 11th the battalion had the opportunity to visit the mobile baths prior to moving to the left sector of the salient to relieve the 1/5th DWR. One man was accidently wounded by a bayonet whilst climbing over his own parapet. On 12 August an intense artillery duel took place and several large shells landed in the trenches. It was noted, no doubt with some satisfaction, that a large German shell dropped short and landed on their own trench.

The battalion casualties were remarkably light with only two men wounded by shrapnel and one man hit in the face by shrapnel from a rifle grenade. On 13 August the battalion snipers shot a German and three men were wounded by the premature explosion of a trench mortar shell. Two other men were wounded by a German trench mortar. On 14 August the battalion was relieved by the 1/8th West Yorkshire Regiment (The Leeds Rifles). During the relief, Private Frank Brady (20), from Keighley, a machine gunner in D Company, was shot in the head and killed. He is buried in Bard Cottage Cemetery. The battalion then proceeded to a tented camp in the grounds of Elverdinghe Chateau. They remained there for two days before becoming the divisional reserve around the farms area. The farms were several fortified strongpoints just behind the front line in the Yser canal area, which were given military names of battles fought during the Second Boer War. A Company occupied Modder Farm, B was on the east bank of the canal, C occupied Malakoff Farm and D took a position at Hulls Farm.

On 17 August 1915, Private Frederick Thornton (23) from Otley Street, Skipton was wounded by shrapnel in the abdomen and arm and died of his wounds on 24 August at No.10 CCS at Abeele and is buried in Lijssenthoek Military Cemetery. He enlisted at Skipton in September 1914.

On 18 August the canal bank area was shelled, causing two casualties, and on the following day Private Harry Wiles from Keighley was killed after being shot in the stomach on a working party.

On 20 August the German shelling was heavier than usual which caused nine casualties from shrapnel. One of the men, Private William George Bradley from Settle, was wounded in both

Private Frederick Thornton. (CPGW)

legs and his left arm whilst he was rescuing a wounded officer. He died of an infection on 9 September 1915 at No.13 Stationary Hospital at Boulogne and is buried in Boulogne Eastern Cemetery. His condition was not initially a cause for concern despite receiving shrapnel wounds to his legs and a broken arm and he was scheduled to be evacuated to the UK, but infection took hold and his condition deteriorated. His mother was summoned to the hospital in France and stayed with him until he died.

As early as June 1915, the Young Men's Christian Association (YMCA) opened hostels near base and stationary hospitals to enable relatives to visit gravely wounded soldiers. A YMCA car and driver would meet the visitors at the port and take them directly to see the injured man. This service was funded by the organisation and as the war progressed they were meeting between 100–150 visitors a day. Most YMCA staff were volunteers, mainly female, but male staff who were over military age or below military medical standards were also appointed.

Private William G. Bradley. (CPGW)

On 21 August the canal bank area was shelled but no casualties were caused. On the 22nd the battalion relieved the 1/7th DWR on the Yser Canal front. Lieutenant Malcolm Colin McGregor Law from Hawksworth Hall, near Guiseley received shell wounds to his right arm and left hand and two other men received shrapnel wounds.

Lance Corporal John (Jack) Middleton Morphett, from Settle, a participant of the 17 June cricket match and one of the 'lucky thirteen', died from a gunshot wound to his chest. He had been repairing a trench parapet and flattening sandbags when he was shot. Lieutenant Edward James C. Supple (33) from Co Wicklow, Ireland, a former master at Skipton Grammar School, had been shot in both thighs and died of his wounds in No.14 General Hospital at Wimereux, France (north of Boulogne). Lieutenant Supple had also played in the 17 June cricket match. Originally from County Wicklow in Ireland, Lieutenant Supple was the former master of the preparatory and athletics form at Ermysted's Grammar School, Skipton and a former master at Skipton Grammar School. In 1909, he joined the 6th DWR as a private but departed the unit in 1912 when he took a teaching position at Lewes in East Sussex. At the outbreak of war, he returned to the battalion as an officer and was a talented sportsman, excelling at cricket and rugby. He is buried in Wimereux Communal Cemetery.

Lance Corporal Jack Morphett.

Lieutenant Edward J.C. Supple.

The 1914-1915 Star, made of bronze (or Mons

Lieutenant Supple's great war medals.

Details on the reverse side of the 1914-1915 Star. (All CPGW)

Star if eligible), British War Medal, made of silver and the Victory Medal, made of bronze, were awarded to all servicemen who saw service in the Great War. Men who served after 1915 were only eligible for the latter two. The medals were issued in the early 1920s and gained the affectionate nickname of Pip, Squeak and Wilfred after three characters in a popular *Daily Mirror* cartoon strip of the same name. Pip was a dog, Squeak was a penguin and Wilfred was a rabbit. On a similar theme, the British War Medal and Victory medal, when worn together, gained the nickname Mutt and Jeff after the newspaper cartoon strip characters of the same name.

In addition to these medals, on 20 April 1920 the British Government instituted the Territorial Force War Medal. Only members of the TF and Territorial Force Nursing Service were eligible for this medal. They had to have been a member of the Territorial Force on or before 30 September 1914 and to have served in an operational theatre of war outside the United Kingdom between 5 August 1914 and 11 November 1918. An individual who was eligible to receive the 1914 Star or 1914/15 Star could not receive the Territorial War Medal. It was made of bronze and in keeping with other war medals, the recipient's name, rank, number and unit was impressed on the rim. This is the rarest of the Great War medals with just under 34,000 issued.

The Territorial Force War Medal 'For voluntary service overseas 1914-1919'.

Lance Corporal John (Jack) Morphett (38) was the school attendance officer at Settle and enlisted at the outbreak of war despite being over the then age limit. He was also a talented sportsman having played professional football for Aston Villa and Burnley and a keen cricketer playing in the Settle team which won the Ribblesdale League Cup in 1914. He is buried in Colne Valley Cemetery near Ypres.

He was the brother-in-law of Driver Benjamin Haygarth (26) from Dent who was serving in the 77th Battery, Royal Field Artillery in India when he died of pneumonia on 25 October 1918. He is buried in Rawalpindi War cemetery in Pakistan.

On 23 August the Germans fired twenty rifle grenades and several small shells towards the British line but no damage or

Private James W. Bell. (CPGW)

injuries were caused. On the same day Private James William Bell (23) from Lower Bentham, Lancashire was shot in the head and killed. Two other men were wounded by a trench mortar.

On 17 September 1915, the *West Yorkshire Pioneer* newspaper reported the death of Private James Bell:

The official confirmation of the death of Private James Bell, of 1/6th Duke of Wellington's, was confirmed on Friday last. Deceased was well known in the

Bentham district, being assistant shopman at the Co-operative Society's Stores at Low Bentham for eight years. He joined the 1/6th Duke of Wellington's at Skipton in November last and along with ten others was picked out and sent to France in April as a crack shot. He was 23 years of age and his mother died whilst he was on his way to the front. His cousin, Cecil Procter, went down with the Good Hope, and his brother-in-law, Richard Townson, is in the trenches in France. The flag was flying half-mast at the Victoria Institute, of which he was a member, all the weekend.'

HMS *Good Hope* was an armoured cruiser with a crew of 900 men. She was sunk on 4 November 1914 by the German armoured cruiser SMS *Scharnhorst* with the loss of all hands during the Battle of Coronel, near the coast of Chile. During the same engagement, the armoured cruiser HMS *Monmouth* with a crew of 735 men, was sunk with the loss of all hands by the German armoured cruiser SMS *Gneisenau* and light cruiser SMS *Nürnberg*.

On 24 August Private George Greenwood (20) from Compton Street, Keighley was killed after being shot in the head and one other man was wounded after being shot in the lower leg. Before the war, Private Greenwood was a pre-war 'terrier', joining in June 1913. He worked as a fitter for Prince Smith & Son, textile engineers of Keighley.

On 25 August at 2.30pm two Germans were shot by the battalion snipers and several allied planes were seen flying over the German lines. The enemy shelled the British lines and the men responded with rifle grenades. One man was wounded when shot in the back. The 26th was a quiet morning, but at 7.30pm, thirty-three heavy calibre German shells fell just behind the British line, although no casualties were caused.

On 27 August Private Fred Young (25) a dyer's labourer, of Springbank Terrace, Guiseley, was shot in the head and killed. He had joined the TF on its formation in 1908 and had completed four years' service before leaving the ranks in 1912. On 5 September 1914, he rejoined the unit at Skipton. He is buried in Colne Valley Cemetery near Ypres.

Private Joseph Henry Stewart (20) from Skipton and Private Richard Dent (22) from Oakworth, were also killed by bullet wounds to the head. Both men are buried in Colne Valley Cemetery.

Two other men were wounded by shrapnel and one man wounded in the head by glass from a trench periscope. The battalion was relieved by the 5th King's Own Yorkshire Light Infantry (KOYLI), and moved to the divisional rest camp where hot baths and church services were provided. On 31 August, a football match between the officers of the 1/6th DWR and the 1/7th DWR was played with the 1/7th officers winning 2-1.

Private Joseph H. Stewart. (CPGW)

CASUALTIES: In the month of August 1915, the battalion had 12 men killed and 47 wounded.

Essex Farm bunkers near the Yser canal in 2016.

September 1915

On 1 September 1915 the battalion was inspected by General Sir Herbert Plumer, Brigadier General H. Mends and Lord Scarborough, the Lord Lieutenant of Yorkshire with 16 officers and 448 men present on parade. The following two days were described as very wet and on 4 September Lieutenant General Sir J.L. Keir, General Officer Commanding VI Corps visited the camp. The men remained in their accommodation whilst the officers and NCOs paraded for the general due to the inclement weather. The bad weather continued for the following days and church parade was cancelled. On 8 September the battalion was inspected by the brigade GOC and sports were played in the afternoon. The battalion CO, Lieutenant Colonel John Birbeck, left for England on twenty-one days leave due to rheumatism and in his absence, Major Cass assumed command.

On 9 September the battalion relieved the 1/5th West Yorkshire Regiment (Prince of Wales's Own) on the Yser canal front. The weather on the following day was hot and a draft of two NCOs and twenty-eight men arrived. On 11 September one man was wounded in the face by wood splinters from a rifle which had been hit by an enemy bullet. On 12 September an artillery duel took place on the trenches and Lance Corporal Percy Brundrett (26) from Middleham was killed and three other men received shrapnel wounds. On 13 September, another fine day, four men were wounded by shrapnel and rifle fire and the next day one man received a gunshot wound to his arm.

On 15 September the battalion was relieved by the 1/7th DWR and proceeded to Elverdinghe Chateau in reserve. The Germans shelled the battalion HQ but no injuries were caused. The 4th Battery, West Riding Field Artillery was requested to retaliate and the German shelling stopped. The next three days were described as quiet, although two men were wounded by shell fire and a rifle bullet. On the 19th multiple church parades were held for Church of England, Roman Catholic and non-conformist faiths. The chateau was still within German artillery range and on 20 and 21 September two men received shrapnel wounds. Later that evening the battalion relieved the 1/7th DWR on the canal.

Lieutenant Colonel Birbeck. (CPGW)

On 24 September a new commanding officer was appointed. Lieutenant Colonel Rodolph Ladeveze Aldercron, formerly of the Cameron Highlanders, took over command of the battalion from Lieutenant Colonel John Birbeck who was invalided home with rheumatism. Birbeck had been a popular commander and was a veteran of the South Africa campaigns. On 25 September, eleven casualties were sustained, mainly by shrapnel, including Lieutenant Malcolm Law of Hawksworth. On 27 September the battalion was relieved by the 1/7th DWR and occupied the canal bank dugouts where they remained for the rest of the month.

CASUALTIES: In September 1915 the battalion had 2 men killed and 32 wounded.

October 1915

On 1 October 1915 three men were wounded by shrapnel and the next day the battalion was relieved on the canal bank by the 1/4th Battalion KOYLI and moved to the divisional rest area. A draft of thirty NCOs and men arrived from the reserve entrenching battalion at Poperinge. Entrenching battalions were temporary units formed during the Great War. Allocated at corps level, they were reserve units of men, from which drafts of replacements could be drawn by conventional infantry battalions.

Inspections and church parades were the order of the day and on 11 October the 49th Division horse show was held, with the 1/6th DWR winning prizes in the following categories: Class C riding horses, 3rd prize was won by Serjeant Field (transport company), and Class 1 chargers jumping, 1st prize was won by Lieutenant Samuel H. Clough (transport officer). The following day regimental sports were held and prizes were presented by Brigadier General E.F. Brereton, GOC 147 Infantry Brigade. The respite was not to last, as the following day the company commanders conducted a reconnaissance of the farms area prior to occupation. The following day, 14 October, the battalion relieved the 7th West Yorkshire Regiment in the farms area. Battalion HQ was at Malakoff Farm, D Company at Pioneer Farm, C at Saragossa and Modder Farms, B in trenches east of Hulls Farm and A on the east bank of the canal.

On the morning of 17 October the CO and company commanders visited the front line trenches east of the canal prior to relieving the 1/7th DWR in the afternoon. On 19 October the Germans fired sixty rounds of large calibre high explosive shells on the battalion front and in several places the trench parapet was blown in. Corporal John Thomas Lomas (28) and Private Alfred William Rooke (20), both from Keighley,

Lance Corporal P. Morgan and Private Fredrick Goodwin (20) both from Oxenhope, were all instantly killed and nine other men were wounded. The dead men were buried at Talana Farm.

On the night of 21 October the divisional bombers were active, throwing 124 bombs and firing ten rifle grenades towards the German trenches. Lieutenant Malcolm Law also rejoined the battalion from hospital and six men were wounded by shrapnel. In the early hours of 22 October, the bombers of D Company threw 207 bombs into the German trenches just 10 yards away. Private Joseph G. Bancroft (26) from Sutton-in-Craven, was killed by a rifle bullet to the head and was buried at Talana Farm Cemetery. He enlisted on the outbreak of war and had been employed in the Sutton Mill Co-operative grocery stores.

Private Joseph G. Bancroft. (CPGW)

Private George Cousins (23), from Otley, received a shell wound to the abdomen and died on 29 October at No.10 CCS; he is buried at Lijssenthoek Military Cemetery. Private Cousins was recruited at Guiseley and was a member of C Company. Although a native of Ripon, he worked as a leather presser at Messrs Wm Barker and Sons and lived on Union Street, Westgate, Otley. He left a widow, Fanny, and one child.

One other man was shot in the neck and wounded. Later that day the battalion was relieved by the 1/5th DWR, and returned to the area of Elverdinghe Chateau where a draft of twenty-five men joined the battalion. Again, being in reserve was no guarantee of safety, as on 24 October several large shells fell in the chateau grounds but no injuries were caused. On 26 October the battalion relieved the 1/7th DWR in the farms. A Company moved to the west bank of the canal, B Company to Hulls Farm, C Company to Modder and Saragossa Farms and D Company to Pelissier Farm. Battalion HQ was located at Malakoff Farm.

Private George Cousins. (British Newspaper Archive

Captain Norman Bairstow Chaffers, commander of C Company, Serjeant Major Orlando Buckley and twenty-five other ranks were selected to provide a representative platoon from the battalion at a parade in honour of HM King George V, who inspected the 6th, 14th and 49th Divisions under the command of VI Corps, GOC, Lieutenant General Sir J.L. Kier, at the aerodrome at Abeele on the French-Belgian border, 6 miles south-west of Poperinge. Meanwhile, the Germans shelled Hulls and Modder Farms for about two and a half hours, but no casualties were caused.

On 28 October, a draft of twenty-five men from the 3rd Entrenching Battalion arrived at battalion HQ and the Germans fired five high explosive shells as a welcome, although no casualties were caused. On 30 October Private Thomas Watmough from Ingrow was shot in the buttocks and died the following day at No.10 CCS.

CASUALTIES: In October 1915 the battalion had 7 men killed and 30 wounded.

November 1915

The weather in the Ypres Salient for 3 November 1915 was showery with a few bright intervals. On that day the battalion relieved the 1/4th DWR in the canal trenches which were in a very bad state. The parapet had fallen in and most of the trench system was impassable with waist-deep muddy water. Sniper activity was again a deadly problem and on 4 November Private Norris G. Dixon (18) from Keighley, Private Albert Toon (20) from Skipton and Private Ernest Thompson from Britannia Street, Keighley, were both shot in the head and killed. One other man was shot in the neck and wounded.

Private Albert Toon. (CPGW)

Private Toon enlisted in January 1915 and was previously employed as a weaver in Skipton. He was also a playing member of Niffany Rovers Football Club and, as was often the case at this stage of the war, his relatives received notice of his death in a letter from one of his comrades, Private John Leslie Berry, also from Skipton. In 1917 Private Berry was commissioned as a second lieutenant in the 9th Battalion of the West Riding Regiment and was killed in action on 12 October 1918.

On 5 November, Private John Thomas Birdsall, from Shipley was hit in the head by shrapnel and killed. He was buried with other fallen comrades in Talana Farm Cemetery.

Private John Thomas Birdsall. (CPGW)

Second Lieutenant John L. Berry. (CPGW)

Three other men were wounded that day and a draft of twenty men from the 3rd Entrenching Battalion arrived at battalion HQ. The weather on 6 November was described as very cold and foggy but in the early hours, a German patrol crawled up to D Company's position and threw a grenade into the trench. Private William Binns (20), from Keighley, was killed and two others seriously wounded by the explosion. Born in Wilsden in 1892, William Binns was a pre-war 'terrier', joining in 1911. He was the son of a stone quarry foreman and raised in the Hog Holes and Glen Lee areas of Keighley. By 1911 he was working as an overlooker for worsted spinners Timothy Hird & Sons, who ran Acres Mill and Fleece Mill. Within a month of attesting for the West Riding Regiment, he was attending the first of his annual training camps at Flamborough. William's younger brother, George Henry Binns, also

Private William Binns. (CPGW)

served in the Great War, fighting with the Northumberland Fusiliers until his death in October 1917 at the age of 21.

Corporal (soon to be Serjeant) James Bury from Barnoldswick was nominated for a gallantry award for his part in driving off the German attack. Private Arthur Greenbank from Stainforth near Settle was killed by rifle fire. Both William Binns and Arthur Greenbank are buried in Talana Farm Cemetery.

Arthur Greenbank joined the army in January 1915 at a patriotic recruiting meeting at Stainforth, on which the *Craven Herald* newspaper reported:

On Monday night, a well-attended meeting was held in the schoolroom. Mr. Duncan Mackenzie presided. Capts. Groves and Brewin and Second Lieutenants Woodhead and McKillop from Skipton were present. Mr. Bibbings, of Sheffield, made a rousing appeal to the audience to enlist now, not to delay any longer. He made special allusion to the German toast 'To-day.' 'It meant,' he said, 'the lowering of our good old English flag and the hoisting of the Teuton in its place.' Mr. Simpson said the village had only added one in 75 of the population to the roll of honour. Mr. Lund, however, pointed out that this was incorrect, and Mr. Simpson readily withdrew the remark. Mr. Farnsworth spoke on the allowances made to wives and children of those who enlisted and Captain Groves spoke on the German people and their military advisers. Five married men volunteered their services. John Greenbank, James Greenbank, Arthur Greenbank, Henry Lund, and John Lund. These were sworn in and heartily cheered. At intervals, patriotic songs were sung by Mr. Thornber, the audience joining in the choruses. In addition to the songs on the sheet, Mr. Thornber sang 'The Flag that never comes down', and 'The boys in khaki, boys in blue'. Mr. Leaworthy accompanied on the piano. The singing of the National Anthem brought a very enthusiastic meeting to a close.'

Private Arthur Greenbank.

Private James Greenbank. (Both CPGW)

James Greenbank, brother of Arthur, died of chest wounds on 1 May 1917 at No.45 CCS at Achiet-le-Grand, aged 31. He was serving in the 2/6th West Riding Regiment at the time of his death and had enlisted with his two brothers at the Stainforth schoolroom meeting in January 1915. He left a wife and five children. The third brother, John, also joined the 2/6th West Riding Regiment, but suffered a hernia during basic training on Salisbury Plain which, in November 1917, resulted in a medical discharge before he saw any overseas service. He died on 6 June 1969 at Stainforth.

On 7 November, between midday and 2pm, the trenches were heavily shelled and mortared. A 20 yard section of the line was blown in and a machine gun buried. It was noticed that many German shells failed to detonate but the bombardment resumed at 4pm. There were no 'duds' amongst the German shells this time, which were mainly shrapnel.

Second Lieutenant Thomas Savile Whitaker (22), son of Mr Thomas Whitaker JP from Walton House, Burley-in-Wharfedale (now Ghyll Royd School) was killed when shot by a sniper. In May of that year his parents had mistakenly received a telegram reporting his death. The telegram should have been sent to the parents of Lieutenant C.F. Whitaker of Horsforth. Unfortunately, this time the telegram was sent to the correct address. His death was a great loss to the men of C Company and he was described as cheery when times were the worst. This description of him undoubtedly understates his leadership qualities and the genuine respect the men under his command held for him. He was educated at Sedborough School in Cumbria and attended Caius College, Cambridge where he joined the Officer Training Corps (OTC). He received his commission in August 1914 and was the commander of the machine-gun section before becoming the battalion bombing officer. He was another participant in the 17 June Fleurbaix cricket match.

Second Lieutenant Thomas S. Whitaker.

Private Richard H. Oldfield (19) from Skipton, was hit in the abdomen by a bullet and died on 9 November in No.10 CCS. Private Charles Hewlett (32) from Barnoldswick was shot in the back and died on 8 November at No.10 CCS. Four other men were wounded.

During this tour in the trenches the front line was so bad that it was impossible to walk upright along the full length in daylight due to the parapet falling in. In most places the mud was up to the waist and in other places up to the knees. Out of the four platoons in a company, only two at a time could be in the front line; the other two were held back in support and were rotated every twenty-four hours, with a hot meal provided to the units going to the front and those returning. The meals were cooked on the field kitchens at the HQ location, transported to the support trench and kept hot using braziers. The rum ration was also issued every day. Introduced in the winter of 1914, the rum was initially given to soldiers to combat the chill and damp of the trenches. A war correspondent wrote:

Private Richard H. Oldfield.

Rum rations are by now probably served out to all sections of our Flanders troops. They were started in some divisions, I know, in November. Some people at home feel very uncomfortable about the small rum ration that the troops receive. Almost every man I have met who has served during the winter is in favour of it. A few convinced tee-totalers use it to rub their feet! To most men the drink comes as a glow of light and warmth.

Private Charles Hewlett. (All CPGW)

An earthenware rum jar held one gallon of spirit, enough for sixty-four men. Each man received approximately one third of a pint each week which equated to about a tablespoon per day. On the side of the jar were stamped the initials 'S.R.D.' thought to stand for 'Service Rations Depot', 'Service Reserve Depot' or 'Service Rum Dilute'. Soldiers, however, said they stood for 'Seldom Reaches Destination', 'Soon Runs Dry' or 'Seldom Rarely Delivers'. Extra rum was also offered to men detailed on unpleasant tasks such as recovering and burying bodies, those about to undertake a trench raid and of course to men about to go 'over the top'.

Despite the efforts made, fifty-seven men had to be hospitalized with exposure, twenty-seven of whom also had trench foot and one man with pneumonia. Thigh-length gum boots were issued as well as three extra pairs of socks to each man. A system was adopted of sending socks back each night to the divisional baths area where they were washed and sent to battalion HQ, where a drying dug-out was established.

The battalion was relieved on 7 November by the 1/5th DWR and was carried out over open ground as the communication trenches were impassable. Luckily no casualties were sustained and the battalion moved to the area of the farms. A Company deployed to Pelissier Farm, B to Hulls Farm, C to Saragossa and Modder Farms, D to West Canal Bank dugouts and battalion HQ to Malakoff Farm. Apart from sporadic shelling, the next few days were relatively quiet.

A First World War era rum jar.

On 11 November the German artillery shelled Pelissier Farm, probably due to the anti-aircraft guns which were firing from the garden of the farm. Lieutenant Leonard Varley (21) was killed when shot in the abdomen whilst examining machine-gun positions. He was born in 1893 and was the only son of George and Sarah Varley of Leyburn Grove, Bradford Road, Shipley. Educated at Belle Vue School, Bradford, at the age of 12, he won scholarships to Bradford Grammar School and Saltaire Higher Grade School. At 16 he won the first 'Isaac Holden' Scholarship to Cambridge, but as he was too young to take up the offer, he went as exchange tutor in English to Rodez College in France. In 1911, he attended Trinity College, Cambridge and a few weeks before the outbreak of war he was appointed language master to The Royal Masonic School in Bushey. He had been a member of the University Officers' Training Corps and on 26 August 1914, he was commissioned into the 1/6th DWR and promoted to lieutenant on 1 June 1915. He is buried in Bard Cottage Cemetery near Ypres.

Lieutenant Leonard Varley. (CPGW)

Later that day the battalion was relieved by the 1/5th DWR and moved by motor bus to the divisional rest camp No.3. The camp was described as very muddy and most of the men were in tents as only three huts were provided. For the men of the 1/6th DWR the rest camp was far from restful. The following day, 12

November 1915, was very wet and a working party of three officers and 100 men were taken by motor bus back to the front line at the farms area. The remainder of the battalion was occupied in constructing huts at the camp. Private Joseph Hudson (23) from Jay Street, Keighley was shot in the back and killed whilst working on a dug-out at Talana Farm. Prior to the war he worked at Prince Smith & Son, textile engineers Keighley. A draft of forty men from the 3rd Entrenching Battalion also arrived at the camp.

Working parties continued on 13 November and the following day, after church services, four officers and 150 men left the camp to work on the front line. On 15 November 150 men were provided again for working parties at the front, whilst the rest of the men were employed building huts, laying a narrow-gauge railway and repairing the road. On 16 November the battalion moved to Elverdinge Chateau where the men were accommodated in tents but the officers were provided with rooms in the chateau. The same day, four officers and 200 men were provided for working parties.

On 17 November, Lieutenant General Sir John Kier visited the battalion and four officers and 200 men were provided for working parties at the front, during which three men were shot and seriously wounded. The weather on 19 November was wet and baths were allocated. The working parties, comprising four officers and 195 men, continued to be provided. On 19 November the battalion relieved the 1/4th DWR in support at the farms area with the deployment as follows: A Company to Pelissier Farm, B Company to Malakoff and Hulls Farm, C Company to Modder and Saragossa Farms, D Company to the west bank of the canal and battalion HQ to Trois Tours Chateau, west of Brielen. They remained here for four days, then on 23 November the battalion relieved the 1/4th DWR in the front line trenches. The relief again had to be carried out across country as the communication trenches were still impassable.

The following day saw artillery activity on both sides of the line with the German shells landing near the farms, except one which fell on C Company dug-out, causing the death of Private Thomas Rencroft (23) from Flax Street, Leeds. He enlisted in September 1914 at the Drill Hall, Guiseley and was buried at Talana Farm Cemetery. Also killed on that day was Private Harry Gillibrand (27), born in Blackburn but lived in Dawlish, Devon. He was recruited at Skipton and was killed by a bullet through the heart, leaving a wife and two children. Private John Donlon (33) born in Street, Co Louth, Ireland was killed by a bullet through the back of the neck. Private Cyril Calvert (20), from Skipton, was shot in the abdomen and killed.

Private Cyril Calvert.

Private Harry Gillibrand. (Both CPGW)

Before the war Private John Donlon was working as a labourer at the Commercial Hotel, Grassington. He had previous military service in the Royal Inniskilling Fusiliers and enlisted at Skipton the day war was declared. During his service in France he was wounded twice. On 22 May he received a minor gunshot wound to his buttocks and on 24 July, a grazing neck wound from a sniper's bullet. Unfortunately, on 24 November 1915, his luck ran out and he is buried in Talana Farm Cemetery.

On 25 November the commander of A Company reported that his men had captured a German soldier who was part of a patrol who were approaching the British lines when they were fired on. One man was captured, one man killed and two others fled back to their own lines. The captured man gave his name as Johannes Rohi (19) of the 250th Regiment and apart from wet clothes, he was described as well fed and clothed. During a trench mortar bombardment, Lance Corporal Ughtred Binns (23) from Beechcliffe, Keighley, was killed. Before the war, he worked as a pattern maker at a washing machine engineering company. He also was a member of the Keighley Celtic, Keighley Caledonian and Beechcliffe football clubs.

At 2.30pm that day a large balloon was observed descending near Hulls Farm and was recovered by men from the 1/4th DWR. Observation balloons were used by both sides for artillery spotting and intelligence gathering. They were filled with flammable hydrogen gas and as such were vulnerable to ground and aircraft fire.

On 26 November, Private William James Morrison from Moss Carr Road, Keighley was shot in the head and killed. He is buried in Talana Farm Cemetery.

Private William J. Morrison. (CPGW)

Example of a rear area balloon station. Note the numerous gas cylinders to the bottom right. (Big Push magazine)

In the early hours of 20 November 1915 the battalion was relieved by the 1/5th DWR and moved back to the farms in the same locations as 19 November. On the 28th, the Germans fired four shells towards Malakoff Farm, two of which went through the roof of the barn but fortunately no injuries were caused. The remaining two days of the month were described as very cold, but no casualties were sustained. One officer and three men from C Company were tasked to find the liaison post where the British lines met the French army.

CASUALTIES: In November 1915, the battalion had 15 men killed and 30 wounded.

December 1915

On 1 December 1915 the battalion relieved the 1/5th DWR in the front line trenches. Again, due to the condition of the communication trenches, the relief was carried out across country. The line was reinforced with barbed wire during the night under the cover of a heavy bombardment and the battalion bombers threw ninety grenades towards the German trenches. On 2 December Private Thomas Fitzsimons (23) from Keighley, but born in Yeadon, and Corporal John Quinn born in Whitehaven, were both shot in the head and killed. Both men are buried in Talana Farm Cemetery.

Private Tom Fitzsimons. (CPGW)

Heavy rain on 3 December caused many parts of the trenches to fall in and the dug-out occupied by C Company in reserve collapsed, but no injuries were caused. The German artillery bombarded battalion HQ but a large proportion of the shells were duds. The bad weather also restricted the activity of the working parties. On 4 December barbed wire was also put up by all companies. Private Geoffrey Hugo Taylor (18) from Preston, was hit in the side by a rifle bullet and died at Hulls Farm, and Private Charles Deighton (20) from Wingfield Street, Bradford, was killed after being shot in the thigh. Both men were buried at Talana Farm Cemetery. Before the war Charles Deighton worked as a warehouseman and originally joined the TF in April 1912 at Bingley. His younger brother, Arthur, turned 18 in June 1918 and joined the 1/6th West Yorkshire Regiment. By the time he had finished his training, the Armistice had been signed and he spent the next fifteen months in Germany as part of the British Army of the Rhine.

Private Geoffrey H. Taylor. (CPGW)

On 5 December the weather was still very wet and 200 German shells landed near battalion HQ but no casualties were caused. Work in the trenches consisted of creating wooden fire steps and *chevaux-de-frise* or 'knife-rests' (a defensive structure consisting of an obstacle composed of barbed wire attached to a wooden frame). The trenches were knee deep in mud and the men had difficulty resupplying the front line. At 10pm the battalion was relieved by the 1/5th DWR and buses were provided at Dawson's Corner to transport the men to rest camp No.3. Fortunately, no casualties were sustained, despite the enemy shelling the area of the farms during the relief.

On 6 December a new draft of thirty-three men arrived in camp. The following day was wet and windy and two working parties of fifty men from A and B Companies were provided. On 8 December Captain Chaffers oversaw working parties erecting huts and C and D companies provided fifty men each for working parties. Heavy rain fell on 9 December and the CO inspected A and B Companies. Baths were allocated to the battalion and 100 men provided for working parties. On 10 December the CO inspected C and D Companies and working parties of 100 men were again provided. The next day men from the newly-arrived draft were instructed in creating barbed wire entanglements and working parties were detailed as usual.

Open air divine service was held on 12 December and no working parties were required. On the morning of 13 December baths were allocated to the battalion and that afternoon the men were bussed to Malakoff Farm where they were issued with rations, a hot meal and thigh-length gum boots. The battalion relieved the 1/4th DWR in the front line trenches with the relief again being carried out across country due to the condition of the trenches. Two platoons from each company took positions at the front and two in support. The Germans shelled the line just before the relief was carried out but no injuries were caused.

The 14th was relatively quiet but there was sporadic machine-gun fire and several bombs thrown at the British lines. At 3.30am a sentry captured a German patrol of four men who had apparently lost their way. A field interrogation was carried out on the prisoners who revealed their leader had been hit in the head by a machine-gun bullet and, owing to the blood streaming from his face, had lost his way. They were from the 240th Regiment and were called up in March, arriving at the front in July. Their uniforms were in good order and the men were described as 'well mannered'. The prisoners were further interrogated at Corps HQ and provided the following information: The 23rd Jägers were alternating with the 240th Regiment. They spent three days in the line, three in support then six in reserve and six in a rest camp. Mail was no longer delivered to the German lines and listening posts were placed in front of the wire. The patrol leader was armed with an automatic pistol but the remainder had rifles and three stick grenades each.

On 15 December Serjeant James Bury saw two Germans in a sap in front of his trench and shot them both dead. (A sap is a trench which projects forward from the main trench system, usually used for observation or listening posts.) Serjeant Bury was to win the Distinguished Conduct Medal (DCM) and Military Medal (MM) and was Mentioned in Despatches, but unfortunately he would not live to see Armistice Day. Wiring was carried out in front of the lines and the new 'corkscrew' wiring pickets were used for the first time. This enabled the men to create barbed wire entanglements without the need to hammer the stakes in. As the name implies, it was screwed into the ground and barbed wire could be threaded through the loops.

Throughout the day, the fatalities continued. Private John West (23) from Settle, was shot in the chest, Private Nelson Holmes (20) from Silsden, was shot in the head and Private David Russell from Skipton was shot in the right side. All these men died almost instantly of their injuries. One other man was slightly grazed on the head by a rifle bullet.

Screw picket near Authuille, still in use 100 years later.

Private John West.

Private Nelson Holmes.
(All CPGW).

Private David Russell

Private John West's original grave marker at Talana Farm Cemetery. (CPGW and Margaret Graveson & Langcliffe Millennium Group)

Private John West enlisted on 8 September 1914, with his brother Amos, at Settle. He worked at Langcliffe paper mill and was a member of the Settle brass band. Amos was medically discharged from the army in March 1919.

Private Nelson Holmes enlisted on 1 December 1914 and was a former member of the 1st Silsden Scout Troop. He was killed when he exposed his head over the parapet whilst fixing a trench periscope. His brother, William Summers Holmes (29) enlisted on 5 August 1914 in the 8th DWR. He served in the Gallipoli campaign, Egypt and France before being posted to Northern Italy. On 29 October 1918 he died of pneumonia at No.29 Stationary Hospital near the Italian town of Cremona and was buried in the military cemetery there. He left a widow and two small children. His other brother, Edgar Holmes, received an arm wound and after transferring to the Labour Corps was medically discharged in February 1918.

Private David Russell of Broughton Road, Skipton enlisted on 4 August 1914 and was employed by the Midland Railway. He was also a prominent player in the Skipton Niffany Rovers Football Club alongside Albert Toon who had been killed on 3 November. He was the brother of Lance Serjeant John Willie Russell, also serving in the ranks of the 1/6th DWR, who died of wounds on 7 May 1918. His cousin Private Clarence Clark (23) from Cromwell Street, Skipton was serving in the 1/5th Essex Regiment when he died of pneumonia in Palestine and another cousin, also named Private David Russell of the 1/6th DWR, was killed on 14 October 1916.

The winter was taking its toll. On 17 December Private John Baxter (22) from Salterforth, near Barnoldswick was shot through the left eye and Private Cyril (Syril) Tomlinson (21) from Ingleton was killed by a rifle bullet. Both men were buried at Talana Farm Cemetery. Six other men were also seriously wounded by bullet and shell fire. Later the same day, the battalion was relieved by the 1/4th DWR and moved back to the farms area. During the relief, Private Asa Brook from Keighley was hit in the head by a bullet and died three days later at the 2nd West Riding Field Ambulance Unit and was buried at Ferme-Olivier Cemetery.

Private John Baxter. (CPGW)   *Private Asa Brook. (Men of Worth)*   *Private Cyril (Syril) Tomlinson. (CPGW)*

It was wet on 18 December and most of the day was spent transporting rations to the 1/4th DWR and cleaning billets. An equipment inspection was also held and two men were wounded by rifle fire.

Chapter 4

The Gas Attack

At the beginning of December intelligence was received that the Germans were planning another gas attack in the Ypres salient. A heavy British artillery barrage was planned for the morning of 18 December to disrupt the German trenches and destroy any gas cylinders that were positioned in the front line. Due to the proximity of the enemy trenches, the plan was for the British to evacuate their own front line positions before the barrage started and then to reoccupy them at the conclusion. Due to poor visibility of the German line, the bombardment was postponed and rescheduled for the following morning. In the early hours of 19 December, metallic banging and coughing was heard by men of the 1/4th DWR coming from the vicinity of the German trenches. There was a gentle breeze blowing from the north-east towards the British lines and by 5am all the men from the 1/4th DWR, except for A Company, had withdrawn from the front line in accordance with the bombardment plan.

Between 5.35am and 5.40am, a sentry in the farms area sounded the alarm by repeated blasts on a whistle. The Germans had released a mixed cloud of phosgene and chlorine gas from hundreds of cylinders positioned in front of the British lines. The quantity of gas released was such that Canadian units some 12 miles to the rear felt the effects. The battalion stood to and received orders to occupy their reinforcement positions in support of the 1/4th DWR. Survivors from the 1/4th DWR described hearing a hissing noise and then seeing a greenish-white cloud appear over the German trenches which began to slowly drift towards the British line. The Germans also launched an artillery and trench mortar bombardment of the British communication and support lines. Fortunately, the British artillery was alert and ready to respond so they were standing by their guns for the prearranged bombardment and as soon as the SOS signal was seen the guns opened fire. A Company from the 1/4th DWR, who had remained in the front line, opened fire on the German trenches, delivering rapid rifle fire until their rifle barrels glowed red hot. They suffered heavy casualties but held their position.

The companies of the 1/6th DWR held the west bank of the canal until around 9am when, with no sign of a German follow up attack, the CO withdrew the men, except for sentries, to an observation trench. During the afternoon, C Company withdrew to a reserve trench for a hot meal and then brought up rations for the 1/4th DWR and the remainder of the 1/6th DWR. At dusk, B Company stood down but D Company relieved A Company of the 1/4th DWR. A Company of the 1/6th DWR returned to the reserve area and for the rest of the night resupplied the front lines with ammunition, hand grenades, gas helmets and rations. About 8.30pm there was a further gas alert and C Company was moved to the front line trenches where they remained for the rest of the night. This was either a false alarm or the gas drifting back towards the German lines. During the rest of the night the enemy fired gas shells near the reserve trenches and PH helmets had to be worn all night. After relieving the 1/4th DWR, Lieutenant Malcolm Law and Second Lieutenant Procter were both tasked with examining no man's land. They reported that the ground was covered in what they described as thick hoar frost which when disturbed gave off gas, which goes some way to demonstrate the quantity of chemicals discharged. Men who were slightly gassed were given brine to drink which caused vomiting, after which they were seen to have slightly recovered.

One man of the 1/6th DWR, unfortunately not named, could not get to his PH helmet in time so he soaked a sandbag in urine, put it round his nose and mouth and positioned his head over the rising heat of an open fire. This happened during the worst period of the gas attack and appears to have worked as he was only slightly affected. A few defects on the PH helmets were also noticed around the breathing tube but most gas casualties in the 1/6th DWR were amongst B Company and the machine-gun section at Hulls Farm dug-outs. These were due to the difficulty in rousing the men from overcrowded dug-outs and it was found that several men were not alerted by the alarm, but by feeling the effects of the gas. This was not due to a lack of effort from the sentries, as Private Walter Butcher from Haworth ran along the company position, rousing the men without waiting to don his own PH helmet. He then stood on the line waiting for the enemy attack, but was subsequently hospitalised suffering from the effects of gas and shell wounds. His actions were brought to the attention of the CO, but there is no record that his selflessness was recognised. He was later discharged from the army because of his injuries.

The German shelling lasted most of the day with a mixture of high explosive and gas shells. The next day the following message was sent to all ranks:

The Divisional Commander is very pleased with the behaviour of all ranks and the promptitude with which all the necessary steps were taken this morning.

Six men from the 1/6th DWR died as a direct result of gassing at Hulls Farm dugouts: Lance Corporal John W. Willan (23) from Skipton, Private Edgar Mallows (23) from East Morton, Private Lynden H. Hall (21) from Keighley, Private Harry C. Taylor (22) from East Morton, Private Maurice Smith (20) from Skipton and Private William Smith (19) from Keighley. Lance Corporal Fred Gallagher from Skipton died from a self-inflicted gunshot wound to the head whilst suffering the effects of poison gas. Corporal Frank Bulcock (25) from Settle was killed by shrapnel in an observation trench. Twenty-five other men were wounded by gas inhalation.

Lance Corporal John Wilson Willan of Otley Street, Skipton enlisted at the outbreak of war and was a member of the machine-gun section. Before the war he worked at his father's boot business and is buried at Longuenesse Souvenir Cemetery, near St

Omer. He was a former pupil of Ermysted's Grammar School, Skipton and had refused a commission in another regiment to remain with this friends in the 1/6th DWR.

Corporal Frank Bulcock, a pre-war 'terrier', was employed as clerk by C.J. Lord, coal agent, Settle. His brother Charles Bulcock also served in the 1/6th DWR and they both landed in France with the battalion on 14 April 1914. Charles Bulcock survived the war and was disembodied (discharged) from full time service on 12 February 1919. His father was Quartermaster Serjeant Bulcock, who was well-known in Skipton through his connection with the 2/6th Battalion, Duke of Wellington's Regiment, and subsequently with the 3/6th DWR, now stationed at Clipstone. He was also the cousin of Gunner John Cokell (23) from Castle Hill, Settle who was serving with the 33rd Battery, Royal Field Artillery when he was killed on 13 August 1917. He was also related to Private Joseph Metcalfe Bulcock (20) of Ashbrook Street, Settle who was serving in the 2/7th Lancashire Fusiliers when he was killed in action at Pozières on 21 March 1918.

Private Lynden H. Hall.

Fred Gallagher (24) of Sheep Street, Skipton was another pre-war 'terrier' who had 'time-expired' in July 1914 but immediately rejoined on the outbreak of war. He is buried at Talana Farm Cemetery. He was a renowned rugby player having played as a forward for both Skipton and Ilkley. He was the brother-in-law of both Private Percy Edgar Smith (28) from Newmarket Street, Skipton who was serving in the 1/7th DWR when he was killed on 16 June 1918 and Private David Russell, who was also serving in the 1/6th DWR when he was killed on 14 October 1916.

Corporal Frank Bulcock. (Both CPGW)

Private Frederick Parker Furness (18) of Brougham Street, Skipton who had been wounded by gas, was evacuated to No.17 CCS near Poperinge but died of his injuries the following day and is buried at Lijssenthoek Military Cemetery. Before the war, he was employed at Marsden & Naylor Iron founders in Skipton. He was another pre-war 'terrier' who joined the TF in 1913.

Private Thomas Hartley (19) had also been evacuated to No.17 CCS suffering from the effects of the gas and died the following day. He lived on Aireworth Street, Keighley with his mother Mary Anne and joined the TF in April 1913. Before the war, he worked as a lathe operative at Prince Smith & Sons of Keighley. He is buried at Lijssenthoek Military Cemetery.

Private Frederick P. Furness. (CPGW)

This attack was part of a German offensive along VI Corps' front, although the enemy, except in one or two places and then only in small numbers, did not leave their trenches. It was speculated that the German failure to follow up on this large release of chemical weapons was due to the lack of panic amongst the British troops who held their positions.

Lance Corporal John H. Willan. (CPGW)

Private Maurice Smith. (CPGW)

Private Fred Gallagher (CPGW)

This was the first use of phosgene/chlorine gas by the Germans. The two gasses were mixed as the lighter chlorine helped to disperse the denser phosgene more effectively. It is estimated that during this attack the Germans released around 88 tons of gas along the Ypres Salient causing 1,069 casualties and 69 deaths. Phosgene affects the human body by preventing the exchange of oxygen in the lungs, thus causing suffocation. Chlorine gas forms hypochlorous acid when combined with water, destroying moist tissue such as the lungs and eyes.

On the evening of 20 December the battalion relieved the 1/4th DWR in the front line trenches. The relief was a difficult one due to early evening heavy rain and then the clouds cleared to reveal a full moon. The following day was relatively quiet with hardly any rifle fire, but a barrage of shrapnel shells was fired over the canal bank during the night, wounding three men. Great difficulty was experienced in getting the men killed in the gas attack to Talana Farm Cemetery due to the wet weather and German shelling. On the evening of 21 December, the battalion was relieved by the 1/5th DWR and moved to the farms area. The deployment was as follows:

A Company to Malakoff Farm, of which No.1 Platoon was sent to Hulls Farm, B Company to the canal bank, C to Saragossa Farm and D to Pelissier Farm. On this day, Private Prince Dawson (22) from High Street, Steeton died in a CCS from effects of the gas attack on 19 December. He was a member of the machine-gun section and had enlisted in October 1914. He was a talented footballer and had played for Sutton United. He is buried at Le Touquet-Paris Plage Communal cemetery, 4 miles east of Étaples.

Private Prince Dawson and his headstone. (CPGW)

Also on 21 December, at 5.20pm, Private Charles Fennerty (26) from Skipton died at the St John's Ambulance Brigade Hospital at Étaples from the effects of the poison gas he received during the 19 December attack. Charles enlisted on 7 November 1914 at Skipton and began training on 1 January 1915. He was posted to France on 14 June of that year and was another member of the machine-gun section. He was due for leave at Christmas and planned to marry his fiancée during his time at home. He is buried at Étaples Military Cemetery.

Private C. Fennerty and his headstone in Étaples Military cemetery. (CPGW)

Private John Hillary (22) from Embsay also died on 21 December at No.10 CCS from the effects of the gas attack. He enlisted just after the outbreak of war, prior to which he was employed in the grocery department of the Co-operative Society. He was the cousin of Private Horace Hillary (20) from Skipton who was serving in the 9th (Service) DWR when he died on 13 July 1916 at 2nd Western Hospital, Pendlebury near Manchester from wounds received in action. John was also the cousin of Lance Corporal Harold Hillary (27) from Skipton who was serving in the 2/6th DWR when he died on 9 April 1917 at No.49 CCS of pneumonia.

Private John Hillary. (CPGW)

On 22 December 22 the men rested all day except for two small working parties. The next day saw the billets cleaned for Christmas Day and six officers, including Lieutenant Colonel Oliver of the 17th Middlesex Regiment, 73 Brigade, 24th Division, arrived to familiarise themselves with the billets prior taking over the line. The weather was very wet and windy. On 24 December, the following message was received from the Second Army GOC, General Sir Herbert Plumer:

> *I have just received the preliminary report of the gas attack and heavy shelling by the Germans on the VI Corps front on the 19th and should be glad if you would convey to the troops of 6th and 49th Divisions my appreciation of their steadiness and behaviour under very difficult and trying circumstances. Owing to their steadiness the attack failed to produce any practical or intentional effect. It was a day which reflects great credit on the whole Corps.*
>
> *The divisional commander has very great pleasure in ordering the publication of the above and announcing the fact that in the whole division there was no case of straggling.*

Captain Sidney Fox Marriner returned from sick leave and took over temporary command of the battalion and the officers from the 17th Middlesex returned to their unit. The weather on Christmas Day 1915 was wet, windy and thankfully quiet, broken only by occasional shelling from both sides. The Padre, Rev. Page, held holy communion in the officer's mess at Malakoff Farm and services were held at Redan Farm (HQ of the 1/7th DWR) and Pelisser Farm (D Company). The CO visited all the billets during the day and the men were made as comfortable as possible. A special dinner was provided consisting of roast pork, apples, tinned tongue, tinned fruits and nuts. The following message was also received from Lieutenant General J.L. Keir, GOC VI Corps:

> *My dear Perceval,*
> *Although I have already expressed to you and your Divisional Commander the admiration I feel for the gallant stand made by the men under their command against the recent German gas attack, I should like to place on record how I highly value the services rendered by all ranks.*
> *I do not think that the importance of their success can be overestimated. It has re-established a complete confidence in our defences which had been severely shaken by the German gas attack gains in the spring, a confidence however which had never deserted the VI Corps.*

The weather on Boxing Day was very windy and wet. Lieutenant Colonel Aldercron returned from leave and resumed command of the battalion. Later that day the battalion moved across country and relieved the 1/5th DWR in the front line trenches.

On 27 December the enemy shelled the area of Colne Valley dug-outs on the east side of the canal, although several shells failed to explode. Patrols were sent out in the evening which reported the German wire was in good condition except in one location, but showed no sign of being cut and the Germans were seen working on the wire opposite the British lines.

Second Lieutenant Thomas Wright Carson (31) from Skipton led a patrol with two men to inspect the German wire and was never seen again. He was separated from the two men who returned on their own. Frequent patrols were sent out but failed to find him. It was thought he might have been taken prisoner, but he was reported missing, presumed killed. He is buried in Sanctuary Wood Cemetery. On 19 May 1916, the *Craven Herald* newspaper reported his fate:

> *Second Lieut. T. W. Carson, 1/6th Battalion, Duke of Wellington's West Riding Regiment, younger son of Mrs. Carson, Salisbury Street, Skipton, who has been missing since December 28th, is now reported killed. The information came from the Inquiry Branch at Geneva of the Queen Victoria Jubilee Fund Association. The letter, dated May 7th, 1916, being in the following terms:*
> > *Dear Sir,*
> > *We are grieved to be the bearers of sad news to you regarding your brother, Second-Lieut. T. W. Carson, 1/6th Battalion Duke of Wellington's West Riding Regiment. The following communication has been received from Countess E. Blucher von Wahlstatt in Berlin:*

'As I see on your last list of inquiries for missing officers the name of Lieut. Carson missing near Ypres, December 28th, I write to tell you that a German officer who came on leave to Berlin in January told me that a few days before he and some of his men had found the body of a young English officer, who could only have been dead a few hours when found, had papers on him with the name Carson. They buried him with military honours and marked his grave. It was somewhere near Ypres and was at the end of December 1915. I am sorry not to have better news to tell the family, but if I can be of any aid in getting any more details for them I will try and find out though the same officer. We have at once informed the Countess Blucher that your brother's photograph will appear on our sheet No.14 in a few days, and asked her to ascertain at the Succession Office of the German Ministry of War what had become of the papers that were found on Lieut. Carson. We notice in the Army list quite a number of officers of the name of Carson, and are, therefore, looking anxiously forward to the identification of the buried officer, either by means of the photograph, or, what would be much better, by the papers found on him. We shall in any case not fail to keep you informed of the progress of the inquiry. We have called the attention of Countess Blucher to the fact that your brother wore glasses.'

This letter was received by Capt. W. B. Carson, 6th West Ridings, who is at present home from Clipstone Camp on sick leave. It will be remembered that Lieut. Carson was reported to have gone out (at his own request) on patrol on the night of the 27th December, accompanied by two bombers. A flare was put up by the enemy and the party had to lie down. When the flare had burnt out Lieut. Carson could not be seen and efforts to find him proved unsuccessful. No shouting was heard and the conclusion arrived at was that he had been made a prisoner. Many attempts have since been made to ascertain the officer's whereabouts, but until last week end no information was forthcoming.

Lieut. Carson joined the Duke of Wellington's Regiment in September 1914, relinquishing an appointment with a firm of solicitors in North Wales. He went to France on November 1st, 1915, and for a time was attached to an entrenching battalion before joining the 1/6th Battalion a fortnight prior to being reported missing. He was 31 years of age and was educated at Lancaster Grammar School and the Merchant Taylors school, Liverpool. In North Wales, he was prominently identified with the Boy Scout movement.

Countess Evelyn Blücher von Wahlstatt was born Evelyn Stapleton-Bretherton in 1876 at Brighton. In 1907 she married Prince Gebhard Blücher von Wahlstatt, an Anglophile Prussian prince descended from the Prussian General Field Marshal Gebhard Leberecht von Blücher, who had contributed notably to the allied victory at the Battle of Waterloo in 1815. Residing in Germany, Evelyn used her influence with the German authorities to conduct enquiries on behalf of the families of missing British officers who were believed to have been captured. The Queen Victoria Jubilee Fund Association (QVJFA) originally had an office in Geneva to aid needy British subjects. Mr S. Goodman, a retired British officer of the Indian Postal Department living in Geneva, was unofficially requested to make enquiries about missing officers with the Red Cross and German sources to establish if they had become prisoners of war. He had a measure of success with his efforts, but in February 1915, the German authorities forbade information on prisoners of war being passed to private agencies so he obtained permission from the QVJFA to use their name and became the honorary manager of the association's enquiry branch.

Private John W. Raw. (CPGW)

Second Lieutenant Thomas W. Carson. (CPGW)

Also on that day, Private Harold Carey (27) was killed by shell fire, Private John W. Raw from Embsay was killed by a rifle bullet through the heart and Serjeant John William Bell from Keighley was shot in the head and killed. The men are buried at Talana Farm Cemetery.

Private Harold Carey of the Copy Nook Hotel, Bolton-by-Bowland enlisted in January 1915 at Skipton and was posted to France on 29 June 1915. He was the brother of Corporal Alfred Carey MM (24) who was serving in the 5th DWR, 62nd Division when he was killed in action on 6 November 1918.

Serjeant John Benjamin Woodcock, who was wounded by shrapnel on 19 December, died at No.10 CCS of his injuries. Originally from Ranskill in Nottinghamshire, Serjeant Woodcock had lived in Keighley for several years. He joined the 3rd (Volunteer) West Riding Regiment in July 1897 at Keighley before transferring to the TF in 1908. He worked as a labourer at the Holmes & Pearson ironworks in Keighley. He was 34 when he died and had been living at Park Avenue in the town. He left a wife, Nellie and a daughter, Emma.

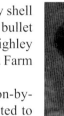

Private Harold Carey. (CPGW)

Serjeant John William Bell was one of five brothers from Haworth who served in the Great War, only one of whom would survive. One of his brothers was also serving as a serjeant in the 1/6th DWR. Serjeant Joseph William Bell was an original member of the 3rd (Volunteer) West Riding Regiment who transferred to the TF in 1908. He was working as a wool sorter before the war and was living at Dalton Street with his wife. He was killed on 23 June 1917.

Serjeant John W. Bell. (Men of Worth)

His other brother, Herbert, served in the 76th Battery, Royal Field Artillery and died whilst a prisoner of war of the Turkish forces after the surrender of Kut-al-Amara in

Mesopotamia (Iraq), aged 20, and is commemorated on the Basra Memorial, on which are recorded more than 40,500 members of the Dominion forces who died in the operations in Mesopotamia from the autumn of 1914 to the end of August 1921 and whose graves are not known. The fourth brother, Lance Corporal Lawrence (Laurie) George Bell, had emigrated to Australia and at the outbreak of war he enlisted in the 4th Battalion, Australian Infantry and was killed on 1 December 1915 at Anzac Cove, Gallipoli, aged 22.

The surviving brother was James Binks Bell. In 1908, aged 22, he joined the 1/6th DWR at Haworth, serving for nearly two years before buying himself out. He also emigrated to Australia and at the outbreak of war enlisted in the Australian Imperial Force as a driver and was posted to France in August 1917. His sister wrote a letter to the Australian authorities pleading for him to be sent home as he was the last surviving brother. The Australians acted quickly and he was removed from the front line and on 10 March 1918 he boarded the RMS *Durham Castle* bound for Australia.

Whilst the 49th Division occupied this part of the Salient, it constructed a whole network of trenches and, in common with the rest of the BEF, used familiar names to identify both trenches and strongpoints. New drafts arriving from Yorkshire would pass along thoroughfares that bore little resemblance to their namesakes back home. Leading towards the front line to the east of the Yser Canal were communication trenches named Colne Valley, Barnsley, Skipton, Huddersfield, Halifax and Strensall Roads. From Coney Street, one could enter Boar Lane, Briggate, North Street, Gawthorpe Road and arrive at Knaresboro' Castle, Clifford's Tower or even the Pump Room (reference to the spa waters of Harrogate).

Tuesday 28 December was quiet, a few trench mortars were fired and the artillery was active on both sides. It was noticed that the first six shells fired by the British guns were duds. At 11.25pm, Lieutenant and Adjutant Malcolm Colin McGregor Law (26) from Hawksworth Hall near Guiseley, was shot and hit in the left side of the abdomen by a sniper's bullet. He was showing five officers from the 5th Battalion, Oxford and Buckinghamshire Light Infantry (Ox and Bucks) around the trench system which they were due to take over. He died at 5am the next morning at the 2nd West Riding Field Ambulance station and is buried in Ferme-Olivier Cemetery, about half a mile west of Elverdinge. Lieutenant Law had joined the TF in 1912 and had been the second-in-command of C (Guiseley) Company. He was working in the family business of Law, Russell & Co. dealers in 'Stuff' (high-quality cloth and house-hold furnishings). As a boy, he attended Streete Court preparatory school in Westgate-on-Sea on the north Kent coast. The headmaster of the school, Mr John Vine Milne, was the father of the children's author A.A. Milne.

At the time of his death, he was the adjutant of the 1/6th DWR and had been mentioned in despatches for distinguished and gallant action. He had also been wounded twice and, prior to becoming adjutant, he had been the battalion bombing officer, which involved planning and co-ordinating close quarter hand grenade attacks on the German lines. The former CO of the battalion, Lieutenant Colonel Birbeck, who had been invalided home, wrote a letter to Lieutenant Law's parents at Hawksworth Hall:

The impressive Law, Russell & Co building located at the junction of Field Street and Chapel Street, Little Germany, Bradford. After years of neglect, the building is being converted into flats.

During the time I was in command, I twice brought his gallant conduct to the notice of the General. He was a most excellent officer and your loss is shared by every officer and man in the Regiment. He had been so very lucky in his escapes that I had almost come to believe he would go on safely through, but it was not to be. You can be justly proud of your son's record which will live forever in the history of the Regiment.

On 7 January 1916, the *Ilkley Free Press* reported his death:

Lieutenant Malcolm C.M. Law who has been mentioned in despatches, was

Entrance to the Law, Russell & Co building.

killed in action on the 29th December 1915. He was the 2nd son of Duncan G. Law of Hawksworth Hall, Guiseley, the principal of the firm of Law, Russell & Co. of Bradford. He was in the Duke of Wellington's Regiment (T.F), and was killed in the fighting subsequent to Sir John French relinquishing the command. He was 26 years of age. He had joined the Territorials in 1912, and had been in France since April 1915, being twice previously wounded. He formed the Guiseley company of the Church Lads' Brigade. In April 1915, the Guiseley company was sent to the front line near Ypres. Lt Law was in charge of a bomb throwing section. In August 1915, he returned home on leave and he took command of a parade of the Church Lads' Brigade. In September 1915 Lt Law received a wound to his face and was hospitalised at Le Touquet.

Lieutenant and Adjutant Malcolm Colin McGregor Law. (Aireborough Historical Society)

He returned to regiment and was appointed Adjutant to his battalion. He was killed by a bullet whilst enquiring on the welfare of his men. One of the men under his command, Pte Dean wrote 'He was always kind and considerate to me and was respected by every officer and man in the battalion for his coolness in every kind of danger'. The church was packed for his memorial service.'

The Rector of Guiseley, the Reverend James Francis Howson held a special memorial service on New Year's Eve and the church bells were muffled. Law was one of three brothers who saw service during the Great War. Kenneth Law served as a Captain in the 2/6th DWR and Ralph Law served as a second lieutenant in the 2nd Yorkshire Regiment (Green Howards). Both men were severely wounded, each losing a leg.

At 6.15 a.m. on 29 December two German soldiers were challenged and shot dead in front of the British lines. Their equipment was recovered and forwarded to brigade HQ. The German artillery was active on the canal bank and some grenades were thrown. On 30 December 1915, the battalion was relieved by the 5th Ox and Bucks and the battalion proceeded to Elverdinge, where they boarded buses to Herzeele in France, 20 miles west of Ypres. The men were being pulled out of the line for extended rest and training, but the journey itself was not without risk as the buses often ended up in water-filled ditches, but thankfully no injuries were caused.

CASUALTIES: In December 1915, the battalion lost 23 men killed and 54 wounded.

There is still evidence of the West Riding Regiment's presence in the Ypres area. The 'Yorkshire Trench' was the name given to a front line position, dug by units of the 49th (West Riding) Division, near the Yser Canal near Boesinghe in 1915. In the mid 1990s, a Belgian archaeology group called The Diggers excavated the site over several years and recovered a lot of material and human remains from the area. Their work was featured in a BBC television documentary called 'The Forgotten Battlefield' and the

Part of the preserved Yorkshire trench, complete with reproduction Livens projectors, on the east bank of the Yser canal.

publicity generated by this programme persuaded the local authorities to preserve a small part of what The Diggers had uncovered. In May 2003, the preserved Yorkshire Trench and Dugout site was opened. An obelisk memorial to the 49th (West Riding) Division also stands on the west bank of the Yser Canal near Essex Farm Cemetery.

Memorial to the West Riding Division, situated on the bank of the Ypres (Yser) Canal near Essex Farm Cemetery, Boesinghe.

Chapter 5

Thiepval

January 1916

On arrival at Herzeele the men were billeted in farms around the town and the routine became one of inspections, route marches, bayonet fighting and gas drill. Specially selected men were trained in the art of bombing, signalling and sniping and on 15 January 1916, the battalion moved into billets in the French town of Wormhout, 5 miles west of Herzeele. The routine here continued in a similar vein, although officers attended a riding school. Instruction was given to the men on the Maxim and Lewis machine guns and lectures on first aid were given by Captain Haddow, the battalion medical officer. On 30 January 1916, the following men of the battalion received decorations for their gallant actions:

Lieutenan Colonel R.L. Aldercron, CO, Distinguished Service Order
Captain A.B. Clarkson, Military Cross
Serjeant Major Orlando Buckley, Military Cross
Company Serjeant Major W. T. Robinson, Distinguished Conduct Medal.

In January 1916, the battalion machine gunners and their serjeants, Fred Stork from Skipton, and J. Watson, transferred to the 147th Machine Gun Company, which came

A Vickers machine gun crew in action at the Battle of Passchendaele in 1917.

A British Vickers machine gun. Water cooled, .303 (7.7mm) calibre, maximum effective range 4,500 yards, rate of fire 450 – 600 rounds a minute. It required a crew of between six to eight men to operate, one to fire, one to feed the ammunition belt and the rest to carry the gun, tripod, ammunition and ancillary parts.

under the command of the newly created Machine Gun Corps. Each infantry battalion had two Vickers machine guns, but after a year of warfare, it was found to be more tactically efficient if the guns were used in larger groups. In October 1915 the Machine Gun Corps was created and three machine-gun companies (each with around nine guns) was created at brigade level. The Vickers guns in the battalion were replaced with four Lewis machine guns which proved to be an excellent infantry support weapon. By the summer of 1918 the numbers of Lewis guns in the battalion had increased to around thirty-five. Unfortunately, Serjeant Stork was killed on 2 July 1916 by a German shell.

CASUALTIES: During January 1916, no casualties were reported.

February 1916
On Tuesday 1 February the men received lectures on trench standing orders and specialist training continued. On the 2nd the battalion moved by train and route march to the small French village of Dreuil-lès-Molliens, 11 miles west of Amiens. The training routine continued and on 10 February the men were issued with the recently designed steel helmets. Initially there were insufficient numbers for personal issue so they were only worn by officers and senior NCOs. The training routine continued but now included trench attacks on specially prepared full-size practice trenches. On 15 February the battalion moved via Bouzincourt to the village of Senlis-le-Sec, 4 miles north-west of the town of Albert. They were preparing to return to the front line once again.

On 18 February 1916 the battalion paraded to hear the verdict of a court martial case against Serjeant Wagstaff. He was reduced to the ranks for using insubordinate language to a senior officer and refusing to obey orders. On 19 February a draft of fifty-eight men and one officer arrived from England and a working party of 150 men from A and B Companies departed to dig a communication trench at Authuille. The next day the men attended a church parade and the CO held a conference with the officers to brief them about his visit to the front line trenches which the battalion was soon to occupy.

On 21 February physical exercise drill and trench attack practice was carried out by the men and the company commanders visited the front line trenches. The day finished with an officers' conference. The weather for the next few days was sunny, but bitterly cold. On 22 February the battalion specialist officers (scouts, signallers, etc) visited the front line trenches and the men continued with company training. Over the next two days, the company commanders visited their 'attack move' or reinforcement positions and a working party of 100 men was provided to make new dugouts at Authuille.

On 25 February a battalion parade was held and every man was given a new set of shoulder titles and a cap badge. Afterwards the Divisional GOC, Major General Percival, watched an open order practice attack across country in a bitterly cold snow storm which lasted all morning. On 26 February a working party of 150 men left to work on the Authuille dug-outs whilst the remainder of the battalion practised attacking from the trenches, observed again by the divisional commander. A church parade was held on the 27th and the following morning was spent cleaning billets prior to handing them over to the 5th KOYLI. In the afternoon, A Company moved to new billets in Bouzincourt whilst the remainder of the battalion marched to Mesnil-Martinsart to occupy the billets of 5th KOYLI.

The 1/6th DWR was now the brigade reserve and on 29 February B, C and D Companies practised advancing to the 'attack move' positions and the company and platoon commanders visited the support and communication trenches. There was an officers' conference in the evening and C Company and half of D Company provided working parties on the Tobermory Street trench system as well as the front line.

CASUALTIES: During February 1916 no casualties were sustained.

March 1916
The first two days of March 1916 were spent working under the cover of darkness on the support and front line trenches. On the 3rd the battalion was relieved from brigade reserve by the 10th Inniskilling Fusiliers from 108 Brigade and marched across country back to billets at Bouzincourt. The next morning men awoke to find the ground covered in thick snow and in the afternoon they received unexpected orders to move into the trenches in the Authuille sector, south of Thiepval. The trenches were in a bad condition and thigh-high gumboots had to be worn. Part of the front line had to be abandoned due to damage by trench mortars that made them practically impassable and in the

evening a draft of sixty-nine men arrived who remained in billets at Bouzincourt until the battalion returned from the front.

On 5 March German trench mortars were active and eight men from A Company were hospitalised due to shock. The bombardment from German trench mortars continued the following day so, in retaliation, an artillery barrage was requested and twenty rounds were fired that silenced the mortars. Later that evening the battalion was relieved by the 15th Lancashire Fusiliers and returned to billets at Bouzincourt. On 7 March, after a few hours' sleep, the battalion marched to Louvencourt, via Hédauville, Forceville and Acheux, 9 miles north-east of Bouzincourt. On 8 March the men were in billets and spent the day cleaning equipment and the new draft of men was inspected by the GOC 147 Brigade Brigadier General Goring-Jones. The next two days were spent on training and inspections and on the 11th a route march was held with 17 officers and 366 men taking part. Church parade was held on the 12th and on 13 and 14 March two drafts of ten men arrived from divisional HQ.

On 15 March a working party of nine officers and 250 men were detailed to work on a new railway cutting at Arquèves, 2 miles from Louvencourt and at midday a mobile field kitchen was sent to provide a hot meal. The work on the railway cutting continued the next day with a working party of six officers and 250 men. On 17 March work on the cutting continued, but seventeen NCOs and men left the battalion due to their becoming 'time expired'. Until the introduction of the Military Service Act (MSA) on 2 March 1916 (otherwise known as conscription) most TF soldiers were engaged for terms of four years. This could be extended in blocks of four years so that a man enlisting in 1908 would 'time expire' in 1912 and a man enlisting or rejoining in 1912 would 'time expire' in 1916 and as such his service was considered finished and he could go home. Unfortunately, if he met the MSA criteria, he could still be conscripted. The MSA commenced on 2 March 1916 for single men and from 25 May 1916 for married men. Any man who was 'time expired' after these dates could also be conscripted and they usually were. The MSA required the man to serve for the duration of the war but for now the fortunate seventeen men were discharged.

Between 18 and 21 March work on the railway continued and a draft of two officers and thirty-two men arrived. On the afternoon of 21 March the battalion moved to billets at Léalvillers, 2 miles south of Louvencourt and the accommodation here was described as poor and dirty. Work continued for the next four days on the railway and on 26 March the men had the chance to visit the baths at Vauchelles and Louvencourt and a church service was held. On 27 March a draft of two officers and forty-nine men arrived. In the morning of the 28th another working party was sent to the railway, but in the afternoon the battalion moved to Toutencourt, 2 miles south-west of Lealvillers. On 29 March, the battalion received orders to proceed to Hédauville, 8 miles east of Toutencourt. They arrived in the evening during a snowstorm to find a tented camp which was pitched in a wood. Ten motor buses were attached to the battalion and the next day was spent moving the camp to another part of the wood. The weather improved and the sun made an appearance.

CASUALTIES: In March 1916, no men were killed but 8 were wounded.

April 1916

The men of the 1/6th DWR spent the first eight days of April 1916 digging trenches in Aveluy Wood. These were the same trenches the men would occupy on the eve of the Somme offensive. The weather was described by the adjutant, Captain Chaffers, as exceptionally hot, making life in the tents most agreeable. On 9 April a Church of England parade was held in the morning and in the afternoon the men visited the baths at Senlis. For the next two days work continued in Aveluy Wood and a case of German measles was discovered in the camp. On 12 April, two officers and fifteen men went on leave, but on 14 April, they were recalled back to camp. The routine of work parties continued until 23 April when the battalion was relieved by the 1/4th DWR and transported by bus to Naours, north of Amiens.

Conditions in rest areas were improving and the billets were described as very good. YMCA and expeditionary force canteens had now appeared, organised entertainments were provided and wire beds were even to be found in some of the billets. Waiting at Naours were Major Charles Malcolm Bateman, one other officer and a draft of eighteen men. On 24 April the battalion attended the baths at Naours and conducted general cleaning and inspections for the rest of the day. During the next two days the men conducted drill parades and bayonet practice. Replicas of the defences of Theipval were constructed and practice attacks carried out. Route marches and attacking the replica trenches occupied 27 to 29 April and on the 30th a church service was held.

April 1916 saw no fatalities or wounded in the ranks of the battalion but four casualties were caused on 24 May by the premature explosion of a rifle grenade during training. The rest of May continued with training, route marches and inspections.

June 1916

On 1 June 1916 the battalion was again on the move. A and B Companies completed a 15-mile route march from Naours to billets at Hédauville whilst C, D and HQ Companies proceeded to the village of Forceville. Working parties were provided for the next two days and on the afternoon of 2 June 1916 the battalion attended church parade, where the two men received decorations. Captain Norman Bairstow Chaffers from Keighley, commander of C Company, received the Military Cross and Serjeant James Bury received the Distinguished Conduct Medal for his actions on 6 November 1915. His citation reads:

Captain N.B. Chaffers MC from the Grange, Sutton-in-Craven survived the war and died on 13 February 1940, aged 52. (CPGW)

When the enemy bombed a post in which he was in charge, causing some casualties, he stuck to the post and bombed the enemy back single handed. This is not the first occasion on which he has shown great courage.

On 5 June C and D Companies visited the baths at Acheux, with A and B Companies having their turn the following day. On the morning of 7 June, the battalion carried out a 12-mile route march and there was a change of command. Lieutenant Colonel Aldercron DSO, was promoted to brigadier general and assumed command of 148 Brigade. He was replaced by Major Charles Malcolm Bateman DSO, who was promoted to lieutenant colonel. Bateman was a popular choice of commanding officer as he had previously commanded the HQ detachment of the 1/6th DWR, and had already proved his leadership in France as a company commander and second-in-command of the battalion. He is described as having fine military judgement and knowledge of his men, who, it was said, would follow him anywhere – high praise indeed, for a man whose leadership skills were soon to be tested. He had been

Lieutenant Colonel Charles Malcolm Bateman DSO. (CPGW)

slightly wounded in the back by shrapnel in October 1915 but recovered from his injuries. Before the war he was living with his aunt, Clara Bairstow, at Royd Hill, Cross Hills near Keighley, now a nursing home. He was the manager of T & M Bairstow, worsted yarn spinners of Sutton and Bradford and a prominent playing member of Skipton Rugby Football Club.

Working parties occupied 8 and 9 June and on the 10th A and B Companies moved to Forceville. The next day was Whit Sunday and a church parade was held and the rest of the day spent on working parties: 100 men to lay cables at Mesnil Cemetery, 100 men to Forceville to make concertina barbed wire and 50 men to work on a road at Martinsart. These working parties were conducted until 22 June. On 23 June, A Company provided 100 men for a working party at Thiepval Wood during which Private Herbert Waddington (19) from Keighley was killed by a rifle bullet and two others were wounded. Private Waddington joined the TF in March 1914 and was the brother of Private Harold Waddington who also served in the 1/6th DWR. Harold was killed on 11 October 1918.

On the afternoon of 23 June, the battalion moved to a brigade concentration area at the town of Contay and the next day a draft of one officer and 102 men arrived. On 25 June the battalion attended church parade and baths were made available at Vadencourt. The next day there was an officers' conference and a draft of 174 men arrived. At

Private Herbert Waddington's grave in Authuille Military Cemetery.

midday on the 27th, the battalion was addressed by the CO, after which they moved en-masse to Warloy.

On 28 June the battalion received orders to move to the assembly trenches in Aveluy Wood where, together with other units of the 49th Division, the 1/6th DWR were to form the reserve of X Corps. The 32nd and 36th (Ulster) Divisions of X Corps were to assault and capture enemy trenches in the Thiepval sector. The 49th Division were then to exploit any gains made by the Corps. However, the weather was very wet and the order to move was cancelled. On 29 June the weather cleared but the battalion remained at Warloy. The bombardment of the German lines had been in progress for several days and shells could be heard passing overhead. On the evening of 30 June the battalion moved up from Warloy into the assembly trenches they had previously dug in Aveluy Wood. The Somme offensive was about to start.

CASUALTIES: During June 1916, the battalion had one man killed.

Chapter 6

Battle of the Somme

An Anglo-French offensive had been in the planning since December 1915, but an anticipated start date in August 1916 had been brought forward due to pressure from the French. In February 1916 they had suffered huge losses when the Germans launched an attack at Verdun and desperately needed to relieve pressure on their army in that area. They hoped that an Anglo-French attack in the Somme area would draw German forces away from Verdun, so a new date was set for 29 June. Heavy rain and poor visibility meant the day of the attack had to be postponed until 1 July.

The 36th (Ulster) Division (Royal Inniskilling Fusiliers, Royal Irish Fusiliers and the Royal Irish Rifles) would take part in the initial assault with an area of responsibility spanning the Ancre Valley. To the north of the river, two battalions of 108 Brigade would advance across the ravine north of Hamel to capture Beaucourt Station. South of the Ancre, the two remaining battalions of 108 Brigade, along with the entire 109 Brigade would attack uphill towards the Schwaben Redoubt. Meanwhile 96 Brigade (15th Lancashire Fusiliers (Salford Pals)), 1st Northumberland Fusiliers (Tyneside Commercials) of the 32nd Division would assault directly towards Thiepval village supported by 16th Lancashire Fusiliers (2nd Salford Pals). Positioned around the village were at least thirty German machine guns in substantial defensive positions that the week-long artillery barrage had failed to destroy. The 16th (Glasgow Pals) and 17th (Glasgow Commercials) Battalions of the Highland Light Infantry and two companies of the 2nd Manchester Regiment would assault the Leipzig Salient.

July 1916

By 2am on 1 July 1916 the 1/6th DWR was in the reserve trenches in Aveluy Wood. At 7.20am 40,785lb (18,500 kg) of explosives was detonated under a German defensive strongpoint on Hawthorn Ridge, near Beaumont Hamel, some 4,000 yards to the north of the 1/6th DWR's position. The explosion at Hawthorn Ridge created initial success, but the enemy quickly responded and the momentum of the attack in that sector stalled. It also gave the Germans along the rest of the line ten minutes' notice of the impending attack. At 7.30am, the main attack commenced and the role of the 1/6th DWR was to exploit and defend any initial gains in their sector.

During the morning of 1 July the battalion was held in reserve but at 11.30am, the men crossed the River Ancre and occupied the northern part of Crucifix Dugouts

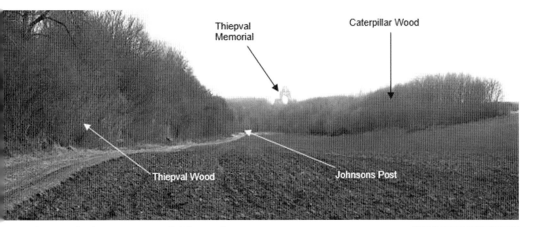

The view looking east towards Thiepval.

Private Henry (Harry) Birch.

situated 100 yards east of the village of Aveluy where the men remained for the rest of the day awaiting orders. The British artillery was active, but the German guns were quiet and the weather was described as fine with hot sun. Three men were wounded by shrapnel and the battalion spent that night at Crucifix Dugouts. Most of the following day was spent in the dug-outs, but at 9.30pm they were ordered to move to the Belfast City trench system in Thiepval Woods where they were to support the 1/5th DWR during an attack on the German trenches opposite Thiepval. This attack was cancelled, but great difficulty was experienced moving to Thiepval Wood. Enemy shelling and a stream of wounded men coming down from the front line caused delays. The battalion spent the night there as best they could but were under constant artillery and machine-gun fire.

Private William Burgess.

Private Arthur Graham, (31) from Bradford, was killed by shrapnel, Private Henry Birch (31) from Skipton, was wounded in the thigh and died of his wound on 7 July. Two other Skipton men were killed: Private William Burgess (24) was killed by a shell and Corporal Edmond Briggs (19) was killed whilst bringing up machine-gun ammunition. Corporal Briggs was the son of Regimental Quartermaster Serjeant Alfred Charles Briggs who died the following year on 29 September. Twenty-six other men were injured including the battalion Medical Officer Captain Haddow.

Private Harry Birch originally enlisted in September 1914, but was medically discharged in December 1915 suffering from pleurisy. By early January 1916 he had recovered sufficiently enough to re-enlist and was posted to France in April 1916.

Corporal Edmond Briggs. (All CPGW)

69

Part of the old trench system in Thiepval Wood.

At 11am on 3 July the battalion was withdrawn from Thiepval Wood and moved to Aveluy Wood where they spent the day, with heavy thunderstorms adding to the problems. At 8.30pm on the 4th the battalion moved from the wood to relieve the 8th South Lancashire Regiment which was holding the front line trenches south of Thiepval Wood. The trenches were in a bad state and numerous British dead were lying in and about the trenches.

Lance Corporal Ernest T Wooff.

Battalion HQ was at Johnsons Post. A Company was to the right, B Company and two platoons of C Company were in the centre. The remaining two platoons of C Company and the whole of D Company were in trenches close to Johnsons Post. The right of the battalion front was Buchanan St, and the left was Thiepval Road. The relief was conducted without casualties. On 5 July the trenches were heavily shelled at irregular intervals by day and night with shrapnel and high explosive shells. Rain fell during the day and many of the British dead from the 1 July attack were buried as practically as possible. On that day Lance Corporal Ernest T. Wooff (22) from Settle, Corporal Wilfred Craven, Private William Feather from Keighley, Private Walter Rawnsley (27) from Crow Lane, Otley (originally from County Durham) and Private John Edward Heyes (37) from Gargrave, were all killed by enemy action. Forty-five men were also wounded. Private Feather had been previously wounded by shrapnel on 12 September 1915.

Lance Corporal Wooff enlisted at the outbreak of war and had been hit in the shoulder by a bullet in July 1915. He spent several months recovering in the UK before returning to the battalion. Before the war he worked at E. Dugdale & Co., tinsmiths, of Settle. His younger brother, Lance Corporal Robert John Wooff, was killed in action on 17 June 1917. He initially joined the West Yorkshire Regiment before being posted to the Durham Light Infantry.

The situation at Thiepval had not improved on 6 July. The trenches were heavily shelled, but during the lulls the trench ramparts were repaired and the dead buried. Rations and ammunition were brought up during the night, but two men were wounded and one man was reported missing. Private William Atkinson Hodgson (19) from Ingleton died at No.44 CCS from multiple shrapnel wounds received the previous day. Despite his youth, he was a pre-war 'terrier' having signed up in May 1913. He had previously been in the cadet corps of the 1/6th DWR and is buried in Puchevillers British Cemetery. He was the brother-in-law of Able Seaman Beauford Henry Creed (26) from Armley, but born in Ingleton, who was serving in the Drake Battalion of the 63rd (Royal Navy) Division when he died in Germany on Christmas Eve 1918.

Private William A. Hodgson. (CPGW)

Between 7.25am and 8.50am on 7 July, the battalion was tasked with performing a 'Chinese attack' in front of the line in their sector. A 'Chinese attack' was the name given to a feint or dummy attack to make the enemy think an attack was underway. This was intended to support a flanking attack on the German positions at Thiepval. Smoke bombs were thrown into no man's land but the wind changed direction and blew the smoke back to the British trenches. In response, the Germans shelled the British trenches and support lines and continued to do so for the rest of the day. The battalion also came under the command of 148 Brigade as 147 Brigade, less the 1/6th DWR, was withdrawn from the line. During the bombardment, Private Edward Ellershaw (26) from Settle was killed and twenty-two men were wounded. Private Ellershaw was an original member of the 3rd (Volunteer) West Riding Regiment and transferred to the 1/6th DWR in 1908 on its formation. He was employed on the Lancashire and Yorkshire Railway at Nelson and was the half-brother of Private Joseph Ronald Lord (22) from Settle who was serving in the King's Own (Royal Lancaster Regiment) when he was killed on 2 March 1916. He was also the cousin of Private Richard Wallbank (18) of Clapham who was serving in the 8th (Service) DWR when he was killed on 23 August 1915 during the Gallipoli campaign.

The next day 147 Brigade came back into the line and the battalion came under their command again. The 1/4th DWR was on the left of the battalion and the 1/5th DWR to the right. The German artillery was less active. Private George William Phillips from Guiseley died of wounds received on 4 July at the British Military Hospital at Étaples, France. His father, George Shillito Phillips, was the landlord of the Station Hotel at Guiseley. Before the war, George was a clerk at a waste cotton factory. He was attested in the regiment on 5 September 1914, departing to France with the battalion in April 1915.

Private George Phillips.

Sunday 9 July was a fine day which allowed the trenches to dry out and the process of burying the British dead continued. Private James

M. Varley, from Skipton, was killed and six other men were wounded. Private Varley had previously served in the 6th DWR and was 'time expired' but at the outbreak of war he rejoined the ranks of the 6th DWR. Before the war he was a weaver at Johnson & Mason, manufacturers, Skipton. He left a widow and three children.

The battalion was relieved by 1/7th DWR and became the brigade reserve at Northern Bluff, just south of Thiepval Wood. The next day the German artillery fired sporadic shrapnel and high explosive

Private Edward Ellershaw. (All CPGW)

Private James M. Varley.

shells and Private Denis Peck (22) from Arthur Street, Barnoldswick was wounded in the chest by a rifle bullet. The 11th was another fine day but the enemy artillery was more active. The battalion was tasked with carrying rations for the whole brigade, during which four men were wounded by shrapnel. The following day was fine but cold and seven men were wounded by shell fire. On that day Private Percy Pawson (33) of Victoria Terrace, Guiseley was killed. He enlisted in the TF on 1 June 1915 at Guiseley and was employed as a boot riveter before the war. His elder brother, Lance Corporal Enos Pawson, served in the 2/6th DWR and the 27th Provisional Battalion and died at Guiseley on 15 November 1915.

Private Percy Pawson.

On the 13th – described as a quiet day – the enemy shelled the ground to the west of the Ancre and two men were wounded. The British artillery was requested to fire a counter barrage which silenced the German guns. On 14 July the British artillery was active, but there was no reply from the enemy guns, although four men were wounded by machine-gun fire. On 15 July McMahons Post was shelled in the afternoon and during the evening and the battalion relieved the 1/7th DWR in the front line which was completed without casualties. It was noticed that the trenches were much dryer and improved since the battalion was last there six days ago. On 16 July the British artillery shelled the German lines opposite the battalion and a few shells were fired in response, but no casualties were caused. Heavy rain filled the trenches with muddy water but, except for a few shells, 17 July was 'quiet', although six men were wounded by shrapnel.

Private Pawson's grave in Authuille Military Cemetery.

The next day was also quiet with no casualties but on 19 July the Germans shelled the front line and three men were wounded. In the evening the battalion was relieved by the 1/7ᵗʰ DWR and relocated to the Northern Bluff, occupying The Mound, McMahons Post and Mill Keep and becoming the brigade reserve. The next day was spent carrying rations for the rest of the brigade and a working party of one officer and thirty men was provided. Two men were wounded by shrapnel on 21 and 22 July.

On the night of the 23ʳᵈ the battalion relieved the 1/7ᵗʰ DWR and took over the line from Union Street to Thiepval Avenue. The next day was fine and a draft of twenty-five men arrived from the 49ᵗʰ Division reinforcement camp who were posted to A Company. On this day, Private Denis Peck (22) from Barnoldswick died of wounds at No.18 General Hospital at Dannes-Camiers, north of Étaples. He enlisted on 25 October 1915 and was posted to France on 10 February 1916. Before the war he worked as a weaver for Brooks & Son in Barnoldswick.

Private Denis Peck. (CPGW)

Tuesday 25 July was quiet up to 12.30pm when the enemy started shelling the front and support lines. The intensity increased and it turned into a heavy bombardment that lasted until 5pm. Johnsons Post was heavily shelled and the trenches were badly damaged in many places, but the damage and total casualties were small considering the intensity of the German fire. The British artillery did reply but it appeared light. Serjeant Leonard Clarkson (21) from Little Coates, Grimsby, Lance Corporal John Thornborough from Unity Street, Riddlesden, Private John Kaye (22) from Milnsbridge, Huddersfield, Private Samuel Bentley from Burley-in Wharfedale, Private Harold Barr from Shipley and Private John H. Holden (19) from Barnoldswick were all killed in the barrage.

Private John H. Holden. (CPGW)

Private Holden's headstone in Lonsdale Cemetery, Authuille.

Serjeant Leonard Clarkson joined the battalion in September 1914 when it was in Healing and before the war he was employed as a clerk at Messrs Robinson & Ward, Grimsby. Private Holden enlisted in November 1914 and was a stretcher-bearer in the battalion. Before the war had worked as a weaver at Nutters & Sons in Barnoldswick. He was in the Calf Hall Road Methodist Church choir and secretary of the church Sunday school. He was one of the Barnoldswick Division of the St John's Ambulance Brigade where he would have learned first aid and, along with many other men from the town, he became a member of the battalion stretcher-bearer company. Others from Barnoldswick who were members of the St John's Ambulance Brigade were recruited into the Royal Navy Sick Berth Reserve. On 30 October 1914, fifteen Barnoldswick men were amongst the 229 medical staff, nurses and crew aboard the aboard His Majesty's Hospital Ship *Rohilla*, originally of the British India Steam Navigation Company. The vessel had been converted to a hospital

HMHS ROHILLA

TO THE MEMORY OF
THE TWELVE MEN
FROM THIS TOWN WHO LOST
THEIR LIVES AT SEA
NEAR WHITBY
ON OCTOBER THE 30th 1914
AND WHO WERE MEMBERS OF
THE BARNOLDSWICK ST. JOHN
AMBULANCE BRIGADE
AND THE ROYAL NAVAL SICK
BERTH RESERVE

Memorial in Barnoldswick to the men lost in the Rohilla tragedy.

The Barnoldswick war memorial.

Corporal Ernest Cowgill.

ship and was sailing from Leith in Scotland to Dunkirk to evacuate wounded soldiers. At 3.50am on that day, during a strong gale, the ship ran aground on submerged rocks at Saltwick Nab, a mile south-east of Whitby, and broke in two. The gale lasted for the next three days and, although the ship was only 500 yards from the shore, the raging sea made rescue exceedingly difficult. The crews of the Whitby, Upgang, Scarborough, Redcar and Tynemouth life boats acted with exceptional bravery but eighty-three people lost their lives. From the Barnoldswick contingent, only three men were saved.

Also on 25 July 1916, three other men were wounded and a draft of twenty-five men arrived from the reinforcement camp who were posted to B Company. Corporal Ernest Cowgill (22) of Primrose Hill, Skipton and Serjeant Fred Stork (23) of Skipton, both attached to the 147th Company Machine Gun Corps, were killed when a German shell hit their dug-out.

Corporal Ernest Cowgill was another pre-war 'terrier' who worked as a weaver at Curl, Kirk & Co. in Skipton. He had three cousins who also died in the Great War. Private Joseph Whitham of the 102nd Battalion, 4th CEF was killed in action on 9 April 1917. He was born in Skipton in 1887 and had originally joined the 3rd (Volunteer) DWR in 1906. He transferred to the TF on its formation in April 1908, serving for one year before emigrating to Canada. Lance Corporal Harold Cowgill DCM (20) from Glusburn was serving in the 15th/17th West Yorkshire Regiment when he was killed on 2 July 1918 and Private Norris Cowgill (19) from Earby was serving in the 2/7th West Yorkshire Regiment when he was killed on 27 March 1918.

Serjeant Fred Stork was another pre-war 'terrier' having joined the TF in September 1913. Before the war he was a weaver at Smith Hartley's Union Mill in Skipton. Both he and Corporal Cowgill are buried in Lonsdale Cemetery near Authuille.

Corporal Cowgill's headstone in Lonsdale Cemetery, Authuille. (Both

The brother of Fred Stork, Private Myles Stork, also serving in the 1/6th DWR, was seriously injured in September 1915 when he lost two fingers and the thumb of his left hand when they were severed by an exploding shell.

The men were buried by Reverend Robert Shipman who, from 1911 to 1925, was vicar at St Mary's Church in Long Preston. In December 1915 he was appointed as an Army Chaplain 4th Class which equated to the rank of captain. On 1 January 1916 he sailed for France, leaving behind his wife Jessica and sons Francis (11) and Robert (7) and was

Serjeant Fred Stork.

Serjeant Stork's headstone in Lonsdale Cemetery, Authuille. (Both CPGW)

posted to a CCS near Saint-Omer. Later he became the regimental chaplain of the 1/6th DWR where he would have known some of the men quite well. He witnessed the preparations and start of the Somme offensive, but in mid-August 1916 he had to return home, suffering from trench fever. After convalescing in Long Preston, he returned to his duties with the army until finally returning home in January 1918.

In a sermon given in Long Preston Church on his return, he spoke of the kindness of the men: *the closer they got to the trenches so much closer was the sense of brotherhood and the nearer they got to the firing line the extraordinary kindness of the men for each other was most remarkable.*

He died in 1958, aged 74, at Harlaxton near Grantham.

St Mary's Church, Long Preston.

In the time before the development of antibiotics, trench fever was the name given to a mystery condition which started to affect soldiers, usually after serving in the front line. The initial symptoms of the illness were often short-lived but a full recovery was slow and casualties were often left feeling depressed. The official name given to the illness was PUO (Pyrexia (fever) of Unknown Origin) but it was after the war when it was discovered that the illness is caused by a bacterium carried in the intestine of the body louse. Infection occurred when a louse defecated whilst feeding and bacterium-infected faeces entered the body via the bite mark, usually by the host scratching the site. The symptoms included sudden fever, lethargy, intense headache, skin rash, pain in the eyeballs, dizziness, muscle ache and constant and intense pain in the shins. After about five days, the symptoms would subside but could re-occur several days later. This cycle could be repeated as many as eight times and complications included relapses of the condition as much as ten years after an apparent recovery.

On 26 July 1916, a draft of twenty-five men arrived from the replacement camp and were posted to C Company. The next day a British heavy trench mortar fired twelve rounds towards the German lines resulting in a brief artillery response which landed in the British trenches causing two casualties. A further draft of twenty-five men also arrived and were posted to D Company. On 28 July the battalion was relieved by the 1/7th DWR and relocated to Northern Bluff, with C Company occupying The Mound, Mill Keep and McMahons Post.

Also on this day, Private Herbert Williams (20) from Guiseley was killed. Herbert lived at Victoria Terrace, Guiseley with his parents Joshua and Annie, brother George (19) and sisters Adie (27) and Kate (21). He was employed as a wool weaver and enlisted at Guiseley on 7 December 1915, initially into the 3rd DWR. He was posted to France on 15 June 1916 and the same week he was transferred to the 1/6th DWR. His service records survive which show in July 1916 he spent several days at No.3 Canadian General Hospital, Boulogne with a severe throat infection. On 19 July he was certified fit and posted to the base depot, so it is highly likely he was in one of the new drafts of men which arrived on or after 25 July. He is buried in Connaught Cemetery, Thiepval.

Private Herbert Williams. (Aireborough Historical Society)

The next few days were quiet and the weather up to the end of the month was hot with only one man wounded.

<u>CASUALTIES</u>: During July 1916, the battalion had 21 men killed and 138 wounded.

August 1916

On 1 August 1916 the battalion provided a working party of five officers and 120 men to dig a new front line trench to the north-east side of Thiepval Wood, during which two men were wounded. Plans had been drawn up to resume the assault in the Thiepval sector but, after the experience of 1 July, it was decided that the expanse of no man's land was too wide to attack across successfully so it was proposed to dig a series of parallel trenches in no man's land which would be connected, thus creating a new front line nearer to the German trenches. The new trenches were to be dug under the cover of darkness from the River Ancre, along the line of Mill Road towards the junction of Thiepval Road. The work was to be carried out by the battalion in support with the battalion in the front line providing covering parties to protect the men doing the digging. German shelling had reduced the communication trenches in Thiepval Wood to mud-filled ditches and the movement of large working parties along them became slow and a lot of time was spent getting to and from the new dig. A combination of this and enemy shelling meant the actual work done on the new trenches was minimal compared with the effort and number of men engaged on the project.

The same routine was followed on 2 August when four men were wounded by shrapnel. On the 3rd the battalion relieved the 1/7th DWR in the front line from Union Street to Thiepval Avenue which was completed at 9pm with no casualties, although one man was wounded later that day.

On 4 August at 9pm, a smoke screen was discharged from the British lines followed by an artillery barrage. The German artillery responded with heavy shelling for an hour during which four men were wounded. On 5 August the British guns shelled the German lines intermittently with little retaliation and work continued digging a new front line between Thiepval points north and south, during which two men were wounded. The following day German trench mortars landed to the left of the battalion line and at 5.30pm, British artillery cut the enemy wire opposite the battalion front and one man was wounded by shrapnel. On the 7th work on the new trench continued and the artillery fire on the German wire continued.

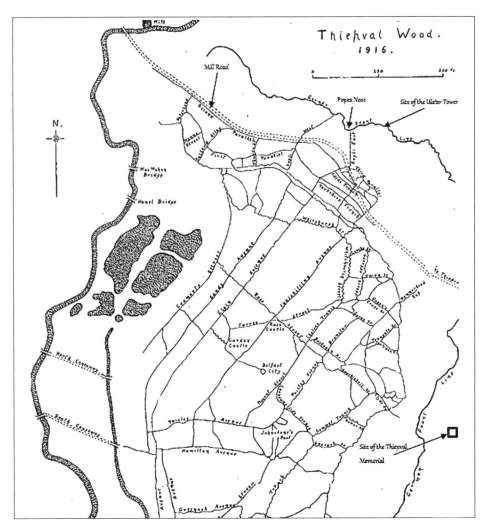

Thiepval Wood map.

Since early July, direct assaults against the German positions in Thiepval had been put on hold, with the emphasis placed on defence. There was, however, constant British artillery and trench mortar fire on the German positions and 147 Brigade issued the following order:

The Army Commander wishes everything possible to be done to keep the enemy in front of the division on alert, make him man his parapets and get him under our shrapnel fire. With this objective, the following demonstration will be made to induce the enemy to man his parapets. At 10 p.m. today, as many bayonets as possible will be shown along the whole front of the Brigade as if an assault is imminent and timed for 10 p.m.

Five or ten minutes previous to this hour, whistles should be blown at

78

intervals along the front as if signals were being made. The tops of trench-ladders should be shown over the parapets. The artillery immediately after 10 p.m. will open a bombardment on the enemy front and support trenches, especially on those trenches which can be taken in enfilade. Any other device which can lead the enemy in the front line to expect an assault at 10.p.m should be employed and machine guns should fire during the artillery bombardment.

At 4am on 8 August a smoke barrage was discharged from the special emplacements which had been dug about every 25 yards along the front line. This was created by throwing smoke bombs into no man's land and which lasted fifteen minutes. It was not always successful due to the changing wind direction which often blew it back towards their own lines. The British artillery shelled the German trenches

Serjeant Rowland Hill.

during the smoke discharge and there was intermittent shelling from both sides all day and night and three men were wounded. On 9 August Serjeant Rowland Hill (20) from Silsden and Corporal Thomas W. Walker (22) from Heywood, Lancashire were both killed by a German shell and three other men were wounded.

Serjeant Hill's headstone in Lonsdale Cemetery, Authuille. (Both CPGW)

Serjeant Rowland Hill from South View Terrace, Silsden joined the 2/6th DWR in October 1914 and was posted to France at the end of June 1915. Before the war he was studying at Bradford Technical College and was assistant scoutmaster of the Silsden Boy Scouts. He was also a Sunday school teacher at Silsden Parish Church.

At 9pm the 1/6th DWR was relieved by the 1/7th DWR and moved back to The Bluff. D Company went to The Mill, McMahon's Post and Mill Keep. On 10 August the battalion provided a working party of 300 men in Theipval Wood, carrying rations to the front at night. A draft of sixty men arrived

Corporal Thomas W. Walker. (CPGW)

from the reinforcement camp and working parties were provided again the next day.

On 12 August a draft of fifty-eight men arrived from the replacement camp and, at 10.25pm, the British artillery bombarded the German lines for half an hour. The next day 300 men were

Corporal Walker's headstone in Lonsdale Cemetery, Authuille.

provided for working parties. On 14 August working parties were provided again but an accident occurred at the Theipval ammunition dump. Five men were wounded when a hand grenade exploded as the men were cleaning them. At 9pm on 15 August, the battalion relieved the 1/7th DWR in the front line with the battalion front extending from Thiepval Avenue to Union Street. On 16 August the British artillery shelled the German lines, prompting the Germans to reply with shrapnel rounds that wounded eight men.

On 17 August at 2.30am the enemy conducted a small raid on the new front line that was being dug between Thiepval points north and south. A patrol of six German soldiers crept up to the trench and opened fire at a working party of one officer and four men. The men returned fire, but it was not known if any Germans were hit. The British casualties were one man killed, one wounded and one missing. The missing man was found dead in no man's land the following evening. Nothing had been taken from his pockets, but his shoulder titles were missing. It is not clear which man was killed immediately and which man was found the next night, but one of the men killed was Private Thomas Edward Mann (26) born in Burley-in-Wharfedale, but residing at Derry Hill in Menston when he enlisted in December 1914 at Guiseley Drill Hall. Before the war he was employed as a house painter in his father's firm. The other man was Private George Cook (20) from Wesley Street, Otley. He enlisted at Guiseley in October 1914 and was one of the original C Company men who landed in France in April 1915. Both men are buried in Lonsdale Cemetery, Authuille. Five other men were also wounded during the day.

It was quiet until 5.20pm on 18 August when, in conjunction with other operations in the south, a smoke barrage was discharged along the battalion front which lasted for thirty minutes. The British artillery also shelled the German front and support trenches and the Germans replied with a heavy trench mortar bombardment to the left of the British line that lasted until 6.45pm. Acting Serjeant Clarence Atkinson (24) of Weston Road, Ilkley was killed by a trench mortar and is buried in Lonsdale Cemetery, Authuille. He enlisted in June 1915 at Skipton and had served as a police officer in the West Riding Constabulary before the enlisting. Ten other men were also wounded.

On 19 August 147 Brigade was withdrawn from the line and relieved by 74 Brigade of the 25th Division. The 1/6th DWR was relieved by the 13th Cheshire Regiment and marched 4 miles to Forceville where they remained overnight. During the relief one man was wounded by a rifle grenade. The next day the battalion marched a mile to Léalvillers where the billets were found to be dirty and the officers' quarters described as being in a poor condition.

On 21 August the battalion paraded under company arrangements, which mainly involved reorganising the companies and platoons. The following day a draft of 161 men joined the battalion. On 23 August the battalion, less C Company, undertook a route march and on the 24th, C Company carried out assault practice in consolidating positions. On 25 August Lieutenant Robinson, who had written tactics on Lewis gun use, was seconded to General Headquarters to roll out the training to the whole army.

Eight officers and sixteen NCOs watched a Bangalore torpedo demonstration (a hollow metal pole, packed with explosives, which is pushed under the enemy barbed wire and detonated to clear a path through). On 26 August, the adjutant and former commander of C Company, Captain Norman Bairstow Chaffers MC, was appointed second in command of the 3rd Worcestershire Regiment. On 27 August the battalion moved to billets at Forceville (which were described as dirty) and C Company departed the battalion to be temporally attached to 57 Field Company, Royal Engineers.

At 1.30am on 28 August the battalion received orders to relieve the 5th West Yorkshire Regiment in the centre sector of Thiepval Woods. The first of the companies departed at 6.45am and battalion HQ was set up at Belfast City in deep dugouts. D Company was at the south-west corner from Oblong Wood to Union Street, B Company from Union Street to Sandy Ave, and A Company in support at Ross Castle and Belfast City. The next day was very wet and soon made the trenches waterlogged. The German artillery was active and gas shells fell on Hammerhead Sap. Corporal Frederick Taylor (22) from Silsden was accidently killed by a rifle bullet.

Corporal Frederick Taylor. (CPGW)

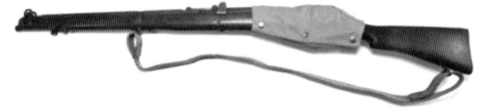

A breech cover was a piece of canvas which fastened around the trigger and bolt action of the rifle to prevent mud and dirt fouling the mechanism.

During the morning of 29 August the firing bay of the trench was blown in by a British shell and buried several rifles. As they were in the process of being recovered, one was picked up and it suddenly fired, hitting Corporal Taylor behind the ear. A court of enquiry ruled that soil had compacted around the trigger and breech cover, making it sensitive to the touch.

Corporal Frederick Taylor enlisted in October 1914 and before the war he was employed as a weaver at Walton's in Silsden. He is buried in Lonsdale Cemetery.

On the same day Corporal Albert Stevenson (21) from Keighley, Private John H. Waters (18) from Keighley and Private Albert W. Tune from Sutton-in-Craven were killed by shrapnel shells. Three other men were wounded.

Corporal Albert Stevenson was born in Holbeach in Lincolnshire but by 1912 he was living at Quarry Street, Keighley with his parents George and Susan, two brothers George junior and Harold, as well as five sisters, Emily, Edith, Ellen, Phyllis and Kitty. He was employed as a labourer for Midgley & Sons and in June 1912 he enlisted in the TF at Keighley. He was promoted to lance corporal in April 1915 but reverted to private in June of that year. By July 1915 he had the stripe back and was made a full corporal in March 1916.

In 1911 Private John Henry Waters was living at the family home on Oakworth Road, Keighley and worked in a textile mill. He enlisted at Skipton in January 1915 and was initially posted to the 27th Provisional Battalion before being sent to France on 6 June 1916. He is buried in Lonsdale Cemetery.

Private Albert William Tune from Sutton-in-Craven enlisted in the 3/6th DWR in November 1915 and before the war he worked as a weaver at T & M Bairstow's Sutton Mill in the town. He received his army training at Clipstone Camp in Nottinghamshire and was posted to France on the 13 March 1916. He had previously received a head wound on 12 August, caused by shell splinters. He is also buried in Lonsdale Cemetery.

Daybreak on 30 August started with rain showers but that did not prevent the German artillery delivering its usual morning barrage, although no casualties were caused. The weather improved on the 31st and trench mortars joined the German artillery in the daily barrage with the result that three men were wounded.

CASUALTIES: In August 1916, 10 men had been killed and 56 wounded.

September 1916

The bombardment of the enemy lines opposite the 1/6th DWR continued on 1 September 1916, which was a fine, clear day. One man had a lucky escape when he was wounded by a fragment of a large calibre British shell which rebounded from the direction of Thiepval and struck his leg. At 3.30pm, D Company was relieved by 1/5th KOYLI and proceeded to Northern Bluff. B Company moved to Paisley Ave as a large attack on the Schwaben Redoubt at Thiepval was planned for the following day. The assaulting battalions from 147 Brigade were to be the 1/4th and 1/5th DWR. The 1/6th DWR was to act as resupply and support and the 1/7th DWR as reserve. It must be remembered that the ground was a steep slope, a mass of shell holes and still covered with the dead from the attack on 1 July.

In the early hours of 2 September Corporal Thomas R. Parker (22) from Skipton and Private Willie Cooper from Keighley were both killed by a German shell and Private Robert Hardisty was wounded in the leg by a bullet.

Corporal Thomas Reid Parker. (CPGW)

Before the war, Willie Cooper from Carr Street, Keighley was employed as a core-maker (prepared moulds for casting) at Clapham Bros Foundry Works on Market Street, Keighley. He was a pre-war 'terrier' who had originally joined up in 1909 and left in 1913. In March 1914 he signed up again in the ranks of the 1/6th DWR but in December of that year he was medically discharged with dyspeptic symptoms. In March 1915 he rejoined at Skipton and was quickly promoted to lance corporal then full corporal. On 1 April 1916 he was sent to France and within days he had voluntarily reverted to the rank of private.

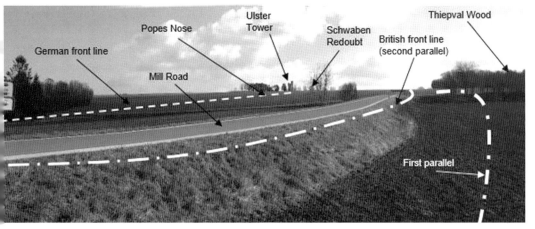

Position of the front line, 3 September 1916

Corporal Thomas Reid Parker from Skipton was a pre-war 'terrier' who in civilian life worked as a plumber. He was the cousin of Private Thomas Davey (19) from Overburn, Sutton-in-Craven who was serving in the 1st Northumberland Fusiliers when he was killed in action on 5 May 1918.

Also on this day Private Robert Hardisty (36) of North Parade, Ilkley, but born in Skipton, died at Queen Alexandra's Red Cross Hospital in Dunkirk from a gunshot wound to his thigh received on 2 September. He enlisted at the outbreak of war and worked as a joiner. He is buried in Dunkirk Town Cemetery and left a widow and six children.

Private Robert Hardisty. (CPGW)

The remains of a German observation bunker on the 'Pope's Nose' looking towards the Schwaben Redoubt south-east of the Ulster Tower.

On 3 September at 5.10am, an intensive bombardment of the German lines commenced and five minutes later the attack began. Without hesitation, the men advanced from the newly dug parallel trenches across Mill Road, towards the Pope's Nose salient. The Germans were immediately on the alert, flares flashed into the sky to alert their artillery and, despite a thorough British creeping barrage, a deadly crossfire of machine-gun bullets opened from the direction of the Schwaben Redoubt and the Pope's Nose. Many men were hit but the troops advanced and halted just short of the German line to wait for the British barrage to lift. The enemy artillery response arrived about ten minutes after the signal flare was launched. It landed on the old British front line at the edge of Thiepval Wood and the newly dug parallel trenches which were soon obliterated. Large calibre German shells landed in Thiepval Wood amongst the men of the 1/6th DWR; as the British barrage lifted, the men of the 1/4th DWR and 1/5th DWR assaulted the German trenches.

There was very little opposition and the objective of 147 Brigade was captured. The German line had been virtually destroyed by the bombardment of the previous two months, but it was riddled with deep dug-outs that had to be cleared. Many prisoners were captured and directed towards the British lines, but most were killed by their own machine guns and artillery. Ammunition and grenades were running low as carrying parties had failed to reach the captured positions, so the only way to replenish was to take them from the dead and wounded nearby. At 6.30am it was apparent that the attack by 146 Brigade, to the left, had failed to reach any of their objectives.

By 7am the only British troops at the correct objective were the 1/4th DWR. The Germans began to counter-attack and at 8am they launched a major assault from the direction of the Schwaben Redoubt. With dwindling ammunition and mounting casualties, the men of the 1/4th DWR withdrew under heavy machine-gun and artillery fire back to the British line. The Germans continued with a heavy bombardment and a shell hit a dug-out at The Bluff, killing six men. Private Fred A. Barnes from Colne, Henry E.C.S. Moorhouse (22), John Turnbull and George Bond (20) all from Skipton, Private Frank Kelly from Keighley and Private Alvara Storey (20) from Hipperholme were killed. Private Henry Warden from Roberttown near Liversedge was also reported missing, presumed killed. Before the war he was working as a dyer's labourer and is commemorated on the Thiepval Memorial.

Private Alvara Storey was living in Sowerby Bridge and was also working as a dyer's labourer when he enlisted in December 1915, aged 19. He was the son of Hubert and Mary Storey of Lower Shelf, Northowram, Halifax.

Frank Kelly was a pre-war 'terrier' having joined in June 1913. Before the war he worked as a fitter at George Hattersley & Co textile machine manufactures of Keighley. On 25 September 1915 he had been wounded by a piece of shrapnel in his shoulder which required treatment at the 3rd Canadian General Hospital but he recovered sufficiently enough to be posted back to the battalion. On 26 August 1916 he was given twenty-eight days Field Punishment No.1 and deprived of twenty-eight days pay after being caught sleeping whilst on sentry duty. The offence occurred on 6 August

Private Fred Barnes.   *Private George Bond.*   *Private Henry Moorhouse.*   *Serjeant James Metcalfe.*   *Private John Turnbull.*

when the unit was in the front line so he could consider himself lucky that the matter was dealt with 'in house' by the CO. A full court martial could have imposed a far greater punishment, including a sentence of death. Field Punishment No.1, often abbreviated to FP No.1 or even just No.1, consisted of the convicted man being placed in fetters or handcuffs and attached to a fixed object, such as a gun wheel or a fence post for up to two hours a day. During the early part of the Great War, the punishment was often applied with the arms stretched out and the legs tied together, which gained it the grim nickname of 'Crucifixion'.

On the same day, another German shell hit a dugout on Paisley Ave and killed Second Lieutenant Frank B. Gill (19) from Birmingham and wounded Second Lieutenant L. Jaques, who suffered a compound fracture to his thigh. Private John W. Robinson from Ingleton was killed by shrapnel and Serjeant James Metcalfe, also from Ingleton, died of wounds. Twenty-five other men were wounded by shell fire.

Private John Robinson.

Second Lieutenant Frank Brooks Gill had been commissioned from the 1/8th Sherwood Foresters Regiment in April 1916 and is buried in Lonsdale Cemetery.

Serjeant James Metcalf from Ingleton enlisted on 5 August 1914 and had had been wounded in July 1915 which required several months recovery in a UK hospital.

Private John W. Robinson was a member of Ingleton Football Club and had worked in a colliery near the village.

Private George Bond (19) enlisted in August 1915 and was posted to France in January 1916. Before the war he worked as an under-gardener at Whinfield on Keighley Road in Skipton.

Private John Turnbull enlisted in May 1915 and was mobilised in September of that year into the 3/6th DWR for training at Clipstone Camp. He was posted to France in February 1916 but almost immediately hospitalised with a severe throat infection. He was eventually posted to the battalion on 1 June.

Private W. Cockshott. (All CPGW)

Private Wright Cockshott (28) from Barn Cottage, Keighley Road, Steeton was also reported missing, presumed killed. He originally signed up under the Derby scheme and was conscripted in April 1916. He had only been in France a few weeks before he was killed. Before the war he was employed at John Clough & Son as a weaving overlooker and was a member of the Steeton and District rose society. He has no known grave and is commemorated on pier and face 6a and 6b on the Thiepval Memorial. He was the cousin of Private Cyrus Cockshott, also from Steeton, who was serving in the West Yorkshire Regiment when he was killed on 21 March 1918.

The Derby Scheme, named after Lord Derby, Director General of Recruiting, was introduced in October 1915. It offered men the opportunity to attest or swear an oath that they were willing to serve in the armed forces without having to enlist immediately. Attested men were placed in administrative groups according to their age and marital status and were issued with khaki armbands bearing a royal crown motif to show their participation in the scheme. The various groups would then be called up when needed, prioritising single men over those who were married. The scheme was abandoned when the Military Service Act (conscription) became law in January 1916.

The casualties of the 1/4th DWR were heavy. During the attack, 9 officers and 336 men out of a total of 18 officers and 629 men who went into action became casualties. Of that number, 7 officers and 115 men were killed, with the others either wounded or missing.

At 3am on 4 September the two companies on The Bluff were relieved by the 5th York and Lancaster Regiment and then marched to Hédauville. They were joined by B Company and were accommodated in billets. The next day was wet and the camp was very muddy. The men were taken by motor lorry to Acheux for baths and at 2pm, C Company rejoined the battalion, having been attached to 57 Field Company, Royal Engineers; a working party of 150 men was provided from A and B Companies.

On 6 September 1916 those who were not on the previous day's working party were engaged in bayonet fighting, arms drill and physical exercise. On the 7th specialist training was provided for the battalion Lewis gunners and bombers and the remainder of the battalion trained the same as the previous day. That night 400 men were provided for a working party on the front line. They left in buses at 6pm and returned at 5am. No training was done on 8 September due to the late return of the men. However, 9 September was a fine day and training as per the previous days was resumed. On 10 September, a brigade parade was held with the divisional band playing. A motor lorry was put at the disposal of the battalion, which transported 2 officers and 31 men to Amiens and 250 men were provided for work on a strongpoint in no man's land.

On 11 September the specialist training continued and the rest of the battalion spent the morning conducting close order drill and in the afternoon practised the formation for attacking from trenches.

Major Alfred Bairstow Clarkson MC was thrown from his horse and broke a bone in his arm. Before the war he was a partner in the firm of Spencer, Clarkson & Co, solicitors of North Street, Keighley and lived at the family home of West Riddlesden Hall. He eventually became the commanding officer of the 1/6th DWR and was awarded the Distinguished Service Order for his actions on 1 November 1918 at

Famars. His younger brother, Lieutenant (later Major) Wilfred Bairstow Clarkson served in the Royal Garrison Artillery and was also awarded the DSO.

On the morning of 12 September baths were allocated at Acheux, 2 miles from the billets. Most of the battalion had to march to the baths, but 120 more fortunate men were transported on lorries. In the afternoon, the men practised close order drill. The Divisional GOC, Major General Percival, visited the camp to observe and commented that he was pleased with the way the battalion performed.

Major A.B. Clarkson MC DSO. (Men of Worth)

On 13 September training resumed and there was a change of command at brigade level. Brigadier General E.F. Brereton DSO, who had commanded since 1912, was replaced by Brigadier General L.G. Lewis DSO, late of the Essex Regiment.

On 14 September those men not on working parties were engaged in physical exercise and bayonet practice. On the morning of 15 September, the CO had just begun an inspection of the battalion when orders were received to relieve 32 Brigade of the 12th Division in the part of the Leipzig Salient that had been captured on 1 July. The battalion proceeded to Martinsart Wood where they had a short rest before meeting guides at Crucifix Corner. Just as the relief started, the Germans commenced an attack on the left part of the Leipzig Salient that was driven back. Heavy artillery barrages were fired by both sides and the battalion was hit hard.

Lance Corporal Lewis Binns.

D Company suffered many casualties before getting to the front. Lance Corporal Lewis Binns from Glusburn near Keighley, Private Sam Cockroft (28) from Queensbury and Private George Hutchinson (30) from Keighley were all killed and thirteen other men from D Company were wounded. In addition, Lance Corporal Thomas Monk from Settle was killed by shrapnel and one other man was wounded. He was the cousin of Rifleman Richard Monk (19) from Albert Hill, Settle who was serving in the King's Royal Rifle Corps when he was killed in action on 11 April 1917 during the Battle of Arras.

Sam Cockroft from West End, Queensbury enlisted in November 1915 at Halifax and before the war worked as a plumber. He was posted to France on 15 June 1916 and sent to the battalion the next day. He had previously served in the 5th West Riding Field Artillery (TF).

Lance Corporal Thomas Monk. (CPGW)

George Hutchinson of Oak Street, Keighley was employed as an electric welder at Jonas Wells Foundry. He enlisted on 8 August 1914 at Skipton and had previously served in the 3rd (Volunteer) West Riding Regiment. Both men are buried in Lonsdale Cemetery, Authuille.

The view looking north from the Leipzig Redoubt.

On 16 September the relief was complete. The distribution of the battalion was as follows: D Company was positioned in the Wonderwork, B Company in the Hindenburg Trench, C Company occupied dugouts in Lemberg Trench and A Company in the Tithebarn dug-outs. In the Leipzig Salient, the Germans had constructed a system of deep dug-outs and fortifications on the reserve line. The Wundtwerk, known to the British as Wonderwork, was a German strongpoint on the reverse slope to the south of the Leipzig Redoubt, out of sight of British ground observers. It was heavily defended with barbed wire and positioned to stop an advance over the spur if the front line trenches were overrun. It was named after the German Generalleutnant Theodor von Wundt, commander of Reserve Infantry Brigade 51.

Hindenburg Trench received heavy shelling, so the CO withdrew B Company to nearby positions. Even so, four D Company men were killed by shell fire: Private John Birkett from Embsay, Private Harry Ellis (20) from Huddersfield, Private Clifford Robinson and Private Harry Barwick (31), both from Oxenhope. Thirteen other D Company men were also wounded by shrapnel and bullets. Second Lieutenant William Balme Naylor (18) of Oaklands, Keighley, the battalion bombing officer, was killed by shrapnel. His father was the manager of the Bank of Liverpool in Keighley. Five other men were also wounded. One of the wounded men was Private Richard Barson (19) from Newmarket Street, Skipton.

Harry Ellis from Fitzwilliam Street, Huddersfield enlisted in December 1915. Prior to the war he worked as an assistant in a restaurant and landed in France on 15 June 1916. He was posted to Étaples, 18 miles south of Boulogne, for induction training. The Étaples training area, known as the Bull Ring, was situated on sand flats and dunes near the main part of the British army camp. It was one of the main centres in France for the final training of British troops before they were posted to the front. *'Etaples was hell,'* said a soldier, *'everything was done at the double and ferocious redcaps lurked in every corner.'* The instructors wore yellow armbands and were known as 'canaries'. They put their charges through two weeks of intensive and often brutal

88

training that lasted from early morning until sunset. It was the setting for the BBC TV series 'The Monocled Mutineer', which was based on the Étaples Mutiny of September 1917.

Harry Barwick from Upper Marsh, Oxenhope enlisted on 7 June 1915 at Keighley and had previously served four years in the 3rd (Volunteer) West Riding Regiment. He was posted to France at the beginning of February 1916 and on his death left a widow, Mary, and five young children.

The view looking south-west towards Leipzig Redoubt.

The view looking north across no man's land towards Leipzig Redoubt.

Private John Birkett of Skipton enlisted at the outbreak of war and had previously worked as a labourer in Skipton. He had also been a member of the Embsay Football Club. He is buried in Blighty Valley Cemetery.

Private John Birkett (CPGW)

On 17 September the German artillery was less active. At 3pm, the men of D Company reported seeing a German machine gun in an open position and an artillery fire mission was requested. The British shells landed right on top of the position and the machine gun was blown into the air; several German soldiers were seen trying to get out of the position and were fired at by battalion snipers. At 6.30pm the 1/7th DWR attacked the German line to the left and succeeded in gaining their objective and straightened the line across the Leipzig Salient. C Company were placed under the command of 1/7th DWR and moved up to Hindenburg Trench, where they were heavily shelled, and A Company was tasked with transporting grenades to the forward lines. No counter-attack was made by the Germans, but they continued to shell the British lines.

Serjeant Hartley Marks (22) from Keighley, Private William Bottomley (23) from Keighley, Private Thomas W. Lemon from Burton-on-Trent, Private Thomas McHugh (aka Stone) from Shipley and Private Frank Smith (21) also from Keighley, were all killed by shell fire and seventeen other men were wounded. The German 5.9-inch artillery fired all night and the battalion contacted the 6th Border Regiment to the right of the line.

Serjeant Hartley Marks was a pre-war 'terrier' who had signed up in June 1912. He was working as a blacksmith at Dean Smith & Grace Engineering Co and was a single man who lived at the family home in Long Lee, Keighley. He was promoted to serjeant at the beginning of March 1916 and had received a minor gunshot wound on 18 August. He is buried in Lonsdale Cemetery.

William Bottomley was another pre-war 'terrier', having signed up in January 1913. He was born in Shipley, but on enlistment he was working at Hall & Stells Ltd, textile engineers at Keighley and resided at Dalton Lane. He is buried in Lonsdale Cemetery

Frank Smith from West Lane, Keighley enlisted in September 1914 at Keighley. He had been admitted to hospital a few times during his time on the Western Front with a sprained knee and scabies, the latter being a condition which affected many soldiers. Before the war, these were hard working men with a decent standard of personal cleanliness and hygiene. The unsanitary conditions in the trenches, the lack of clean clothes and washing facilities must have been an extra burden for them to cope with. The rear area bathing facilities and steam cleaning of uniforms helped, but it did not take long for the lice and highly infectious scabies to return. Some of the men bathed in the River Ancre, but the thick weeds and German shelling made this a dangerous pastime and bathing was forbidden altogether after a man drowned in July 1916. Thomas William Lemon enlisted in October 1914 at Keighley and is buried in Lonsdale Cemetery.

On 18 September the German artillery was quieter but fired in salvoes at irregular intervals. At night, listening posts and patrols were sent out and a German soldier was captured by D Company. Captain Cedric Fawcett Horsfall (26) of Crosshills, Keighley, the commander of D Company, was killed by shrapnel whilst supervising the digging of a connecting trench towards the 6th Border Regiment. He was a popular officer and was well liked by the men under his command.

Captain Cedric Fawcett Horsfall. (CPGW)

He was educated at Streete Court School in Westgate-on-Sea, Kent, the same prep school Lieutenant and Adjutant Malcolm C.M. Law had attended. He matriculated at King's College, Cambridge, obtaining an MA. On leaving Cambridge he went into business with his father, Sir John Cousin Horsfall, 1st Baronet Hayfield, in the family textile business at Hayfield Mills, later becoming a partner in the firm. He was also interested in educational work and was a member of the general council at the Glusburn Technical Institute and a member of the Science and Art Committee. At the outbreak of war he was president of the Craven Association of Village Institutes. He was interested in politics and had presided over numerous meetings of the Liberal Party in the Crosshills district. He was also a member of the Sutton Baptist Church, had officiated as chairman at several public gatherings at the Church, and gave lectures to the young men's bible class at the church. He was commissioned at the outbreak of war and was soon promoted to captain and later became a company commander. He had been wounded twice and on one occasion he had been buried by a 5.9-inch German shell, known as a 'Jack Johnson', and had to be dug out by his men. He is buried in Blighty Valley Cemetery, Authuille Wood.

His brother, John Donald (known as Donald), also served as an officer in the 1/6th DWR and ended the war as a captain. Donald succeeded to the title of 2nd Baronet Horsfall of Hayfield on 18 October 1920. He was the chairman of John C. Horsfall & Sons, worsted spinners and held the office of High Sheriff of the West Riding, Yorkshire in 1927. He also held the office of Justice of the Peace for the West Riding of Yorkshire in 1928. He died in 1975 aged 84. One of his sons, Cedric Michael Horsfall, born in 1918, served as a captain in the British 1st Airborne Division in the Second World War and died of wounds received at Arnhem on 20 September 1944. His other son, John, served in the Second World War as a major in the DWR and won the Military Cross for action against the Japanese Army in Burma. Sir John Donald's other son, Patrick, also served in the DWR as a captain during the Second World War.

'Jack Johnson' was the nickname given to a German 5.9-inch (150mm) medium artillery shell, named after the popular African-American world heavyweight boxing champion who held the title from 1908-1915. The gallows-humour of the men in the trenches likened the detonation of a 5.9-inch shell, which exploded with noticeable black smoke, to being on the receiving end of a punch thrown by Mr Johnson himself.

Private George Sanderson (22) from Bradford, Private Willie Hewitt from Cowling near Keighley, Private Herbert Lake and Private James Whittaker, both from Keighley, were all killed by shell fire. Nine other men were wounded.

George Sanderson of Raven Street, Bradford, was working as a warehouseman in the wool trade at the outbreak of the war. He was a newly married man when he enlisted at Bradford in November 1915. He had married Augusta at St Patrick's Church, Bradford on 26 June of that year. He mobilised on 7 April 1916, initially into the ranks of the 3/6th DWR. This was a training unit which, on completion of their basic training, sent men to fill the ranks of the 1/6th DWR and later the 2/6th DWR. He was posted to France on 14 July where, after induction training at the Étaples Bull Ring, he was posted to the 1/6th DWR on 9 August.

Herbert Lake of Carlisle Street, Keighley was a pre-war 'terrier' who joined the TF in June 1913 when he was working as a blacksmith at George Wilkinson & Son, Engineers of Braford Road Keighley. In July 1915 he was promoted to lance corporal but in May 1916, after several minor infractions (late for parades), he was deprived of his stripe. He also had suffered from several bouts of pyrexia (high fever) which resulted in his being admitted to hospital.

Private Willie Hewitt enlisted in May 1915 and was posted to France in February 1916. Before the war he was employed as a warp dresser at Royd Mills, Cowling. He is buried with his comrades in Lonsdale Cemetery, Authuille.

Private Willie Hewitt. (CPGW)

On the night of 19/20 September the Germans attempted a counter-attack to the right of the line. The SOS signal rocket was sent up which alerted the artillery to open fire and the attack was repulsed. The Germans replied with their own 5.9-inch shells and when things quietened down, patrols were sent out and reconnoitred Josephs Trench which was found to be strongly defended. During the day, C Company replaced D in the front line. D Company had spent five tough days at the front and lost many good men. Before they left, Private C. Shackleton discovered a map in a dug-out in the Wonderwork which showed the disposition of all the German forces in the Leipzig Salient and Thiepval areas. His name appeared in divisional orders and he was recommended for an award.

The rest of the day passed much quieter with only three men wounded by shell fire. On 19 September Private Richard Barson from Brown's Court, Newmarket Street, Skipton died of a gunshot wound to his chest, received on 16 September. He died at No.49 CCS and is buried at Contay British Cemetery. He enlisted on 13 November 1914 at Skipton and commenced his basic training on 25 October 1915 at Clipstone Camp near Mansfield. He was posted to France in April 1915 and was wounded on 29 September 1915. He spent the next five months convalescing in the UK. On 1 February 1916 he rejoined the battalion in France.

On 21 September Corporal Cecil Rhodes captured a German who had been hiding under a waterproof sheet in the corner of a trench. The prisoner tried to escape but was soon stopped and sent to brigade HQ for interrogation. The prisoner was found to be from the 209th Reserve Regiment. At 3pm, German troops were seen in Josephs Trench and were engaged by the battalion snipers and two were seen to fall. Private Fred

Barker from Todmorden died of wounds in a CCS and four other men were wounded by shell fire.

On the evening of 21 September the enemy launched a heavy bombardment of the front line. They fired high explosive, shrapnel and chlorine gas cylinders from trench mortars which landed to the rear of the Wonderwork, although no casualties were caused. A German machine gun was found in a dug-out and taken to brigade HQ. In the early hours of 22 September the battalion was relieved by 1/7th DWR, and proceeded to Crucifix dug-outs, 200 yards east of Aveluy. Later that day the Germans launched a counter-attack to the right and the line was heavily shelled. Serjeant John Stone Hepworth MM (25) from Snettisham, Kings Lynn, Norfolk, was killed by a shrapnel wound to the head. He joined the 1/6th in September 1914 at Settle and was a participant in the 17 June 1915 cricket match at Fleurbaix. He was also one of the 'lucky thirteen', photographed at Riby in 1914 and is buried in Blighty Valley Cemetery.

Serjeant John S. Hepworth. (CPGW)

Serjeant Fred Chadwick (31) of Guiseley died from shrapnel wounds to his leg at a CCS. He had previously been wounded by shrapnel on 20 July 1915 on the bank of the Yser Canal. Before the war he lived at 7 Henry Terrace, New Scarborough, Yeadon and worked as a case maker. He had worked as a moulder's labourer at the Sykes & Shaw iron foundry at Ghyll Royd, Guiseley and had seen service in the 3rd (Volunteer) DWR. He was a pre-war 'terrier' having joined in 1909 and served for five years, leaving in early 1914. On the outbreak of war, he rejoined on 5 September 1914 and is buried at Varennes Military Cemetery, 9 miles west of Thiepval.

Serjeant Fred Chadwick. (Aireborough Historical Society)

Captain A. Driver, the officer commanding C Company, and Private Stanley Sowrey from Burley-in-Wharfedale were both wounded in the head by shrapnel. Two other C Company men were also wounded. On the night of 22 September, A and B Companies were conducting working parties and at 3.30pm on 23 September, the battalion was relieved by the 10th Essex Regiment, of 53 Brigade, 18th Division. They then marched to 7 miles west to the village of Léalvillers via Hédauville.

At Hédauville men suffering from trench foot were transported onwards by lorry and the following day at 11am, the battalion marched 11 miles north-west to Mondicourt via Louvencourt, Authie and Pas-en-Artois. A midday meal was served at Authie from field kitchens and the men arrived in billets at 7pm. The packs and heavy equipment were delivered by lorry.

The Divisional GOC, Major General Percival, watched the battalion march through Pas-en-Artois and was reportedly highly pleased with what he saw. On 25 September the day was spent cleaning equipment, weapons and clothing and on 26 September, the Brigade GOC, Brigadier General Lewes, visited the battalion and spoke to the company commanders. The rest of the battalion was inspected by the CO, Lieutenant

Colonel Bateman and the next day, 27 September, the battalion marched 3 miles east to St Armand via the villages of Grincourt and Gaudiempré, where comfortable billets awaited them. The next day saw the battalion move to the front line again. They marched 5 miles south-east, via Souastre and Bienvillers, to the trenches in the Foncquevillers/Gommecourt sector. The battalion relieved the 5th Scottish Rifles in the trenches from Second Road to Colchester Street. The next day passed quietly with only one or two trench mortars fired at the British line, as was 30 September with one man wounded by a rifle bullet in the shoulder.

CASUALTIES: During September 1916 the battalion had 35 men killed and 96 wounded.

October 1916
The first day of October passed quietly with no casualties. At 8pm on 2 October the battalion was relieved by the 4th KOYLI and marched the $2^{1}/_{2}$ miles to Humbercamps where the men were billeted in huts. Heavy rain fell the next day and on 4 October the battalion visited the baths at Gaudiempré. The following day specialist training was conducted in the morning and close order drill in the afternoon. On 6 October Brigadier General Percival inspected A and B Companies who were in full marching order. The war diary records that he did not appear to be pleased but the reason for his displeasure is not recorded. The problem appears to have been rectified because the next day, 7 October, he inspected the whole battalion again and was reportedly this time very pleased with the turnout of the men. The next day was wet and the brigade church parade had to be cancelled due to the weather. That night, A and B Companies provided eighty men each for working parties in the front line trenches.

Chapter 7

Gommecourt

On 9 October 147 Brigade relieved 148 Brigade in the front line trenches. The battalion, having had more than its share in the trenches, was placed in support at Bienvillers and relieved the 1/4th York and Lancaster Regiment. D Company was detached to support the right battalion and provided men for tunnelling. Four shifts, each of six hours, was worked, with the entire shift spent putting the excavated earth in sandbags and moving it away from the tunnel shaft in the form of a human chain. Two platoons of C Company were detached to 21st Field Company, Royal Engineers at Foncquevillers for wiring duty. The remainder of C Company were in billets at Bienvillers.

Tuesday 10 October was a fine day, but in the evening the Germans shelled the area of Bienvillers with heavy artillery and continued to do so all night but miraculously only three men were wounded by shrapnel. The bombardment continued on the next day when 200 German shells fell to the south of the village. The weather was wet and cold and on 12 October, specialist training was conducted by the Lewis gunners and bombers with the remainder of the companies having target practice on the rifle range. Five officers and ninety men were required for working parties in the front line and two men were seriously wounded by a German rifle grenade. One of the wounded men was Private David Russell from Skipton. The routine was the same for 13 to 15 October but on the 14th, three men were wounded by shrapnel.

On that day Private David Russell (28) died of his wounds at No.4 General Hospital at Étaples and was buried in the military cemetery there. Prior to the war he was employed at Belle Vue Mills, Skipton, and was widely known in the town and district as a playing member of the Skipton Rugby Football Club, the Cononley Association Football Club and the Skipton Church Institute Cricket Club. He was the brother of Lance Serjeant John Willie Russell who also served in the ranks of the 1/6th DWR, who died of wounds on 7 May 1918. He was the cousin of Private David Russell, also a serving member of the 1/6th DWR, who was killed on 16 December 1915 and the brother-in-law of Lance Corporal Fred Gallagher who died on 19 December 1915.

In the early hours of 16 October 1916 the battalion relieved the 1/4th DWR at the front in the Hennescamps sector. The next day was quiet with rain most of the day and night and in the early hours of the 18th the battalion was relieved by the 5th West Yorkshire Regiment and returned to the billets at Humbercamps. On 19 October the day was spent in fitting new uniforms and cleaning weapons and equipment and on the 20th close order drill, physical exercise and bayonet fighting were the order of the day. The next day the battalion marched, via St Amand, to Souastre into billets in barns but there were plenty of estaminets (cafes) and a YMCA hut. On 22 October the battalion was allocated baths all day, while those men not bathing attended a church service in the YMCA hut. In the afternoon the brigade GOC inspected the billets and inter-platoon football matches were held.

On the morning of 23 October close order drill, bayonet fighting, physical exercise and specialist training was held and, in the early afternoon, PH helmet drill was practised. Every available man was on this parade, including runners and orderly room staff. At 3pm a football match took place between the battalion and the 19th Lancashire Fusiliers. The war diary states that it was a good match for the first half, but the second half developed into somewhat of a scramble with the Lancs winning 4-0.

On 24 October the battalion moved back into the front line at Foncquevillers, relieving platoons from the 1/6th and 1/7th West Yorkshire Regiment. It was another dull, wet day. The following day was relatively quiet but the Germans shelled the area of battalion HQ at Foncquevillers where one man was wounded in the head. On 26 October the Germans shelled the front line trenches and fired trench mortars for over three hours in the morning and again in the afternoon but only one man was wounded. The weather on 27 October was wet all day and a few German shells landed. The main excitement that day was the accidental detonation of a flare pistol cartridge causing two injuries.

On the morning of 28 October the British artillery bombarded the German lines and in the afternoon the Germans replied with trench mortars. During this bombardment Corporal William Henry Maddocks (21) from Keighley was killed. He was a pre-war 'terrier' having enlisted in March 1913. In civilian life he was a labourer at George Hattersley's textile machine engineering Co of Keighley and lived at Spring Row in the town. An original member of the 1/6th DWR who landed in France in April 1915, he is buried at Foncquevillers Military Cemetery.

The weather on 29 October was overcast with rain all day and night. The German trench mortars were quiet, but the German artillery shelled the Foncquevillers area around the church and one man was wounded in the face by a German rifle grenade. The battalion was relieved the next day by the 1/7th West Yorkshire Regiment. C and D Companies moved to huts at Souastre and A and B Companies moved to billets at Foncquevillers to supply night time wiring patrols and daytime ammunition carrying parties. On 31 October, the companies at Foncquevillers spent the morning bathing and cleaning equipment and in the afternoon the brigadier general inspected the huts. C and D Companies provided a party of 111 men for work on the front line.

CASUALTIES: In October 1916, the battalion had 2 men killed and 12 wounded.

November 1916
Another wet day followed on 1 November when the battalion was allocated baths and during the morning the men were issued with clean uniforms. That evening a working

party of 100 men was provided and one man was wounded in the leg by a shell. The next day was wet again and those men who were not on the night time working party practised bayonet fighting, arms drill and physical exercise. Another 100 men were provided that night for working parties, during which one man was wounded in the head by shrapnel. The weather on 3 November had improved and the routine was the same as the previous day. On 4 November working parties were only provided in the morning as the battalion was moving up to the front line.

The enemy artillery fired a barrage of high explosive and phosgene gas shells onto the rear area. Five men were wounded, one hit in the leg by shrapnel, one had his legs crushed by a collapsing bunker and three other men suffered the effects of gas poisoning. On 5 November the battalion relieved the 1/7th DWR in the front line. A, C and D Companies occupied the trenches from Gommecourt Road to La Brayelle Rd. B Company were at Snipers Square and battalion HQ at Foncquevillers. The next day started off wet and the German trench mortars were very active between 2pm and 3.30pm Private Fred Brooks (23) from Low Moor, Bradford was killed by a trench mortar and one other man was wounded.

At 11.30pm the British artillery commenced an intense bombardment of the German lines to the right of the battalion, in conjunction with a raid by the men of the 31st Division on the German trenches. The weather on 7 November continued wet, with rain falling all day. Even though hand-operated water pumps were used, the trenches flooded. Apart from a few shells near Foncquevillers, the sector was quiet but Private Fearon G. Walker, from Kendal, received a shrapnel wound to the stomach and died of his injuries.

It was wet again on 8 November. Both the divisional and brigade commanders inspected the front line trenches during the morning and Foncquevillers was shelled between 11.30am and 2pm by enemy artillery. The next day was bright and sunny and aircraft from both sides could be seen flying over the front lines. There was a little German shelling and one man was wounded in the head by shrapnel. Generally 10

The view from the German front line at Gommecourt, looking across no man's land towards the British line near La Brayelle Road.

The view looking north-east across no man's land from the Foncquevillers/ Gommecourt road towards the British front line.

The road junction was the location of the German front line at Gommecourt.

November was a quiet day with a few trench mortars and a little rain, but on the morning of the 11th the enemy trench mortars were active and two retaliatory barrages were requested.

At 1pm on 11 November, the battalion was relieved by the 1/7th DWR and marched 3 miles west to Souastre into billets. During the relief one man was wounded by a trench mortar. On 12 November 100 men attended a church service taken by Major General Llewellyn Gwynne, Deputy Chaplain General of the British Army and the second Bishop of Khartoum. Later 210 men were provided for working parties during the day and night. On 13 November the CO, Lieutenant Colonel Bateman DSO, proceeded to the UK on leave and the battalion was allocated baths in the morning. The divisional GOC inspected the billets and found them to be in good order. A working party of 200 men was also provided to transport rations and ammunition.

On 14 November a short course in engineering was held. Two officers and six NCOs per company were given one hour's instruction on revetting (support for trench walls) and constructing dug-outs, followed by four hours practical work. A working party of 250 men was also provided and at 2.45pm, a German aircraft flew low over the village, probably on a reconnaissance mission. Between 6pm and 8.30pm that evening a concert was held in the YMCA building in Souastre at which the divisional band played. The engineering course continued the next day and working parties were provided as usual. Those men not working were sent on a short route march and then practised close order drill and bayonet fighting. On 16 November working parties were provided as usual, plus forty men to construct wire entanglements for the units at the front. The war diary notes that this was the first time the battalion in reserve had been tasked with this type of work. Those men not working went on a short route march and then had the chance to view the engineering work.

The battalion returned to the front line on the 17th and on 18 November heavy rain returned which continued all night. German trench mortars were fired in the morning and again in the afternoon but no men were injured. The weather on 20 November had improved and the clouds parted. At 8pm that evening a raid on the German lines was conducted by the 1/5th DWR. The raiding party comprised two officers and ninety-five men and two men from the 1/5th were killed, although many Germans were killed or captured. During the raid the Germans launched SOS warning rockets from a sap in front of the 1/6th DWR and the bombardment landed mostly on the centre of the line. Serjeant William Hudson (23) from Brighouse was killed and four other men were wounded. Corporal Thomas Allsopp (22) from South Milford (originally from Ingrow), Lance Corporal Arthur H. Scott MM (20) Lance Corporal Charles Lowndes and Lance Corporal Joseph W. Tatton MM, all from Keighley, were killed by a trench mortar.

Arthur Heaton Scott was a pre-war 'terrier' who originally signed up in 1913 when he was working as an iron borer at the foundry of Ward, Haggas & Smith.

William Tatton and Charles Lowndes were childhood friends who grew up together on Belle Vue Terrace in the Parkwood area of the town. They were also friends with the two other men from the Keighley area, Thomas Allsopp and Arthur Heaton Scott. In January 1916, the *Keighley News* reported on the death of William and Charles:

It is a pathetic coincidence that they met their death instantaneously by the explosion of a trench mortar. Both young men had been comrades since boyhood and joined the Territorials, going out to the front together in April 1915. In the bitter defence of Ypres, fighting before overwhelming odds, they would be found together and during the summer they were both on leave at home and only a few weeks ago they were promoted to a non-commissioned rank. Both fellows were of a pleasant disposition and highly esteemed.

On 1 December 1916, the *Craven Herald* newspaper reported the death of Corporal Allsopp:

Mrs. Allsopp, of Beech Street, Crosshills, received a letter on Sunday morning from Lieut. B. Godfrey Buxton, informing her that her son, Corporal Tom Allsopp, of the Duke of Wellington's West Riding Regiment, had been killed in action in France. Lieutenant Buxton pays a glowing tribute to the memory of Corporal Allsopp, and says:

'Dear Mrs. Allsopp, I deeply regret to have to inform you that your son, 2595, Corporal T. Allsopp, was killed in action last night. He had just received his promotion and was doing particularly good work. We all join in sending you our deepest sympathy in this great loss and pray that you may indeed have comfort through it. He was buried this afternoon by the Chaplain with some of his comrades in the British cemetery behind the line. His personal belongings will be forwarded to you as soon as possible. Again, with our deepest sympathy in the loss of so brave a son. I remain, yours sincerely, B. Godfrey Buxton, Lieutenant, D Company.'

Corporal Thomas Allsopp. (CPGW)

Corporal Allsopp enlisted in the month following the outbreak of war. He went out to the front with his regiment in April 1915. About last Christmas he and others were coming home on leave and were resting at a farmhouse near the firing line, when they were ordered by their officer to put on their gas helmets at once, as the Germans had launched a gas attack. They were then marched in single file into the trenches again, first into the reserve trenches, and then into the front-line trenches. When they got to the first line trench they found all the men who had been in the trench at the time of the gas attack were dead.

Corporal Allsopp (then Private Allsopp) and several of his comrades were then picked out to go on guard on the canal bank. They were on guard three successive days and nights, and it was at this time that Corporal Allsopp contracted gas poisoning. For his work on this occasion he was promoted to Lance Corporal and was granted leave, and came home to Crosshills. He returned to France about New Year's Day. When he arrived back in France he fell ill from the effects of the poison, and was sent to a war hospital in France, where he was seriously ill for several weeks. He should have come home on one of the hospital ships, but was too ill to be moved. When he was fit to be sent across the sea he was sent to a war hospital in Ireland, and afterwards to a convalescent hospital at Blackpool. After being at Blackpool for some time he received a ten days' leave, at the expiration of which he went to his depot at Clipstone, shortly afterwards being drafted out to France again.

He was made Corporal about six weeks ago, was the eldest son, and was about 22 years of age. He was closely connected with the Crosshills Wesleyan Church, and is the first whose name is on the church's roll of honour to fall in action. He was a lad who was held to high esteem for his sterling qualities, and his parents have received numerous expressions of sympathy in their sad bereavement.

Two other D Company men were wounded, one in the arm by shrapnel and one shot in the jaw by a sniper. A patrol from B Company was attacked on La Brayelle Rd and three men were wounded by a German hand grenade.

On 21 November a few German artillery salvos were fired at Foncquevillers but apart from that the day was misty and quiet. The mist allowed daylight patrols to be sent out and one patrol from D Company encountered a German patrol working in no man's land and engaged them with Lewis machine-gun fire. Second Lieutenant Frederick Lawrence Wilson (22) from London was wounded in the thigh by shrapnel and died on the 23rd. He was born in 1894 at Edgeware Road, London and was the son of Frederick and Ruth Wilson of College Road, Winchmore Hill, London. He enlisted as a private on 14 September 1914 in the Sherwood Foresters Regiment. He served with the British Expeditionary Force from June 1915 and was commissioned into the 1/6th DWR in May 1916. Before the war he was studying theology at the Society of the Sacred Mission college at Newark with a view to taking holy orders. In a letter to his parents, Lieutenant Colonel Bateman wrote:

I always found your son a very willing and hardworking young officer, and he was one in whom I placed the greatest trust and confidence. Although rather young, he always carried out his duties thoroughly and cheerfully, and we can ill afford to lose such fine young fellows. I can assure you his death is deeply felt in the battalion. I sent over and had a very nicely painted wooden cross placed on his grave, as a last token of respect from myself, his brother officers, and his non-commissioned officers and men.

Captain Sam H. Clough wrote*:*

The battalion has lost one of its keenest and most efficient officers, one who put his heart into everything he did, and one that it could ill afford to lose. Such officers as he are very hard to replace. It is some consolation to know that he gave his life for his country's cause, which is the biggest sacrifice that a man can make.

Private Thomas Watson (35) from Wellington Road, Undercliffe, Bradford, was killed by a shell and one other man wounded. Thomas Watson was a wool comber before the war and enlisted on 9 December 1915. He was mobilised on 3 April 1916 when he was posted to the 3/6th DWR for basic training. On 19 June he was posted to the 34th Infantry Base Depot at Étaples, where he would have experienced the 'bull ring'. He was finally posted to the 1/6th DWR on 3 August 1916 and is buried at Foncquevillers Military Cemetery.

The German machine guns were active at night time and it was noticed that flares were launched in conjunction with the machine guns. The 22nd was another misty day, but cleared towards the evening. Major General Percival and Brigadier General Lewis inspected the front line in the morning and were pleased with the work done by the battalion during its time in the trenches. A British aircraft was brought down by enemy fire near the village of Hébuterne, about a mile south-west of Foncquevillers, but the crew were seen to alight safely from the craft. At 5am on 23 November the line was on the receiving end of a heavy trench mortar bombardment. Five men were wounded including Private Fred Thornton from Skipton. Later that morning the battalion was relieved by the 1/7th DWR. C and D Companies moved to Foncquevillers and A, B and HQ companies moved to Souastre in support. The next day was spent cleaning kit and equipment and bathing.

On 25 November the CO, Lieutenant Colonel C.M. Bateman, and Major A.B. Clarkson rejoined the battalion from England. The weather was wet in the morning but brighter later in the day. A church service was held on the morning of 26 November in the YMCA hut at Souastre. The CO had been called away to a conference, when the VII Corps GOC, Lieutenant General Thomas D'Oyly Snow KCB, KCMG (great-grandfather of the television historian and author Dan Snow) visited the battalion and conducted an inspection of some of the billets. He found them to be in an unsatisfactory state and 100 men were provided for a night time working party.

On 27 November, between 2pm and 7pm, 120 men were required for working parties. The rest of the companies practised the rapid deployment of wire and on 28 November, working parties were again provided. On the morning of 29 November the battalion relieved the 1/7th DWR at the front between Gommecourt Road and La Brayelle Road. The relief was completed at 11.45am and a few German shells landed in Foncquevillers and Calvary Road during the day. One man was wounded in the arm by rifle fire. On 30 November 1916 more shells fell on Foncquevillers between 4pm and midnight. One man was wounded in the shoulder by rifle fire.

CASUALTIES: During November 1916, the battalion had 9 men killed and 20 wounded.

December 1916

Thick fog shrouded the front line on 1 December 1916 and all the companies managed to put wire entanglements in front of their trenches. The fog also enabled the battalion scouts to patrol the area of no man's land and twenty-four pay books, known as AB64s, were recovered from the British dead. A few shells also landed around Foncquevillers.

The weather on 2 and 3 December was fine, but a hard frost had settled. It was a quiet day except for shelling around Foncquevillers. Night time patrols were ordered, so three patrols comprising one officer and ten men, were sent into no man's land, primarily to check on the condition of the German wire. The next two days passed quietly, the only thing of note was the return of the CO from his conference.

On 6 December, starting at 8am, the battalion was relieved by the 7th Sherwood Foresters (Nottingham and Derby) Regiment (Sherwoods). The war diary notes that this was a remarkably quick relief, completed by 12.30pm. One of the company commanders of the Sherwoods was Major Geoffrey Vickers VC, who won his award for his actions on 14 October 1915, when he held a barrier across a trench in the Hohenzollern Redoubt in France, against heavy German bomb attacks. He ordered a

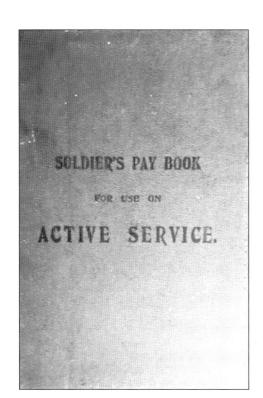

Example of a form AB64. This booklet would be kept in the breast pocket of the soldier's tunic.

Instructions to Soldier.

1. You will produce this book whenever you require an advance of cash on account.

2. You will give a receipt, on the acquittance roll of the Officer paying you, for all cash advances made to you. The Officer making the payment will sign the corresponding entry in this book on the page for Cash Payments.

3. You will make no entries in this book, except to sign your name on pages 3 and 7 and to make your will, if you so desire on page 14.

4. Should you lose your book you will at once report the loss to your Commanding Officer. A new book will be obtained, if possible, from the Accountant, but it must be understood that no pay can be issued in respect of the period before the date on which you report your loss, until you are finally settled with.

Regiment or Corps *3 WRB. RFA*

Squadron, Battery, or Company *9 Batt y*

No. *426* Rank *Gunner*

Name in full *George W Lewis*

Date of Attestation *1908 March 2nd*

Age on Enlistment *20*

If appointed to a Unit formed on Mobilization the designation of such unit should be clearly stated here—

3rd West Riding Bde. R.F.)

NOTE.—The account of the soldier while on active service will be kept in the Office of the Accountant paying the Base Depôt of his Unit, and to that Officer all communications relating to his accounts should be addressed.

second barrier to be built behind him to secure the safety of the trench, regardless of the fact that his own retreat would be cut off. He held the enemy back long enough for the second barrier to be completed and then escaped to a friendly trench. He survived the war and lived to be 87.

The battalion marched by platoons 2 miles to Souastre, then by companies marched 3 miles to Warlincourt, having dinner en route. The war diary recorded that the men marched well after seven cold days in the trenches. The accommodation they found was not at all good as half the battalion was in tents in a muddy field. The next day, 7 December, the battalion marched 4 miles to a brigade camp at the village of Halloy. The 1/4th, 1/5th and 1/6th and 1/7th Battalions of the DWR were all billeted at Halloy, so it was rather crowded and good accommodation was at a premium. The following day was spent cleaning weapons and equipment and the weather was described as wet and cold.

The weather on 9 December did not improve and the 10th was just as bad, but a church parade was held. In the evening a British aircraft crashed close to the camp after hitting a tree. The pilot was understandably shaken but not seriously injured. Also on 10 December, Private Fred Thornton (22) from Skipton died at No.20 CCS from wounds to both arms, both legs and face, received on 23 November. He enlisted in December 1915 and was posted to France in May 1916. Before the war he was employed as weaver at Sackville Mills, Skipton. In September 1916 he had been wounded in the leg which required admission to a base hospital. He is buried at Warlincourt Halte British Cemetery, near Saulty, France.

Private Fred Thornton (PGW)

On 11 December the battalion was allocated baths at Pas-en-Artois and on the 12th snow fell but that did not stop a battalion route march. By the morning of 13 December the snow had thawed and A Company spent the morning on a nearby shooting range. The other companies practised wiring, physical drill and bayonet fighting and in the afternoon a football competition was held. The following day the weather was better and training as per the previous day continued. The VII Corps GOC, Lieutenant General T.D. Snow, watched the training and inspected the camp. Unlike his last visit, he stated he was pleased with what he saw.

The 15th was a wet day and the men of the battalion spent the day being issued with and fitting the new Small Box Respirator (SBR). This was a huge improvement on the previous PH gas helmet. The SBR was made of thinly rubberized canvas with a canvas-covered rubber hose connecting it to a filter which was all contained in a square canvas bag. The SBR worked by filtering dangerous chemicals through a canister of charcoal and gauze impregnated with neutralizing chemical agents. Every SBR issued was tested to ensure a correct fit by the wearer walking into a sealed hut, in which a chemical called lachrymatory was ignited to form a gas cloud. (Lachrymatory was an early form of CS gas).

The 1916 issue Small Box Respirator or SBR.

From 16 to 21 December the battalion provided working parties and on the 22nd normal training resumed. The weather was very wet in the morning and a route march was undertaken in the afternoon when the rain had eased. The weather on 23 December was heavy showers with strong winds. Second Lieutenant Grears left the battalion to become the town major of Puchevillers and Second Lieutenant Drewery returned from a posting as town major of Foncquevillers. (A British Army town major was responsible for liaison between the civilian authorities and the military).

On Christmas Eve the battalion visited the baths at Pas-en-Artois and a church service was held in the evening. The weather on Christmas Day 1916 was fine but windy and football matches were played in the morning. Christmas dinner was at 1pm and the men were served ham, beans and potatoes followed by plum pudding with rum sauce. They also received a bottle of English beer, some chocolate and a cigar. Messages were received from HM King George V, the Commander-in-Chief General Sir Douglas Haig and the Brigade GOC, Major General Lewes. The Divisional Commander, Major General Percival made a telephone call to wish the men of the 1/6th DWR a happy Christmas.

Training resumed on Boxing Day with one company on the shooting range whilst the rest of the battalion trained in bayonet fighting, drill and physical exercise. Specialist training was also done by the Lewis gunners, bombers and sharpshooters (snipers). Training continued on 27 December and in the afternoon the officers from 147 Brigade played the officers of 146 Brigade at rugby. The 147th lost 20-3.

On 28 December, the battalion inter-platoon competition was held to select representatives for the brigade competition. The categories were drill and turnout, rifle and Lewis gun shooting.

The winning results were as follows:

Drill and turnout: 15 platoon, D Company; Rifle shooting: 1 platoon, A Company; Lewis gun: 14 platoon, D Company,

A draft of 211 men also arrived. The weather on the 29th was wet and the CO inspected the new arrivals. The brigade drill and turnout competition was held on 30 December and those men not involved took part in a route march. The results for the drill and turn out competition were as follows:

1st – 1/4th DWR, 97 points; 2nd – 1/7th DWR, 91 points; 3rd – 1/6th DWR, 89 points; 4th – 1/5th DWR, 74 points.

On New Year's Eve 1916 a church service was held in the morning and the brigade rifle and Lewis gun competition was held. The rifle competition was won by the 1/5th DWR, with the 1/4th DWR taking second place. The Lewis gun competition was won by 1/7th DWR with 78 points, with the 1/6th DWR taking second place with 77 points.

CASUALTIES: In the month of December 1916, the battalion was fortunate not to suffer any casualties.

The Lewis machine gun.

January 2017

Training resumed on 1 January 1917 and between 5.30pm and 7.30pm, one company and the battalion sharpshooters provided a working party. Training continued on the 2nd and on the afternoon of 3 January, a team of officers and men from the 1/6th DWR played a rugby match against the 24th Motor Transport section, Army Service Corps. The 1/6th DWR were victorious, winning 5-3. Between 4 and 6 January, training continued and on the 7th, the battalion moved 4 miles to the village of Humbercamps in preparation for a return to the front.

Chapter 8

Berles-au-Bois

At Humbercamps the battalion went into billets as the reserve of 147 Brigade who were relieving 89 Brigade which comprised the 17th, 19th and 20th King's Regiment (Liverpool) and the 2nd Bedfordshire Regiment. On 8 January medicals, SBR drills and kit inspections were the order of the day and the CO and adjutant visited the trenches at the front. On 9 January the company commanders visited the trenches and the men spent the day performing physical drill, route marches and close order drill. On the 10th the men were allocated time at the baths in Berles and eighty men were used for working parties, but the village of Humbercamps was shelled and one man and a civilian were wounded.

The next day the battalion moved to the front line in the Berles-au-Bois sector when they relieved the 1/7th DWR. C and D Companies took a position in the front line trenches with B Company in close support and A Company in reserve. The battalion front reached from Francis Street to Renfew Road with the 1/4th DWR to the right and 146 Brigade to the left. On 11 January one man was wounded in the arm by a machine-gun bullet. The trenches and dug-outs were described as very muddy and snow fell on 12 January that later turned to rain. A few shells fell on brigade HQ and on 13 January, the British trench mortars fired thirty-five rounds which provoked a short retaliatory German barrage but no casualties were caused.

On the 14th the brigade and divisional GOCs visited the front line trenches and, not surprisingly, saw that they were very muddy. During the visit, one of the battalion men was wounded by a bullet in his leg. On 15 January the battalion was relieved by the 1/7th DWR and went into reserve. HQ and two companies were billeted at Berles, with the remaining two companies at Humbercamps. The 16th saw every man in the battalion on working parties, both day and night, which continued for the next two days with persistent heavy snow storms adding to the problems.

On 19 January the battalion relieved the 1/7th DWR at the front. The 20th was a quiet day and the trenches were cleaned and repaired. There was only a little machine-gun fire but no casualties were caused. A sharp frost appeared overnight the next day and the enemy fired a considerable artillery barrage on the British lines but again, no casualties were caused. On 22 January the battalion was relieved by the 1/7th DWR and moved to Humbercamps in reserve. During the relief, Private William Wyman from Brighouse was killed by a rifle bullet. William Wyman was living at Clayton Buildings, Brookfoot when he enlisted at Brighouse in December 1915. He was 19

A British Army stores depot. Stores like these trench duck-boards were transported to dispersal depots and eventually had to be taken to the front line units by hand.

and working as a dyer's labourer. Initially posted to the 3/6th DWR at Clipstone for basic training, he was then sent to France on 15 June 1916. He joined the 1/6th DWR on 26 June after induction and battle training at the Étaples Bull Ring. He is buried in Berles-au-Bois Churchyard Extension Cemetery.

The temperature had dropped again on 23 January and a sharp frost lay on the ground. The weather was clear and aircraft were seen flying over the line which were engaged by anti-aircraft guns. About eight German shells fell into Humbercamps and one man was killed by an anti-aircraft shell that hit the battalion first-aid dressing station. As a retaliation, around 150 heavy shells were fired into German held Douchy-lès-Ayette, 4 miles to the east. The dead man was Private James Southern, from Whins Terrace, Ingrow near Keighley who before the war was working as a mechanical engineer. He enlisted in September 1914 and was posted to France at the end of June 1915. In December 1915, whilst in the Yser Canal sector, he was evacuated to the UK suffering from trench foot and spent six months convalescing before returning to France at the beginning of June 1916. He is buried in Warlincourt Halte British Military Cemetery.

On 24 January 147 Brigade was placed under the temporary command of XVIII Corps and its commander Lieutenant General Sir Ivor Maxse. A performance of the divisional concert party, The Tykes, was arranged for the battalion at the town of Bavincourt, some 3 miles north of Humbercamps and 350 men marched there and back for the performance. The weather on 25 January continued to be fine and cold and the GOC Brigade, Brigadier General Lewes gave a lecture to officers and senior NCOs. At 6am on 26 January the battalion commenced the relief of the 1/7th DWR in the front line. The relief was completed by 10.30am without any casualties and the rest of the day was quiet.

The weather on 27 January was fine and quiet except for German trench mortars firing on the rear areas, which, the war diary notes, might have been to celebrate the

Kaiser's birthday. German machine guns were also active at night and the freezing cold weather continued into the 28th. On the 29th the British medium and heavy trench mortars bombarded the German wire to good effect, destroying large swathes of entanglements. The battalion was relieved by the 1/7th DWR the next day. HQ, C and D Companies went to Berles in support and A and B Companies went to Humbercamps. On 31 January the CO, adjutant and company commanders were taken by motor transport, to the area of the village of Wailly to conduct a reconnaissance of the front line. They were shown round by 7th Rifle Brigade from 41 Brigade, 14th Division. One man was wounded in the back by shrapnel at Berles.

CASUALTIES: During January 1917, the battalion had 3 men killed and 5 wounded.

Chapter 9

Wailly

February 1917

The frost continued on 1 February 1917 and the day was spent cleaning and preparing kit and equipment. On the 2nd A and B Companies marched 4 miles from Humbercamps to the village of Rivière. The battalion then moved the short distance to the village of Wailly where they relieved the 1/4th DWR and occupied support posts at Factory Keep, Petit Moulin Keep, Wailly Keep and Petit Chateau, areas collectively known as the 'keeps'.

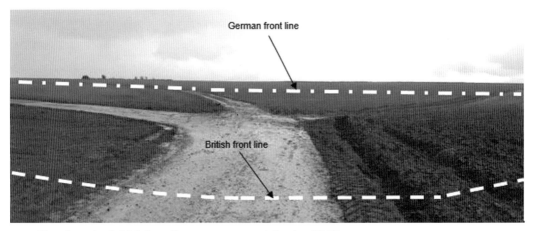

View from the British front line across no man's land at Wailly.

HQ, C and D Companies were relieved by the 5th South Staffordshire Regiment, after which they marched to Rivière. Once the battalion was reunited, they became support for 41 Brigade of the 14th Division. The 'attack move' positions were reconnoitred in the afternoon and on 3 February at 10.30am, the battalion moved up to the trenches and relieved the 7th Rifle Brigade at the front line between French Street and Friary Street. The relief was completed by 2.30pm during which the enemy fired trench mortars, but no casualties were caused. Here 147 Brigade took over responsibility for the sector from 41 Brigade; 148 Brigade was to the right and 42 Brigade was to the left.

Modern day location of Wailly Keep.

It was cold again on 4 February, but enemy activity was light and there was only one casualty when a man accidently shot himself in the arm. The 5th was fine and cold and several German rifle grenades landed but no casualties were caused. The cold weather continued on 6 February and German machine guns fired on the rear areas. Both sides used indirect fire from the machine gun to hit targets that were out of sight, in the same way artillery was used to hit indirect targets. The machine gun is elevated and fired at a given angle. The flight path of the bullets takes a curved trajectory and eventually hits the ground in a spread called a beaten zone.

On 7 February the battalion was relieved by the 1/7th DWR and moved into divisional reserve at the village of Bailleulval, 4 miles to the east. The 8th was spent cleaning kit and equipment and the SBRs were treated with glycerine to prevent the rubber from perishing. In the afternoon the divisional GOC gave a lecture on attacking from the trenches, which required the attendance of all the officers and NCOs. The next day part of the battalion attended the baths and the rest of the men practised attacking from the trenches. In the afternoon the brigade GOC inspected the billets and gave a lecture to officers and senior NCOs. The battalion departed Bailleulval on 10 February at 10.30am to relieve the 1/7th DWR in the Wailly sector trenches. The relief was completed by 3.15pm without casualties.

On 11 February the weather became milder and the Germans fired thirty light mortar rounds at the support lines but no injuries were caused. The thaw continued on the 12th; a few light mortars fell on the front line and a retaliatory barrage was launched by British light mortars. The following day was quiet, with a few shells falling at the junction of French Street and the support line. It was reported on 14 February that the enemy had been sweeping no man's land with a searchlight the previous night, probably to try and catch a wiring party in the act. On 15 February the battalion was scheduled to be relieved but it was cancelled. The German light trench mortars were more active, but no casualties were caused. The battalion was eventually relieved the following day by the 1/7th DWR and marched 3 miles to the village of Simencourt to act as divisional reserve. During the relief one man was shot in the right arm. The morning of 17 February was spent cleaning kit and equipment and in the afternoon, parades were held under company arrangements. The mild weather continued and the ground and roads were in a muddy condition. On the 18th B, C and D Companies commenced training for a large-scale attack on the German lines. A Company was not required for the raid and continued with normal training.

On 19 February the men of A Company departed Simencourt for the front line at Wailly to relieve B Company of the 1/7th DWR who, on being relieved, moved to Simencourt. B, C and D Companies of the 1/6th DWR continued training for the proposed raid and were visited by the corps and brigade GOCs. Later that day, D Company and two platoons of C Company were allocated baths. Training for the raid continued the next day and B Company with the remaining two platoons of C Company were allocated baths. B Company of 1/7th DWR spent the morning cleaning kit and equipment and conducted normal training in the afternoon. Rain fell most of the day and the roads and training area were in a bad state.

An officers' conference was held in the evening and orders were received to cancel the proposed raid. On 21 February, despite the cancellation order, B, C and D Companies carried out a dress rehearsal of the raid on the training area. The Brigade GOC, Brigadier General Lewes was present and expressed regret at the cancellation but felt great satisfaction in the way the battalion had trained and the enthusiasm shown by all ranks.

At 6am on 22 February D Company of the 1/7th DWR departed Simencourt to relieve A Company of the 1/4th DWR in the 'Keeps' area of the front at Wailly. At 9.15am B, C and D companies of the 1/6th DWR also departed Simencourt to relieve the 1/7th DWR at Wailly. D Company was on the receiving end of a trench mortar bombardment as they moved into position and four men were injured. The relief was completed at 4pm and the Germans continued to bombard the front line and support trenches. At 7pm an enemy raiding party entered the British trenches but they were immediately ejected, although two men were wounded by a German grenade. The next day was quieter and the weather was fine, but the trenches were in a bad state. A few light mortar bombs fell around Fleet Street trench but no injuries were caused.

On 24 February a trench raid was undertaken. At 2am Serjeant James Bury DCM MM and seventy-five men from D Company left the trenches and crawled through the German wire towards a sap. They waited in a shell hole until a party of Germans entered, then Serjeant Bury and the party of men jumped in the sap and encountered two Germans who were bayoneted and shot. A third raised the alarm by a whistle and on hearing this, the British party threw grenades towards the saphead, where it joined the main trench. The signal was then given to withdraw and the party returned at

4.30am. One of the men, Private Scott from Keighley, became entangled on the German wire and was taken prisoner by a German officer. He was taken into a dug-out and searched but they failed to find his identity disc. As he was led to the rear of the German line, his escort was distracted and he managed to escape and make his way back to the British lines, arriving back at 6am. He reported the Germans had the number 98 on their shoulder straps, the dugouts were well stocked with food and drink and lit by oil lamps. On his way back, he counted seven dead Germans near the sap and two wounded near the gap in the wire. The rest of the day passed quietly after the early morning excitement.

On 25 February the Divisional GOC Major General Percival visited the lines and congratulated Serjeant Bury and the men who raided the German sap. He was very pleased and said it showed excellent spirit. The British artillery was active between 3pm and 4pm and several aircraft were seen flying over the British lines. The German machine gunners were firing flares to illuminate no man's land during the night. That night the German forces withdrew from the Ancre sector of the front, 15 miles to the south of Wailly. A close watch was kept on the enemy lines and a patrol of three officers was sent out but the only thing they noticed was a tape leading from no man's land towards the British trenches where the Germans entered during the raid of 22 February.

On 26 February the battalion was relieved during the morning and B, C and D Companies went in to billets at Rivière. The platoons of A Company went in to the 'Keeps' at Wailly: Petit Chateau, Wailly Keep, Petit Moulin and Factory Keep. B, C and D Companies were due to move to Simencourt to train for a new proposed raid on the German trenches, but again it was cancelled, causing disappointment amongst the men.

On the 27th the battalion was relieved by the 2/9th London Regiment (TF), 58th Division and marched 8 miles west to the village of Saint-Amand. A Company was relieved in the 'Keeps' and made its way to Saint-Amand. The transport and quartermasters stores made their way from Bailleulval. On arrival, the battalion was comfortably accommodated in huts and the next day was spent cleaning weapons and equipment and inspections.

CASUALTIES: In February 1917, the battalion had no fatalities and 8 men wounded.

March 1917
At 9am on 1 March 1917 an unexpected operational order was received from 58th Division to the effect that the battalion was to be relieved at Saint-Amand by the 8th Sherwoods. The billets were cleared by midday and the men marched 5 miles to Halloy via the villages of Pas-en-Artois and Henu. The war diary reports that not a single man in the battalion fell out during the march. The unexpected move was a result of the enemy's withdrawal from Gommecourt. It was a planned withdrawal to new positions on the shorter, more easily defended Hindenburg Line which took place between 9 February and 15 March 1917. It eliminated the two salients or bulges in the line which

had been formed in 1916 between Arras and Saint-Quentin and Saint-Quentin to Noyon during the Battle of the Somme.

The British referred to it as the German Retreat to the Hindenburg Line but the operation was a strategic withdrawal rather than a retreat. Railways and roads were dug up, trees felled, wells polluted, buildings destroyed and large numbers of mines and other booby-traps planted. The Germans had had plenty of time to construct the new defences of the Hindenburg line. Thick-walled concrete bunkers and belts of barbed wire, often up to 30 or 40 yards deep, had been constructed. Machine guns had been placed in tactical supporting positions and the line was built in depth often with several support trenches behind the front line.

The battalion arrived in Halloy at 4.30pm and moved into the same billets they had occupied at Christmas 1916. The following day was spent cleaning equipment, weapons and kit and in the afternoon the men went on a route march in full kit. On 3 March C and D Companies visited the baths at Pas-en-Artois whilst A and B Companies played football, with A Company winning 8-4. On this date, Private Harry Downs (21) died in Grantham Military Hospital from shrapnel wounds to the back and right ankle he received on 3 September 1916. He enlisted on 8 December 1915 and lived at 350 Girlington Road, Bradford. Before the war he had worked as the manager of his father's grocery shop. He is buried in the Heaton Baptist Burial Ground.

Sunday 4 March was cold and frosty and a church parade was held, the first for some time, with men from the 1/6th and 1/4th DWR attending. The service was a short one due to the cold weather for there had been a heavy snowfall overnight. Another short notice move occurred on 5 March when the men marched 5 miles north-west to the town of Bouquemaison via Lucheux. The morning of 6 March was spent on a route march, preparing kit and inspections. In the afternoon, Serjeant James Bury and Private J. Scott were awarded Military Medals for their gallantry during the trench raid at Wailly on 24 February.

On 7 March the battalion departed at 7.15am and marched 4 miles to the town of Doullens, arriving at 9am. The intention had been to board a tactical train which was supposed to depart at 10am (tactical trains were for military use only and had priority at signals, junctions etc) but it did not arrive as planned, so the men had to wait at the roadside in the freezing cold wind for six and a half hours. The train eventually arrived at 3.30pm and the battalion was transported to Merville, thirty-one miles to the north-east, back towards Flanders. The men entrained at 4pm and the scheduled journey time was four hours but the train eventually reached Merville at 4am the next day, some eleven hours after setting off. The war diary records that the journey by tactical train was a complete failure. The men detrained at Merville, were given hot tea, and marched 4 miles through thickly falling snow to the hamlet of Le Bout Deville, a mile north-west of Neuve Chapelle.

Chapter 10

Neuve Chapelle

The men marched via Lestrem, with the battalion transport and stores arriving in the afternoon on a later train. The CO and company commanders made their way up to the front line trenches to make arrangements for the following day's relief. At 2pm on 9 March 1917, the battalion moved to the front line and relieved the 1/4th London Regiment (Royal Fusiliers), 168 Brigade, 56th Division. The battalion had to cover a front of 2,600 yards, from the left of Frère-du-Bois to the outskirts of Neuve Chapelle. The relief was completed by 4.45pm, with the last two hours of the relief carried out in a snowstorm. The rest of the night passed quietly except for the German machine guns. The 10th was quiet until 7pm when the Germans fired eighty trench mortar bombs, most of which landed in the British wire in front of the trenches, but one man was slightly wounded by shrapnel. The next day was stormy in more ways than one; the weather was cold, rainy and windy and at 8am the Germans fired trench mortars at Port Arthur. At 10am they fired twenty-five rifle grenades at the Church Road area and between 12 – 3pm about thirty 5.9-inch shells landed near Church Road. Trench mortars were used again which landed along the rest of the front, as well as the machine guns which were active at dusk. Despite the bombardment, only five men were wounded by shrapnel. The enemy started early on 12 March. From 8am and lasting the whole day, they launched a continuous barrage of trench mortars, 4.2-inch and 5.9-inch artillery shells. The British artillery was slow to react, with the British 6-inch guns only becoming effective late in the afternoon. Private William Troughton (20) from Settle, was killed by a trench mortar and one other man was wounded in the face. Private Lawrence Western (22) from Skipton was killed by a bullet.

Private William Troughton.

Private Western from Gladstone Street, Skipton, enlisted in September 1914 and was appointed as a Lewis gunner. Before the war he was employed in the grocery department of the Skipton Co-operative Society and was a member of the hand bell ringers association of Skipton Parish Church.

Private Troughton enlisted in September 1914 and before the war had been a projectionist at Settle Picture Palace. He had previously been wounded in the right shoulder by shrapnel in July 1916 and spent five

Private Lawrence Western. (Both CPGW)

115

months recovering before returning to the battalion. He is buried with Lawrence Western at St Vaast Post Military Cemetery, Richebourg-l'Avoué.

As darkness closed in, the trench mortar bombardment continued. It was suspected the enemy were preparing a raid, so the British artillery was informed that if the front line platoon officers fired red flares followed by the SOS rockets; it was a signal that a raid was in progress. At 8.30pm C Company sent up the SOS rockets and the artillery immediately opened fire but it was some time before any information was received at battalion HQ. The Germans had entered the British trenches near Hun Post as part of a planned raid at the point on the line where it was thinly held. When the dust settled, five men were missing, presumed captured and several 10-inch square boxes of explosives, complete with a gun cotton fuse and detonators were found. These were presumably part of a failed attempt to demolish the post. In any case, the trenches were in an awful state after two days of bombardment and nearly all the communication trenches had caved in or were thick with liquid mud.

During the attack Private Harold Boothman from Wilsden and Private Granville Beaumont (30) from Stainland, near Huddersfield, were both killed by shrapnel. Private Herbert Robinson (19) from 144 Hollins Road, Walsden near Todmorden died two days later at No.7 CCS from a gunshot wound to his shoulder which he received during the attack. Thirteen other men were wounded and five men were missing, presumed captured. Six of the wounded and all the missing men were from C Company.

Granville Beaumont enlisted on 20 February 1916 and was called up on 19 July for basic training. Before the war he was employed as a clothes presser and was sent to France on Christmas Day 1916. On Boxing Day he was posted to the 34th Infantry Base Depot at Étaples, where his stay was short as he was sent to the 1/6th DWR on 29 December 1916. He is buried in St Vaast Post Military Cemetery near Richebourg, alongside Harold Boothman.

Herbert Robinson enlisted on 22 February 1916 at Halifax and was mobilised on 29 August for basic training. Like Granville Beaumont, he was posted to France on Christmas Day 1916 where he was posted to the 34th Infantry Base. Again, his stay was a short one as he joined the 1/6th DWR on 29 December 1916. He is buried at Merville Communal Cemetery Extension.

The remainder of the 12th and early morning of 13 March were relatively quiet and the battalion was relieved that morning by the 1/7th DWR completed by 11.30am. The battalion then moved back into support. C Company was in close support and the rest of the battalion moved a mile west to the hamlet of Croix Barbee (La Croix Barbet) with only one platoon provided for a working party. On 14 March the battalion marched a mile south to the village of Richebourg St-Vaast for baths and 100 men were required for working parties at night. The next day was bright and sunny with the men carrying out practice platoon attacks and other training in the morning. Two companies were provided for working parties that night and Private William Hampton from Keighley, who was wounded by a rifle grenade in the legs on 12 March, died at No.7 CCS at Merville.

William Hampton was pre-war 'terrier' who originally joined the TF in 1910 and was living at Hall Street, Oakworth. He was working as a labourer at George Hattersley's Engineering works in Keighley and in June 1915 he was posted to the 24th Provisional Battalion for coastal defence. This unit comprised men with a lower medical category or members of the TF who, for whatever reason, declined to serve overseas. In June 1916 he was serving at Clacton-on-Sea when he was deemed medically fit enough to serve overseas. Like the other men, he was posted to France on Christmas Day 1916 with a short stay at 34th Infantry Training Base before joining the 1/6th DWR on 28 December 1916. He is buried in Merville Community Cemetery Extension. He left a wife and young daughter.

Training continued and SBRs were checked on 16 March which was another fine day. A court of enquiry was held regarding the five missing men and working parties were provided at night. At noon the next day the battalion relieved the 1/7th DWR at the front with the relief completed at 3.30pm and the rest of the day passed off quietly. The next day was fine in the morning with light rain in the afternoon. The artillery was active that day with shells from both sides landing mainly behind each other's lines. Patrols were sent out at night to examine the German wire, but when one of the British patrols was observed, the Germans shelled their own wire although no casualties were caused.

On 19 March the divisional and brigade GOCs inspected the front line and one man was wounded by shrapnel. The following was a wet day with a strong wind. The German artillery was active, with shrapnel shells bursting around Copse Street and Rue-de-Bois. During the night the SOS signal was sent up by the brigade to the right of the battalion, but it appears the Germans opposite thought it was the 1/6th DWR who had fired the rocket and launched a barrage of shells and machine-gun bullets towards the battalion's position which wounded three men.

Wednesday 21 March started with a snowstorm that cleared by mid-morning and the German artillery shelled the area of La Bassée Road. On the 22nd two men were wounded in the head by rifle fire. The battalion was relieved the next day by the 1/7th DWR, with the left company being relieved by the 1/5th York and Lancaster Regiment from 148 Brigade. The 147 Brigade line had been shortened with Curve and Neb Posts, Church and Hill Redoubts and the B Line (reserve line) north of Sandbag Alley now the responsibility of 148 Brigade. Before the relief was complete, Corporal George Hoyles (34) of Duckett Street Skipton suffered a fractured skull from shell fire and died the next day at 1st/2nd CCS. He enlisted in November 1915 and was posted to France in March 1916. Before the war he was employed as a gas stoker at Skipton Urban District Council's gas works. He is buried in Merville Community Cemetery Extension. George Hoyles was one of three brothers who were killed in the Great War. His younger brother, Serjeant Ernest Hoyles, had emigrated to Canada in 1912. He was an experienced man who had seen service in the Second Boer War and at the outbreak of the Great War, joined the 15th Battalion, The Canadian Highlanders and was killed in action near Ypres on 3 June 1916, aged 30. He has no known grave and is commemorated on the Menin Gate Memorial. Their older brother, Richard Hoyles (37), served in the East Lancashire Regiment and was killed in action near Gheluvelt, east of Ypres on 5 October 1917. He also has no known grave and is commemorated on the Tyne Cot Memorial.

Corporal George Hoyles. (CPGW)

Two other men were wounded on the 22nd by shell fire, and one man by a self-inflicted gunshot wound to his hand. The battalion then proceeded to billets at Croix Barbee.

Cleaning kit and having baths at Richebourg St Vaast took place on 24 March. A demonstration of listening equipment was given in the afternoon and 150 men were found for working parties. The next day was fine and church services were held in C Company's billet. A special party of men also began training under Captain Samuel H. Clough for a proposed raid on the German lines. Working parties of 200 men were provided for the Royal Engineers and carrying rations. Training for the raid continued on the 26th and a full-scale ground plan of the German trenches was made by removing the turf. A night practice was also held and the usual working parties were provided by the rest of the battalion. Heavy snow fell on the 27th and a rehearsal for the raid was held during the afternoon. Another rehearsal took place that evening and two Bangalore torpedoes were detonated under a replica section of wire which worked perfectly, creating a gap 18-yards wide.

The weather on 28 March was fine and in the morning, a final practice for the raid took place. The usual working parties were provided at night. Around nightfall it started to rain and continued until about 12.30am. The final approval for the operation was received and last preparations were made. A section of the German line, named Mitzi Trench, had been chosen for the raid.

Looking west towards the front line that the 1/6th DWR held at Neuve Chapelle.

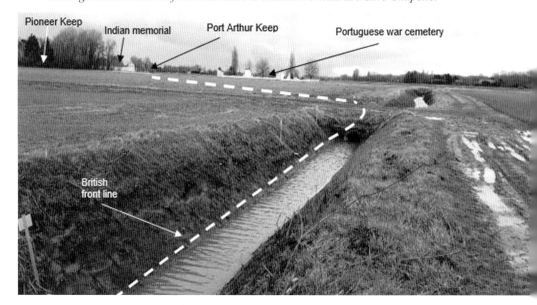

Pioneer Keep   Indian memorial   Port Arthur Keep   Portuguese war cemetery

British front line

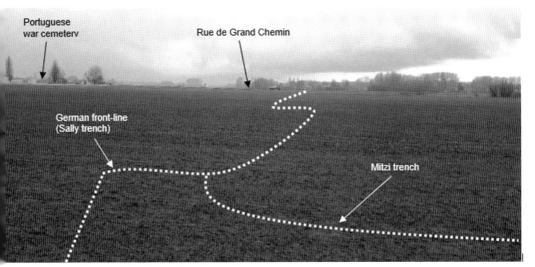

Portuguese war cemetery

Rue de Grand Chemin

German front-line (Sally trench)

Mitzi trench

The view of Mitzi Trench from the west.

Mitzi Trench

Shepherds Redoubt

German front line (Sally Trench)

British front line

Looking towards Mitzi Trench from the British front line.

The raiding party comprised the following men:

Raid Commander: Captain Samuel H. Clough

Bangalore torpedo party: Second Lieutenant J.W. Denison and four Royal Engineers.

Mitzi Trench raid party: Serjeant Bury DCM MM and eleven men from D Company.

Right hand party: Serjeant Driver and eleven men from B Company.

Clearing party: Second Lieutenant T.G. Brown and twenty-one men from C Company.

Left hand party: Second Lieutenant J.G. Butler and eleven men from A Company.

Parapet party: Captain S.H. Clough plus six bayonet men, two runners, three signallers, two stretcher-bearers and two buglers.

The raiding party left the billets at Croix Barbee at midnight and paused at Windy Corner. Each man had a hot drink, no doubt laced with a drop of SRD rum, rifles were made ready and bayonets fixed. Empty sandbags were tied over the bayonets to prevent glare from flares and moonlight. They moved off down Copse Trench towards Copse Street. Each man carried five Mills bombs (hand grenades) and the rifle grenadiers carried twelve No.23 rifle grenades.

The men wore belts and bayonet scabbards and a white identifying armband on the left arm. The officers wore other ranks tunics with a white cloth disc sewn on the back. All identifying marks were removed from tunics and pockets were emptied. Each man was to carry a wire cutter and six clips of rifle ammunition (each 'clip' held five .303 calibre rounds). The objective of the raid was to capture prisoners, obtain identification and kill Germans.

The plan was to enter the enemy line at Mitzi Trench, proceed 40 yards along it to the rear, and 30 yards to the left and 90 yards to the right of the Sally Trench and a detailed artillery fire plan had been worked out for the raid. Before the raid, a barrage was to land on the German objective and adjacent trenches as the men were breaching the German wire with Bangalore torpedoes. The barrage was then to shift to the German rear and support lines leading to the objective trench to prevent a German counter-attack. The British wire had been covertly cut in two places and a ditch bridged by men from A Company. The Bangalore torpedo party had crawled in front of the British wire and were waiting in no man's land.

Zero hour for the operation was 2am and the raiding party formed up at Mole Post. Due to faulty timekeeping, the artillery barrage started two minutes early and the shells landed short of the German lines. The raiding party, on hearing the barrage, climbed out of the trenches and made their way towards the German wire. Several British shells landed amongst the Bangalore torpedo party, causing one of the devices to explode and damaging the other. When it detonated, two Royal Engineer sappers who were part of the demolition team, were killed.

Company Serjeant Major Giles of 57 Field Company, Royal Engineers, managed to repair the damaged Bangalore torpedo and a runner was sent for replacement men to carry it to the German wire. It detonated at 2.09am, five minutes later than planned, but created a good-sized gap in the wire, allowing Captain Clough to lead the raiding party towards the German trenches. As the men entered Sally Trench, no Germans, either dead or alive, were found. A few were seen withdrawing through support trenches and were fired at with rifles and grenades. A telephone wire had been taken across no man's land with the raiding party but failed to work. Several German SOS rockets were launched as the men entered Mitzi Trench and after staying for twelve minutes, the code word 'Clough' was passed to the men, signalling the withdrawal as the Germans shells began to land on their own lines. When the raiding party was clear, Captain Clough lit a red signal flare to indicate all his men were clear from the German lines. The code word 'Clough' was used instead of 'withdraw' or 'retire' to prevent the Germans shouting those words in the confusion and noise of the raid.

Whilst returning to the British lines, Second Lieutenant John Goodwin Butler (20) from Newport Pagnell was fatally wounded by shrapnel. Serjeant James Bury and Private Victor Proctor of Eric Street, Keighley were helping Private John E. Pickup DCM from Barnoldswick who had been wounded. A shell landed near the three men and Private Proctor and Private Pickup were killed. In the darkness and confusion their bodies were not recovered, despite a search being carried out later that day. All that was found in the area where they fell were two steel helmets and a rifle. Private Pickup's DCM was awarded on 14 November 1915 and his citation reads:

Private J.E. Pickup DCM. (CPGW)

For conspicuous gallantry as a stretcher bearer during operations he has shown the greatest pluck and disregard for danger when repeatedly tending the wounded under heavy shell fire.

He enlisted at the outbreak of war and was employed as a weaver at Albert Hartley and Co.'s sheeting works in Barnoldswick. He is buried in St Vaast Post Military cemetery, Richebourg alongside Victor Proctor.

Captain Clough was wounded by shrapnel in both legs but insisted on walking to the aid post. The battalion stretcher-bearers, under the command of Serjeant Whitely, were singled out in a debrief report for their gallantry in evacuating the wounded. In total, five men were killed and nineteen wounded. The raid was partially successful, in so much that the objective was reached, but failed to obtain any prisoners or obtain identification. The brigade and divisional GOCs were both pleased with what the men had achieved despite everything seeming to go against them. It was established the failure of the raid was entirely due to the inaccuracy and poor timing of the artillery, which as well as causing fatalities and casualties amongst friendly forces, caused the delay in breaching the German wire that in turn alerted the Germans. One artillery battery was identified as the one which fired early. When the men of the 1/6th DWR saw the shells landing, they left the British trenches as per the plan, which meant that when the other batteries fired at the correct time, the men were caught in no man's land with only shell holes for cover. Combined with British shells falling short and the Germans shelling their own line, it is a miracle that so few men were killed.

That afternoon the battalion relieved the 1/7th DWR in the front line and the relief was completed at 4.45pm without incident. B and C Companies were in the front line, A Company in support and D Company in reserve. The 30th was a wet day and passed quietly. Major Wilfred Claughton departed the battalion to join the 2/6th DWR in the 62nd Division. He was the son of Hugh and Jane Claughton of Claybank, Guiseley and uncle of Hugh Marsden Claughton. He was the former commander of the Guiseley Company and would have been a familiar face in the 2/6th Battalion as many Guiseley men were

Major Wilfred Claughton. (CPGW)

121

serving in the ranks. Unfortunately, Major Claughton did not live to see the end of the war. He died on 24 March 1918 whilst commanding a contingent of the Chinese Labour Corps and is buried in Boulogne Eastern Cemetery.

The last day of March passed quietly except at 11am when a few shells and trench mortars landed near Huns Post. That night the support company worked on strengthening the B line and the reserve company worked on the front line and Huns Street. Two platoons of 1/7th DWR were engaged on a wiring party.

CASUALTIES: In March 1917, the battalion had 11 men killed, 56 wounded and 5 missing.

April 1917
Sunday 1 April passed quietly until about 2.30pm when trench mortars landed on Lansdown Street causing damage to the trench and about 11.30pm, the bright moonlit night was disturbed by a heavy snowstorm. On the 2nd at 10am the German trench mortars launched a bombardment of the front and support line. British howitzers were tasked with a counter-barrage on the small gauge train line which was suspected of supplying the ammunition to the mortars. This appeared to be successful as the German mortaring stopped, but one man was wounded by a machine-gun bullet. Heavy snow fell overnight into 3 April and continued for the rest of the day.

At midday the British artillery bombarded the village of Lorgies, a mile behind the German lines. About 11.15pm fifty German shells landed near Copse Street and one man was wounded in the leg by shrapnel. On the 4th the battalion was relieved by the 1/7th DWR and proceeded to billets at Croix Barbee in support. The next day was fine and two companies were provided for working parties during the day and night. Those men not working had baths at Richebourg and Rue-de-Bois and the rest of the day was spent cleaning kit and equipment. The good weather continued between 6 and 8 April and working parties were increased to three companies. The working hours were 9am to 1pm and 2.30pm to 4pm, with the remainder of the battalion conducting training.

On the 9th working parties and training continued, but in the early hours the distant rumbling of artillery could be heard. This was the attack at Vimy Ridge near Arras, which was undertaken by the Canadian Corps of the First Army. On 10 April, five men who took part in the trench raid on 28th/29th March were awarded the Military Medal. The recipients included Serjeant Whitely (stretcher bearer) and Company Serjeant Major Giles of the Royal Engineers. Four other men, including Captain Clough, received a mention in despatches.

In the afternoon the battalion relieved the 1/7th DWR in the front line. A and D Companies were at the front, C in support and B in reserve. At 10.25pm a raid was carried out by 148 Brigade to the left of the battalion and, in conjunction with the raid, the Boars Head salient of the German line was bombarded by the British artillery. The SOS signal was sent up by the defenders and a large-scale bombardment of the British lines commenced. It was noticed that a number of the German shells and trench mortars fell in no man's land, as if they were anticipating an infantry attack. Private Roland Fishwick (35) from Barnoldswick and Private Walter Jeffrey from Keighley were both killed by a trench mortar. Two other men were wounded.

Wednesday 11 April started off dry, but at 4pm heavy rain began that lasted until 8pm and the rest of the afternoon and evening passed quietly. On the 12th a strong wind blew in which helped to dry out the trenches and, apart from a few trench mortars, the day passed quietly.

Private R. Fishwick. (CPGW)

The next day a company of the 22nd Regiment of the Portuguese Expeditionary Force (PEF) was attached to the battalion for twenty-four hours. The party consisted of six officers and 200 men. The Portuguese company was made up of three platoons, two of which were attached to the front line companies and one in support. Portugal did not form part of the alliances which led up to the start of the Great War and was initially neutral but tensions arose due to the German U-boat blockade of the UK, which was an important trading partner of Portugal. Clashes also occurred with German forces in Portuguese Angola near to German South-West Africa (Namibia) and in German East Africa (Tanzania). On 23 February 1916 the Portuguese government complied with a British request to seize thirty-six German and Austro-Hungarian ships that had been interned at Lisbon. On 9 March the Germans declared war on Portugal, with the Austro-Hungarian Empire following suit on 15 March. The Portuguese government sent about 56,000 men to the Western Front, of whom nearly 12,000 were killed.

A few trench mortars landed around Pioneer Keep, wounding four men, including one Portuguese soldier. The 14th was a clear, fine day which passed quietly apart from a little shelling in the early morning. The next day started overcast and wet, which lasted all day. At 9am, the Portuguese company departed the line, apparently having enjoyed their first visit to the front. On 16 April around midday, the Germans began a bombardment with large calibre trench mortars around Landsdowne Post but no casualties were caused. The battalion was relieved in the afternoon by the 1/7th DWR which was completed at 4pm. The men then marched to billets at Croix Barbee to take up the support position. Heavy rain started at 6pm, lasted all night and continued into the next day. Half the battalion bathed at Croix Barbee and Rue de Bois with the rest of the men on working parties. The remaining half of the battalion bathed on the morning of the following day and the afternoon was spent training in the tactics of open land warfare. Small platoon-sized attacks were practised involving Lewis gunners, rifle grenadiers and bombers (specialist grenade men). Working parties were provided on 19 April with the remaining men engaged in training. The divisional and brigade GOCs observed the training and inspected the billets. Both commanders expressed their pleasure at the battalion's performance.

The morning of 20 April was sunny and warm with working parties and training continuing as normal. The men competed in various sports during the afternoon to celebrate the second anniversary of the battalion arriving in France. Each company fielded a team with events consisting of the 100 yard sprint, 200 yard relay and the

Portuguese Stokes Mortar crew in action.

tug of war, which was won by B Company. There was also a 2-mile cross-country steeplechase, the winner of which was the first team to get six men across the finish line. The first man across the line by a long way was Private Carter of C Company, but the eventual result was a draw between B and D Companies. After the sports, all ranks were given two eggs, a tin of potted meat and some French bread, all paid for out of regimental funds.

Working parties and training continued as usual on 21 April and on the 22nd the battalion relieved the 1/7th DWR in the Ferme-du-Bois sector of the line. About ten German observation balloons were seen during the relief, but fortunately it passed off unmolested. To the satisfaction of the men, the closest balloon was destroyed by a shell from a British artillery gun. During the relief one man was shot in the arm.

On 23 April a company from the 15th Regiment of the PEF was attached to the battalion for the day, which, apart from a few trench mortars, passed quietly. The fine weather allowed the aircraft of both sides to be active. The 24th was another fine day and the divisional and brigade GOCs inspected the trenches, as well as the CO of the PEF, Captain Amaral who was attached to the battalion for four days. The enemy artillery was active and a German plane was shot down and landed intact behind British lines at La Touret, a mile south-west of Neuve Chapelle.

On the morning of 25 April, a company of the 28th Regiment of the PEF joined the battalion for forty-eight hours of instruction in trench warfare. The German mortars were active during the day, particularly at Pioneer Keep, and the German artillery shelled the B Line around Whiskey Corner for most of the day with a mixture of high explosive and phosgene gas shells. Seven men from C Company were wounded by trench mortars and one man from A Company was shot in the hand. On the 26th the German artillery was active in the afternoon and evening. Two men were wounded and a soldier from the PEF was killed by a shell. The PEF Company departed the trenches around 9am on 27 April and fortunately the morning was quiet which allowed the men to withdraw without incident. Captain Amaral from the PEF left in the afternoon.

The British artillery was active during the night, firing on the German light railways. The 28th was fine and sunny and the battalion was relieved by the 1/7th DWR and marched to billets at Croix Barbee in support. The relief was completed by 11.30am and the men visited the baths. The 29th was another sunny day and an open air church service was held at 11am with the non-conformists holding a service in one of the billets. The last day of April was spent training in open warfare tactics around Richebourg St-Vaast. The strength of the battalion on this day was 40 officers and 923 men.

CASUALTIES: During April 1917, the battalion had 2 men killed and 12 wounded. A member of the PEF was also killed.

May 1917
Training in open warfare continued on 1 May which was sunny and warm. In the afternoon the CO, Lieutenant Colonel Bateman, gave a lecture to all ranks on constructing listening posts in no man's land and numerous aircraft were active during the day. A German plane was seen to be brought down in flames after being shot at by anti-aircraft guns. The good weather continued the following day with training continuing in the morning. In the afternoon, an inter-company football tournament was held; A Company beat C Company 2-1 with B and D Companies drawing 0-0 after twenty minutes of extra time.

The next day continued sunny and training resumed. The CO inspected the troops in full marching order and, in the afternoon, British and German aircraft were seen overhead. The weather was fine again on the 4th and the morning was spent inspecting SBRs, PH helmets as well as thirty minutes gas drill. In the afternoon, the battalion relieved the 1/7th DWR in the front line.

The rest of the day and night passed quietly and on 5 May two companies of the PEF, some 400 officers and men, were attached to the battalion for forty-eight hours and one man was wounded by shrapnel. The next day passed quietly with no casualties and the fine weather continued into the 7th, which again passed quietly, apart from one man being wounded by shrapnel in the arm. The men of the PEF departed in the morning. Tuesday 8 May was another fine quiet day, but at 11 pm that night things changed.

British troops in training at Porton near Salisbury preparing Livens projectors for firing. (IWM Public domain)

During the previous days men from M and F Special Companies of the Royal Engineers had placed 1,000 Livens projectors just behind the British trenches. A Livens projector comprised a 7.6-inch diameter steel cylinder which was dug in to the ground at a 45-degree angle. These were then loaded with a projecting charge and a steel drum containing chemicals. When fired, the steel drum was launched towards the enemy and a small rupture charge detonated on landing, dispersing the contents. Stokes mortars, similar in appearance and use to modern mortars, were also to fire 1,260 rounds of 4-inch gas bombs. All the projectiles contained either irritant chemicals or lethal phosgene. In total, 38,820lb (17,608kg) of chemicals were to be launched against the German lines. The signal to fire was given by launching three rockets from battalion HQ at Lansdowne Post. The target area stretched from Shepherds Redoubt, north-east to the Bois-de-Biez woods. The wind speed was 3mph to the east which gave perfect conditions. The British machine guns, artillery and trench mortar batteries also added to the barrage of the German lines. Those men who were in the battalion at the time of the Yser Canal gas attack on 19 December 1915, must have looked on in satisfaction. German retaliation was practically non-existent, which indicated the effectiveness of the operation in neutralising the enemy, but the plan did not include a follow-up attack.

On the morning of 9 May two companies of the PEF were attached to the battalion for twenty-four hours and the German artillery was active, with the area of St Vaast the target. The 66th Division to the right of the battalion launched a raid on the German lines, but the night passed quietly for the men of the 1/6th DWR with only a few gas shells landing on the support lines. The next day the battalion was relieved by the 1/7th DWR and moved to the billets at Croix Barbee and the 11th was spent bathing and cleaning kit and a working party of 100 men was provided. Training in open warfare continued on 12 May, overseen by the brigade GOC. In the evening men from battalion HQ played brigade HQ at football. Honours were even with a 2-2 draw.

The 13th was a fine sunny day and a church parade was held, but halfway through the service, German artillery shells began to land in the area. The first two landed on battalion HQ at Penin Mariage, about 40 yards from the parade. The barrage lasted from 11am to 2pm and around 300 4.2-inch shells were fired. Several casualties

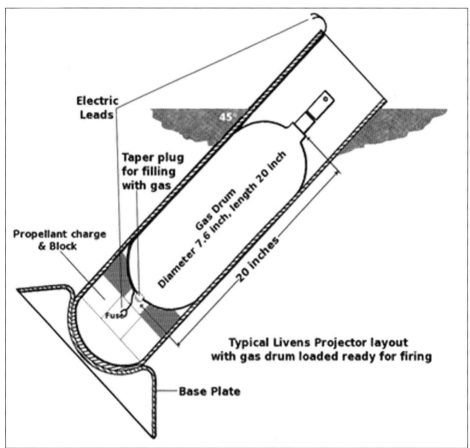

Simplified diagram showing typical layout of a Livens Projector embedded in the ground at an angle of 45 degrees, with gas drum loaded ready for firing. The thin electric leads run from the fuse in the base of the tube, up the inside of the tube and from the barrel muzzle to an electric generator. When the generator plunger is depressed the electric current sparks the fuse in the base of the tube, which ignites the propellant charge and the expanding gas pressure launches the bomb out of the tube. (Public domain, courtesy of R.C. Butcher)

resulted from the two shells which hit battalion HQ. Private Willie Marsden from Ovenden and Private Ernest Baxter (29) from Golcar were killed and ten other men were wounded. One of the wounded men was Private William Wallwork from Skipton, who subsequently died of his wounds on 15 June 1917.

A thunderstorm broke overnight into 14 May but training and working parties continued as normal. On the 15th the battalion played 246th Battery, Royal Field Artillery at football with the battalion winning 2-1. On 16 May the battalion relieved the 1/7th DWR in the Ferme-du-Bois sector which was completed by 11.45am without incident. Rain fell overnight into the 17th and the day passed quietly apart from British trench mortars bombarding the German lines. The 18th started fine and warm and the divisional GOC visited the front line. A barrage of British 2-inch 'toffee apple' mortars and Stokes mortars was launched against the German trenches and wire but surprisingly there was no retaliation. The 19th was another fine day and the British artillery targeted the enemy communication lines as it was suspected the Germans were rotating their units at the front. At 11.30pm a patrol of one officer and five men left the British trenches and headed towards the German lines to try to snatch a prisoner. This type of action was known as 'winkling' and, despite the danger, there was great competition between the companies to capture the most prisoners. The German wire was found to be very thick, but a route was carefully cut. The German trenches were reached at 1.35am and a group of four sentries was seen but it was decided to look for a more vulnerable subject. A lone sentry was located towards the rear of the trench, but he moved off as the group were trying to outflank him. At 2.45am, the party started to return to the British lines but as the men were being withdrawn, the Germans opened fire and Lance Serjeant William A. Hodgson was shot in the buttocks and was assisted back to the British trenches by Private Dickinson.

The next day was very hot and about 1.10pm British aircraft dropped bombs on the area of Bois-du-Biez. Three of the bombs landed short on the British lines but no casualties were caused. Both the British and German artillery was active in the afternoon, a few trench mortars landed in the British trenches and one man was wounded by a rifle bullet. The fine weather continued into 21 May and the day passed quietly but rain started at 10pm and lasted all night. One man was shot in the head and wounded. The rain cleared at midday and the battalion was relieved by the 1/7th DWR, which was completed by 5pm when the battalion returned to billets at Croix Barbee. The next day was fine and sunny and spent cleaning kit and equipment. On 24 May training resumed and the divisional GOC visited to observe it. The fine weather continued and on 25 May the day was spent as follows: A Company conducted training, C Company were on working parties, two platoons of B Company attended the brigade training school and the remaining platoon relieved a platoon of 1/7th DWR in support. D Company also relieved a company from 1/5th DWR at the front.

On 26 May A Company resumed training and C Company provided working parties. Several German aircraft flew over the British lines but were driven off by anti-aircraft fire. The 27th was fine and sunny and church parades were held in the morning while in the afternoon SBRs and PH helmets were checked. The following day A and

C Companies resumed training but working parties were cancelled. On the 29th the PEF relieved the units of the 1/6th DWR that were at the front. The remainder of the battalion at Croix Barbee was relieved by the 1/7th DWR, and the battalion marched 2 miles west to billets in the village of Paradis. On 27 May 1940 this village was the scene of a massacre of British troops by German units from SS Division Totenkopf during the Battle of France, when the British Expeditionary Force was attempting to withdraw through the Pas-de-Calais region during the retreat to Dunkirk. Ninety-seven British troops died but two survived with injuries and hid until they were captured by Wehrmacht forces several days later.

Lance Serjeant William A. Hodgson. (CPGW)

The morning of 30 May was spent on cleaning kit and inspections with a short route march after lunch, followed by target practice. On this day Lance Serjeant William Atkinson Hodgson (27) from Skipton died of wounds he received during the trench raid of 19 May. He enlisted at the outbreak of war and, although living in Skipton, he was a native of Blackburn. He was employed as a gardener on the Skipton Castle estate. He was an accomplished long distance runner and had won numerous prizes. A well respected NCO, he had been offered a commission and recommended for the award of a DCM. He is buried in Boulogne Eastern Cemetery.

The last day of May was spent bathing in the morning , then open warfare training in the afternoon. A and D Companies received inoculations and a draft of thirty men arrived.

CASUALTIES: During May 1917 the battalion had 3 men killed and 11 wounded.

June 1917

Training resumed on 1 June with bayonet drill and specialist training by the battalion marksmen, Lewis gunners, bombers and signallers. This was followed by a route march and open warfare training. Private Dickinson was awarded the Military Medal for his gallantry and devotion to duty on the trench raid on 19/20 May. The training routine continued on the 2 June and on the 3rd, a Church of England divine service was held at 9am on the parade square. The non-conformist parade was held in a billet at 9.30am and the Roman Catholic service was held in Paradis Church at 8.30am. A rehearsal was also held for a parade and march-past for the corps GOC.

On 4 June a full rehearsal was held in front of the brigade commander for the forthcoming parade and the weather was described as warm and sunny. On the 5th the Corps GOC, accompanied by the Portuguese Army GOC, inspected the 1/6th and 1/7th DWR and congratulated the men on their turnout. B and C Companies were inoculated in the afternoon and a YMCA tent erected. In the days before the creation of the NAAFI (Navy, Army and Air Force Institute), organisations such as the YMCA, The Church Army, The Salvation Army and Talbot House (Toc H) provided the soldiers with hot drinks, refreshments and reading materials. On 6 June the men visited the divisional swimming pool at La Gougue and in the afternoon the YMCA tent was opened for business.

The next five days were spent conducting training, shooting and church parades. The 13th was a very hot day and the battalion, less C Company, marched 4 miles east to Laventie as the battalion was now attached to 146 Brigade. This was a result of the 1/8th West Yorkshire Regiment having been selected for a special operation. The trenches in the Fauquissart sector, north-east of Neuve Chapelle, were visited by the CO and other officers prior to the battalion taking over. On 14 June the battalion relieved the 1/8th West Yorkshire Regiment in the sector. A and D Companies were in the front line, with one platoon each at Elgin and Erith posts with battalion HQ north-west of Crab House at Temple Bar. B Company was in support in the B Line. The relief was completed at midday and two men were slightly wounded by shrapnel. Apart from a few trench mortars, the night passed quietly.

The morning of 15 June started hazy but it soon cleared into a hot sunny day. Word came through that the operation in which the 1/8th West Yorks were due to participate had been cancelled, so the battalion was to be relieved and returned to the command of 147 Brigade. The relief was completed at 5pm and the battalion marched back to Paradis in the cool of the evening with only two men dropping out of the march.

On this day Private William Wallwork (33) from Ermysted Street, Skipton, died from wounds he received on 13 May. He had been transferred to a military hospital in Whitstable, Kent and is buried at Pendlebury Christ Church Graveyard, near Manchester. He enlisted in October 1914 and was posted to France in April 1916. In June of that year he was wounded in the leg and after several months recovering in hospital, returned to the battalion. On 13 May 1917 he was hit by shrapnel on the same leg as his previous wound and evacuated to England where his leg was amputated. During this procedure, a severe hemorrhage occurred that led to his death. Originally from Pendlebury in Lancashire, he moved to Skipton in the early 1900s to work for the English Sewing Co. at Skipton.

On 16 June the battalion set off at 10.30am to march 3 miles south to the town of Béthune via Hinges. This was the hottest day of the year so far and many men suffered from heat stroke. Frequent rests were carried out and the men eventually arrived at 2pm and were billeted at a tobacco factory. The next day, 17 June, the battalion marched 2 miles south-east to billets in the village of Sailly-Labourse.

Chapter 11

Hulluch

Aparty of men consisting of the CO, adjutant, two officers and three NCOs proceeded in a motor lorry to the St Elie sector, north of Loos, to conduct a reconnaissance of the trenches. On the morning of 18 June time was spent inspecting SBRs, and the men visited the baths at Labourse. In the afternoon the battalion moved to the trenches in the St Elie sector and relieved the 9th Norfolk Regiment. The relief was completed at 1.30pm without incident. The southern boundary of the sector was the Vermelles to Hulluch road and parts of the defences here were opposite considerable stone quarries which consisted of an elaborate system of tunnels, cut out of solid chalk in which troops could be housed. They were lit with electric lights and ventilated by fans which led to most of the front line posts. The tunnels were upwards of 40ft deep and provided excellent cover. A little to the north of the sector was an enormous slag heap named Fosse 8 which was the dominating feature in the area and used by the Germans for observation. The British had positioned a heavy trench mortar in one of the tunnels some 40ft below the surface, which fired out of an aperture similar to a chimney cut out of the chalk.

Later in the day the Germans fired a heavy barrage of trench mortars and grenade-throwers, wounding a man in the stomach and Serjeant James Bury was slightly wounded on the arm by a grenade. The German artillery and trench mortars were active all day on 20 June and heavy rain fell for most of the day and night. The German barrage continued on the 21st and 22nd but the deep tunnels and bunkers prevented any casualties. On 23 June the German trench mortars appeared to be specifically targeting the British defensive strongpoints and several German aircraft flew over the British lines on an apparent reconnaissance mission. This all pointed to a hostile raid being planned so extra sentries were posted. Despite the protection of the tunnels, the men above ground were as vulnerable as they were in any other location along the line. Serjeant Joseph James Bell (40) from Haworth, one of four brothers killed in the war, and Private James Mitchell from Albert Street, Lockwood, Huddersfield were killed by a trench mortar. The mortaring and shelling of the line continued on 24 June and Lance Corporal Willie Hargreaves (23) from Sutton-in-Craven was killed by a shell, with six other men wounded.

Second Lieutenant James Robinson Darragh (26) from Northern Ireland was wounded in the knee by a shell and died from his wounds on 5 July. He is buried in Choques Military Cemetery, Pas de Calais and is also commemorated at the 1st

Ballymena Presbyterian Church. He was the son of the late Samuel and Jane Darragh of Ballycraigy, Ballymena and was one of three brothers who were to lose their lives in the Great War. His brother, Second Lieutenant Matthew Sloan Darragh was commissioned into the 1/6th DWR in October 1915 and just before his death he was attached to the 1/5th DWR. He was killed on 20 March 1917 whilst leading a patrol into no man's land at Neuve Chapelle. He has no known grave and is listed on the Loos Memorial to the Missing.

Matthew and his other brother, John McClelland Crombie Darragh, had emigrated to Canada, but at the outbreak of war they both returned to Northern Ireland and all three brothers enlisted in the 6th Inniskilling Dragoons (Service Squadron No.128). Matthew and James applied for a commission and in February 1916 they attended No.24 Officer Training Battalion at Oxford and were both commissioned into the 1/6th DWR in July 1916.

Their other brother, John McClelland Crombie Darragh, was posted to France in October 1915 and was attached to the HQ of the 36th (Ulster) Division. On Christmas Eve 1915 he died as a result of a self-inflicted gunshot and is buried in St Riquier British Cemetery.

Lance Corporal Willie Hargreaves enlisted in September 1914 and was employed at T. & M. Bairstow's Sutton Mill. At the time of his death he was part of a Lewis gun team and is buried in Sailly-Labourse Communal Cemetery Extension. He was the brother-in-law of Lance Corporal Norman Riley, from Holmfield, Sutton-in-Craven who was serving in the 9th DWR when he was killed on 21 December 1915.

Lance Corporal Willie Hargreaves. (CPGW)

Monday 25 June was quiet apart from a few trench mortars and shells. The battalion was relieved that night by the 1/4th DWR and marched 3 miles west to billets at Philosophe, south of Vermelles. The men arrived in the early hours of the 26th and a breakfast of fried bacon was provided. Later that day they visited the baths and 250 men were required for working parties.

At 3.50am on 27 June the battalion received the SOS call and prepared to move in full kit. The Germans had launched a raid on the St Elie sector that the 1/6th DWR had just vacated, but after an hour they were stood down and went back to the billets. The rest of the day was spent on physical exercise, bayonet fighting and inspections. A further 250 men were also provided for working parties.

At 2.14am on 28 June, seventeen men and an officer crawled towards the German wire and detonated a Bangalore torpedo. Pieces of uniform identifying the regiment were also left for the Germans to find. This was part of a distraction operation to make the Germans suspect a raid was imminent in the sector and to give the impression the 49th Division had taken over the sector. To add to the feint, the battalion departed Philosophe and headed towards the front line in an exposed communication trench to give the impression of troops massing for an attack. The real attack was to be made by the 46th Division to the south and at 7.10pm a heavy German bombardment commenced which lasted most of the night but no casualties were caused. By the 29th June the battalion had returned to billets at Philosophe and spent the morning training. A working party of 100 men was also provided.

On 30 June the battalion marched back to the tobacco factory billets at Béthune and returned to the command of 49th Division having spent fourteen days under the command of the 6th Division of the First Army. On this day, the strength of the battalion was 39 officers and 996 men.

CASUALTIES: During June 1917, the battalion had 3 men killed and 11 wounded.

July 1917

On 1 July 1917 at 6am the battalion marched 4 miles to the village of Le Grand Pacault, on the southern outskirts of Merville. They marched via the villages of Locon and Paradis and arrived in billets at 10.30am. The weather was cool and dry and the 2nd was spent cleaning kit and training. Several German planes flew over the area that night and dropped a number of bombs, but no damage or casualties were caused. The weather had improved on 3 July and the men bathed at Calonne, a mile to the south-west. The fine weather continued into the 4th and the first part of the morning was spent training in attacking from the trenches, then specialist training was conducted in the afternoon for stretcher-bearers and scouts. The CO, Lieutenant-Colonel C.M. Bateman DSO, also went on leave to England. The next twelve days were spent training and preparing kit. On 10 July, a special performance by The Tykes concert party was given and 140 seats were made available for the battalion.

Chapter 12

Nieuport

On 13 July at 5.55pm the battalion boarded a train at Merville and were transported to Dunkirk, arriving at 10.45pm. The men then marched to a tented camp on the sand dunes between St Pol and Fort Mardyck on the west side of the town. There was a shortage of tents, so there was a bit of a rush to find a space before heavy rain set in. On the morning of the 14th the battalion bathed in the sea, but this was short-lived when several of the men were on the receiving end of small stinging jellyfish. Later a church parade was held, with training in the afternoon.

On arrival in this area the 49th Division became part of the Fourth Army, XV Corps, alongside the 1st, 32nd and 66th Divisions. The Fourth Army GOC was General H. Rawlinson. The 16th July was a fine, sunny day and training began for a large-scale planned attack of the German lines known as Operation Hush. The CO returned from leave and the battalion code name was also changed due to the move to the XV Corps. It became 'Vend' having previously been known as 'Thorn'.

Operation Hush was a British plan to make amphibious landings on the Belgian coast, supported by an attack from Nieuport and the Yser bridgehead. Several plans were considered in 1915 and 1916, but were shelved due to operations elsewhere. Operation Hush was intended to begin when the main offensive at Ypres had advanced to Roulers and Thourout, linked by advances of the French and Belgian armies in-between. The German command anticipated the British plan and on 11 July 1917, launched their own attack on Nieuport using the Marinecorps, leaving the British with only a small bridgehead on the east side of the town.

Tuesday 17 July was a hot, sunny day and training for the attack continued. Flags were placed in the sand dunes to represent the German trenches and at 5am on the 18th the battalion marched 12 miles east to the town of Bray Dunes where they were accommodated in tents which, it was observed, were greater in number than at St Pol and nearer to the sea. On 19 July the battalion was to have marched 14 miles east along the coast to the town of Oostduinkerke in preparation for the attack, but the move was cancelled, although training for the attack continued.

On the morning of 20 July the battalion marched a mile south to the village of Ghyvelde where the men were accommodated in tents. Training continued in the afternoon and on the 21st skill at arms (as specialist training was now to be known) was carried out in the morning. The company commanders conducted reconnaissance on a system of trenches dug on the training ground which represented the German trenches near Lombardsijde, east of Nieuport. A practice battalion attack was also carried out in the afternoon with three objectives.

At 9.30am on the 22nd church parades were held and then at 10.30am the battalion practised an attack out of trenches, this time with four objectives. An artillery barrage was simulated by using the battalion side drummers and the next four days were spent practising the attack. On 26 July after training the men bathed in the sea at Bray Dunes, after which they were provided with clean uniforms. On the morning of the 27th, training for the attack continued. The men bathed in the sea in the afternoon and the next day the CO, two company commanders and eight platoon commanders (four of whom were serjeants) travelled by lorry to Nieuport to conduct a reconnaissance of assembly points for the impending attack. The rest of the battalion practised the attack in the morning, then had specialist training in the afternoon.

On 29 July at 3.50am a practice attack was carried out by 147 and 148 Brigades, which was, in terms of a training attack, a success. The battalion was back in camp by 6.30am, and church services were held later in the day. The 30th was again spent training for the attack and a 'skeleton' enemy force was provided who counter-attacked the positions gained by the battalion. The counter-attack was successful, but the enemy forces were soon driven out of the position which was retaken. The afternoon was spent on skill at arms training and at 6am on 31 July 500 men from the battalion were transported by lorry to Oostduinkerke. On arrival, it was found that no billets were available, so the men spent the day on the sand dunes.

The battalion was attached to 257 Tunnelling Company, Royal Engineers, and 200 men were immediately sent up the line to Nieuport to work on the tunnels. The remaining 300 men formed a working party at the tunnelling companies' depot at Oostduinkerke. To add insult to injury, the men had to build their own billets out of prefabricated huts.

On this day, the strength of the battalion was 38 officers and 979 men.

CASUALTIES: In July 1917, apart from a few jellyfish stings, no casualties were reported.

August 1917
On 1 August Operation Hush was cancelled. This caused a lot of disappointment amongst the ranks, although now the battalion was overwhelmed with working parties and 700 men were sent to various locations. It was a very wet day and three men were wounded by shell fire. The 2nd was a day of changes; numerous working parties were sent in all directions to live and work at various railheads and ammunition dumps unloading freight trains. At 2pm that afternoon, a twenty-four-hour warning order was issued to the effect that the battalion was returning to the front line. The battalion was to be relieved by the 1/5th York and Lancaster Regiment and proceed to the area of Coxyde-les-Bains to re-form but a party of sixty men, working at an ammunition dump near Nieuport, were not relieved. Heavy rain fell, making the relief very wet, and three men were wounded by shell fire.

Friday 3 August was a wet and windy day, but the battalion was fortunate to be in good billets. At 8pm the men moved off and relieved the 2/6th Manchester Regiment of the 66th Division and became the reserve battalion of 147 Brigade which had taken over the Lombardsijde sector from 199 Brigade. The relief was completed at 12.15am on 4 August and the battalion was holding the west and part of the east bank of the Yser Canal, the same canal they had been holding in 1915 some 30 miles to the south. During the relief, Private Hubert Pickering (29) from Kelbrook was killed by a shell. The men were fortunate to complete the relief when they did, as a heavy artillery barrage commenced after the relief which, along with the rain, lasted the rest of the night.

Private Hubert Pickering. (CPGW)

The Redan sector was, in its simplest terms, a bridgehead some 1,370 yards wide and 1,000 yards deep. It was bounded on the east by a flooded area named Bamburgh Polder and to the west by the flooded Bamburgh Brook. The conditions in this sector were described as appalling and, given what the men had encountered up to date, this area must have excelled. The water table was so high that only breastworks of earth could be made as the trenches were almost destroyed and flooded beyond use. On the south side of the sector was a nineteenth century earthwork and stone defensive structure that protected the canal locks. Its official name was Palinbrug, but to the troops it was known as the Redan. The thick walls of the structure had been converted into bunkers for reserve troops and provided safety from all but the biggest shells. It contained six rooms which were home to battalion HQ. The shelling became sporadic during the day, but picked up again at about 6pm. Around midnight, B Company began moving along the canal bank to relieve men from the 2/8th Manchester Regiment and for the first time, the men of the battalion were to encounter a deadly new weapon. The German artillery began a barrage of mustard gas shells (chemical name of dichlorodiethyl sulphide, these shells were marked by the Germans with a with a yellow cross).

Within twenty-four hours of exposure to mustard gas, victims experience intense itching and skin irritation that gradually turns into large blisters filled with yellow fluid wherever the chemical contacts the skin. These are chemical burns and as such are very debilitating and painful. Mustard gas vapour easily penetrates fabrics such as wool or cotton and if the casualty's eyes are contaminated they become sore, starting with conjunctivitis after which the eyelids swell, resulting in temporary or permanent blindness. Inhalation of the chemical causes severe bleeding and blistering of the respiratory tract and loss of voice.

It was so named due to the smell of the chemical being similar that of mustard or horseradish. The chemical agent that forms mustard gas was mainly delivered by artillery shells and aircraft bombs and has the appearance of thick brown liquid which pools on the ground. Depending on weather conditions, it can remain for days or weeks and continue to be effective.

Contaminated men and their equipment could transfer the chemical to other soldiers or medics by direct contact with the casualty. It was used tactically by the Germans on ground that they had no intention of occupying and was mainly used to wound rather than kill, although prolonged exposure to the chemical in sufficient amounts was often fatal. In conjunction with the mustard gas, the Germans often used 'Blaukrauz' gas, an irritant which could penetrate the filter of a SBR, causing the wearer to suffer extreme irritation of the nose and throat resulting in sneezing and coughing fits. These shells were marked with a blue cross. Phosgene gas shells were marked with a green cross, and CS (or tear gas) shells were marked with a white cross.

The relief was not completed until after daylight on 4 August and the Germans began to fire 11-inch shells from a massive siege howitzer. Two of the shells fell near battalion HQ, blowing the front off the orderly room and signal office, but causing no casualties. The shelling lasted until about 5am, after which things calmed down a little. On the 5th three men were killed by shell fire: Private Bertie North from Baildon, Private Frank Hiles (34) from Manchester Road, Bradford (who had rejoined the battalion in April 1917 after spending the previous fourteen months in hospital with a bullet wound to the leg) and Private George Marsh (35) from Holmfirth, Huddersfield. Three other men were wounded by shell fire. Thirty-eight other men were suffering the effects of mustard gas. Most of the gas casualties were sustained by the men of B Company during the relief and sixteen men from C Company, who were in trenches on the west bank of the canal near Putney Bridge.

There were three bridges in this sector connecting the west and east banks of the canal, named Putney, Vauxhall and Crowder. Units of Royal Engineers were permanently stationed near the bridges to repair the damage caused by shelling. They were bridges in the loosest sense of the word, constructed of cork-filled frames; they floated on the surface of the water like a pontoon bridge but were affected by the ebb and flow of the tide. At low tide, the bridge sagged at a steep angle to the bank, making it virtually impossible to cross. Loitering near bridges was discouraged as they were a priority target for the German gunners, but crossing them at night gave protection from German observation. This was a double-edged sword as often they were covered in unrepaired shell holes which could not be seen in the darkness. Burdened down with rations and ammunition, there was little hope of rescue if a man fell into the water.

Just before dawn, the Germans frequently fired a heavy artillery barrage on the support trenches to neutralise any troops massing for an attack, then about 8am they would bombard the bridgehead for the rest of the day. During the night the enemy fired mustard and phosgene gas shells at the Redan and practically all communication was carried out by runners. Except for artillery bombardments, the Germans showed little activity. Trench mortaring was minimal, as was machine-gun fire and sniping was almost unheard of. The worst feature of this sector had to be the German artillery. Two factors combined here to make a perfect storm of misery and death for the British troops. First, the strength of firepower which could be brought to bear on the British forces was immense. German coastal batteries between Nieuport and Ostend, which often had little to do, could rotate their guns and fire at the line. Secondly, the small size of the bridgehead restricted movement and meant that the German shells had an increased chance of hitting a target. On the plus side, the British gunners were also noticeable by their numbers. After the German attack of 11 July, a large deployment of artillery had been positioned in the area west of Nieuport. Guns of every calibre had specific firing plans to ensure shells were always landing on the enemy and on one occasion, when the SOS signal was sent up, the British gunners fired over 8,500 rounds in thirty minutes.

Orders were received to prepare a trench raid for the night of 7/8 August. The object of this raid was to capture prisoners, kill Germans, to destroy defences, to capture and hold an enemy bunker and to gain information.

The dress for the raid was belt with bayonet, SBR, rifle with nine rounds loaded and one in the breech; all ranks carried two clips of ammunition (ten rounds) in pockets and officers carried revolvers. A white armband was to be worn on the left upper arm and officers had an additional 6-inch square patch sewn on to the rear of the tunic. The raid would be led by Captain Barclay Godfrey Buxton. All pockets were emptied of personal items except a piece of paper with the soldier's name, rank and number. Each man carried two grenades in the bottom pockets and specialist bombing squads of four men each carried a sandbag of five grenades as well as four extra men carrying buckets containing eight grenades each, giving a total of fifty-two extra grenades. The rifle grenade section had four men, each with five rifle grenades. Three explosive charges were also carried for the destruction of concrete dug-outs.

The raid had a platoon of extra men supplied by the 1/4th DWR, as an enemy bunker, opposite the left side of Nose Trench, was to be spared destruction and captured and occupied by the 1/4th DWR contingent, who were the resident battalion in the line at the time. The password for troops meeting each other in the German trench was 'Keighley' and the withdrawal command 'Buxton'.

The German artillery was active overnight of 5/6 August and mustard gas shells landed, but these were mainly confined to the town of Nieuport. Around 270 men were found for working parties and seventeen men were hospitalised with gas poisoning. The 7th was a quiet day and final preparations were made for the raid. Wire cutters, grenades and extra ammunition were issued to the raiding party and, at 4pm, 125 men from D Company under the command of Captain Barclay Godfrey Buxton, Second Lieutenant Dyer and Second Lieutenant Lacey moved off across the canal in small groups and formed up in the tunnels of the Redan. Just after they arrived it was heavily shelled, but no casualties were caused. At 11.30pm the raiding party moved out of the Redan and formed up just behind the front line, during which Second Lieutenant Dyer was hit in the shoulder and badly wounded. At 1am a barrage lasting four minutes landed on the German front line and as it lifted, the leading platoon rushed the German trench and captured a machine gun with its crew of six from the German 199th Regiment.

The barrage shifted to the German support line for a further four minutes and two other platoons moved through to the connecting trenches, which were found to be very badly smashed up by artillery, although a few dug-outs were found and dealt with using grenades. The men from the 1/4th DWR followed the raiding party, but most of the men became disorientated in the dark and confusion, causing the platoon to separate. The majority of the men went as far forward as the German second line and started to consolidate, thinking they had reached the right location. Eventually they realised their mistake and withdrew some forty minutes after the main raid started. The platoon commander from the 1/4th DWR, Second Lieutenant A.J. Robb, reached the correct objective and found he had only one NCO and six men but set about fortifying the bunker whilst a runner unsuccessfully tried to locate the rest of his platoon. Not long after, the raiding party from the 1/6th DWR withdrew and the Germans advanced to reoccupy the post.

The captured enemy bunker was fiercely defended by Second Lieutenant Robb and his men, causing the Germans to withdraw, but two of his men were wounded. The Germans would undoubtedly return in greater numbers so, with dwindling ammunition and two wounded men, Second Lieutenant Robb ordered a withdrawal back to the British lines. Just before daylight, the Germans reoccupied the post.

Private Edwin Wilkinson (19) from Lees near Oldham was killed by a shell and Serjeant Grainger from D Company was so badly wounded that he had to be left in the German trench. Six other men were missing and twenty-five others were wounded by shell fire. The brigade GOC signalled his pleasure at the success of the raid. In the early hours of 9 August, Livens projectors launched a barrage of phosgene gas towards the German trenches. A retaliatory German artillery bombardment prevented the battalion relieving the 1/4th DWR at the front so the men managed to get a good night's rest.

At 9.30pm that night the battalion started to relieve the 1/4th DWR in the Lombardsijde sector. Fortunately, the night was one of the quietest for some time and the relief passed off relatively smoothly and was completed at 9.30pm. During the relief, one man was wounded by gas inhalation. The battalion deployment on 10 August was as follows: A Company with four Lewis guns were holding Nose Trench, Nose Support and Nasal Trench; C Company were holding Nasal Support and Nasal Walk, B Company had two platoons in Nasal Lane; and two in the Redan, and D Company had two platoons in the Redan and two attached to the Royal Engineers. At 9.45pm the Germans launched a barrage on the British front and support lines which indicated a raid was imminent, so the SOS signal was sent up. The British artillery opened fire, but by 10.30pm, with no sign of a German attack, the men were stood down.

Overnight into the 11th an attempt was made to place barbed wire in front of the British lines, but this was abandoned and one man was wounded by shrapnel. The remainder of the day passed quietly with only sporadic shelling of the canal bank and bridges. The German artillery was more active in the evening with most of the shells landing on the Redan. The wiring of the front line, which divisional command insisted must be done, was hampered by German shelling, trench mortars and mustard gas shells. Private Charles Meynell Gant (39) was killed by shell fire and two other men were wounded. One man was wounded by gas poisoning.

At the outbreak of war, Charles Meynell Gant was living in Christchurch, New Zealand. He returned to the UK and enlisted at Skipton.

British 18lb Mk2 field gun in action with Royal Field Artillery gunners.

Also on this day, Private Moses Baxter (33) from Skipton died of wounds at No.39 CCS and is buried at Adinkerke Military Cemetery in Belgium.

On 12 August the German artillery was active in the morning with several German 11-inch howitzer shells landing in Nieuport. Mustard gas shells also landed around the area of battalion HQ and the battalion war diary records, in a classic case of British understatement, that *'things became very unpleasant'*. As night fell, the German artillery became more active, firing 4.2-inch and 5.9-inch shells containing high explosive and mustard gas.

Private Moses Baxter. (CPGW)

Serjeant William Ireland (36) and Serjeant Charles Victor Child (32), both from Skipton, and stretcher-bearer Private Bertie James Wilkin (24) from Barnoldswick, were killed by shell fire. Three other men were wounded by shrapnel, two men were gassed and one man wounded by a rifle bullet.

Serjeant William Ireland was one of four brothers from Skipton who served in the Great War. He was employed as a weaver by John Wilkinson of Park Shed, Skipton. He was a member of the Otley Street Baptist Church and was connected with the Sunday School at the church. He was in the same dug-out as Serjeant Victor Child when it was hit by a large calibre German artillery shell, killing both men instantly. He was the brother-in-law of Gunner Harold Ervine Lewthwaite (25) from Skipton who was serving in the Royal Field Artillery when he was killed in action on 24 August 1917.

Serjeant W. Ireland.

Serjeant Charles Victor Child of Clitheroe Street, Skipton was a pre-war 'terrier' who was employed as a dyer at Belle Vue Mills in Skipton. He was 'time expired' in March 1916 but re-enlisted in June. A member of the Skipton Congregational Church Brotherhood, he left a wife and five children. Both men are buried at Coxyde Military Cemetery.

Serjeant C.V. Child.

Private Bertie James Wilkin, from Philip Street, Barnoldswick, like many of his fellow 'Barlickers', was a battalion stretcher-bearer. He enlisted at the outbreak of war and was employed as a weaver at Ormerod's Moss Shed. He was a member of Barnoldswick Football Club and had been wounded twice. He is buried at Adinkerke Military Cemetery.

On 13 August the German artillery was active before dawn and then eased off, but in the afternoon the Redan and canal bridges were the targets. At 10.30pm the battalion was relieved in the front line trenches by the 1/4th DWR and took up position in the Redan. During the relief at about midnight, the Germans launched a heavy bombardment with high explosive and gas shells which lasted for two hours. The relief was completed at 2.10am, during which two men were gassed and one wounded by shrapnel. On 14 August twenty men were sent to hospital suffering from the effects of the mustard gas they had received several days before, one man was wounded by shell fire and 210 men were found for working parties. On the 15th, between 6am and 8am, the

Private B.J. Wilkin. (All CPGW)

enemy shelled the area of Putney Bridge with 15-inch shells and twenty-two men were hospitalised with the effects of mustard gas. The CO of the 5th Scottish Rifles, who were due to relieve the battalion, arrived for a reconnaissance. The Germans fired a barrage of 5.9-inch shells on the bridges and 170 men were found for working parties.

On the advice of the Medical Officer, thirty-seven light duty men were sent to the rear at Coxyde-les-Bains (Koksijde). At 12.15am on 16 August Royal Engineers launched phosgene gas from Livens projectors onto the enemy lines and three men were wounded by retaliatory shelling. At 2.15am a further Livens projector bombardment was launched from the rear of the battalion lines but there was little retaliation from the Germans. At 9am the company commanders from the 5th Scottish Rifles arrived for a reconnaissance and, as a welcome, the Germans shelled the bridges and approaches for most of the day. At 11pm the bridges and approaches to them were again shelled with high explosive and mustard gas which finally destroyed Putney Bridge. At 2am on the 17th the relief from the 5th Scottish Rifles commenced and the Germans launched a barrage of the bridges and surrounding area that lasted for about thirty minutes and during which two men were wounded.

After the relief, the battalion formed up and marched 6 miles west to Coxyde-les-Bains and relieved the 2/8th Lancashire Fusiliers who were conducting costal defence. C and D Companies were in the defences and A and B were in billets. This part of the coast had been favoured by wealthy Belgians in peace time and the men were billeted in abandoned villas and summer houses. The Germans shelled the coast between 11pm and 4am but there were no casualties. The 18th was spent bathing and cleaning kit, with every man receiving a clean uniform. Practically every man had suffered with the effects of the mustard gas, so the line for sick parade was exceptionally long. The 19th was a fine day and was spent conducting kit inspections and church services. Five men were awarded the Military Medal for bravery during the raid on 7/8 August and ten other men were mentioned in despatches.

It was another fine day on 20 August which was spent training and bathing in the sea but the stinging jellyfish continued to cause problems. Training continued on the 21st and that evening a concert was held in the Hotel Terlinck, which was attended by all ranks. The 22nd was fine and sunny and training continued in the morning and the CO had an inspection of billets in the afternoon. On 23 August A and B Companies relieved C and D on coastal defence. A few shells fell in the area, but no casualties were caused. The 24th was a stormy day with heavy showers and sunny periods and the battalion visited the baths at the town of La Panne, about $1\frac{1}{2}$ miles west of Coxyde-les-Bains. The baths were well organised, with a disinfecting plant for men and their uniforms as well as heated baths and showers. There was also a barber's shop, quite an attraction as nothing like this had been seen so near the front.

Acting Captain Barclay Godfrey Buxton was awarded the Military Cross (MC) for his gallantry and leadership during the raid of 7/8 August and a DCM was awarded to Corporal G. Driver for his actions when his platoon serjeant and officer had become casualties. He led his men during the raid and brought them safely back to the British lines. He then returned to no man's land to help a comrade who had been wounded in the eyes. Private J. Bibby also received a DCM for his gallant action when he rushed a German machine-gun post and killed the occupants using hand grenades. His bravery undoubtedly saved the lives of many of his comrades.

On 25 August at 9am several shells and aircraft bombs landed in and around the town but training and bathing continued as normal. On the 26th church services were held and during the afternoon, the CO inspected C and D Companies in full marching order but the inspection was interrupted by heavy shelling. On 27 August the battalion was relieved at 9.30am by the 2/6th Manchester Regiment. Training was conducted in the morning and the men bathed in the sea in the afternoon. At 3.30pm the divisional gas officer, who had received training and instruction on chemical weapons, gave a lecture on the new German mustard gas. Training was attempted on the 28th, but heavy rain and strong wind made it impossible.

On this day Second Lieutenant Harry Frank Dyer died at No.7 Stationary Hospital at Boulogne from infected wounds he received during the trench raid of 8 August. His right arm had been amputated but infection had set in which resulted in his death. He was born in Bridgnorth, Shropshire, where his father was Baptist minister, and educated at Bridgnorth Grammar School and Corpus Christi College, Cambridge. After graduation he became a schoolmaster, teaching in Cardiff and later at Giggleswick School. He is buried in Boulogne Eastern Cemetery.

A draft of forty-six men arrived, mainly transferees from the Army Service Corps (ASC) were responsible for transport and logistics). The vicinity of the billets was shelled during the afternoon but no casualties were caused. On a daily basis the heavy shells of the German siege guns could be heard above the camp, tearing across the sky on their way to Dunkirk. The 29th was another wet and windy morning, making training outside pointless. At midday the battalion marched to new billets at La Panne, with A and B Companies billeted in a chateau, but C and D Companies drew the short straw and were billeted in huts close by. The officers were billeted in the Grand Hotel, La Panne, where an officers' mess was established. The 30th was another rainy day with heavy showers at frequent intervals. The battalion formed up on the sand for a practice ceremonial parade and a few aircraft bombs landed on the town in the afternoon. The last day of August was again showery with a battalion parade practice on the sand flats in the morning and specialist training in the afternoon. The strength of the battalion on 31 August 1917 was 37 officers and 892 men.

CASUALTIES: During August 1917, the battalion had 10 men killed, 146 wounded and 7 missing.

September 1917

On 1 September the battalion was inspected by the XV Corps GOC, Lieutenant General Sir John DuCane. He congratulated the men on their performance at Nieuport which, he mentioned, had been commented on by the GOC 32nd Division, Major General W. Rycroft. He then presented Acting Captain Godfrey Barclay Buxton with the Military Cross and DCMs to Corporal Driver and Private Bibby. Military Medals were also presented to Serjeant James Bury and four other men for bravery.

The next twenty-three days were spent training and preparing to go back into the line. During this time there was only one casualty who was wounded by shell fire. At 9am on 23 September, the battalion bid farewell to La Panne and marched 8 miles, via Bray Dunes, to the French village of Uxem, arriving at 1.30pm. The men were accommodated in farms around the village. After six weeks out of the war, the battalion was going back to the front to take part in their greatest test to date.

On 24 September, after an early start, the men marched 13 miles to Wormhout, via the hamlets of Teteghem and Wylder. The day soon warmed up and many men were affected by the late summer sun and had to fall out. Battalion HQ and many of the men were accommodated in the same billets they had occupied in January 1916 and some of the local population still remembered the men and welcomed them with open arms. Their stay in Wormhout was a brief one, as at 6.30am the next day an early start was made on the next leg of the march to avoid the midday heat. The men marched 8 miles to Broxeele via Rubruck, where good billets were found. The day turned out to be very hot and the early start prevented a repeat of the previous day's occurrence.

The 26th was another fine day and was spent cleaning kit and training. A brigade tactical exercise was held in the afternoon and on 27 September two companies visited the baths whilst the remainder of the battalion carried out a practice attack.

At 9am on the 28th the battalion marched 11 miles to Setques via Saint-Omer and

Wisques. They arrived at Setques at 5pm with HQ, C and D Companies billeted in the nearby hamlet of Fersinghem. Training, including attacking pillboxes and continued on 29 September which was another sunny day. Fifteen lucky men were granted leave in the UK which was the largest allocation for over two years. Also on this day Regimental Quartermaster Serjeant Alfred Charles Briggs died at Skipton and was buried in Waltonwrays Cemetery in the town. His son, Corporal Edmond Briggs, also of the 1/6th DWR was killed on 3 July 1916 and has no known grave. He is commemorated on the Thiepval Memorial in France and on his father's headstone.

Regimental Quartermaster Serjeant Alfred C. Briggs. (CPGW)

Headstone in Waltonwrays Cemetery, Skipton.

At 7.15am on 30 September, the battalion marched 15 miles to Ebblinghem via Arques, Fort Rouge and Rennescure. It was another hot day and on arrival the billets were found to be scattered round the outskirts of the village. On 30 September 1917, the strength of the battalion was 41 officers and 932 men.

CASUALTIES: During August 1917 the battalion had 1 man wounded.

Chapter 13

The Third Battle of Ypres (Battle of Passchendaele)

T he Third Battle of Ypres commenced on 31 July 1917 with a combined attack by two British armies. The Second Army attacked on the right and the Fifth Army on the left supported by a French Army Corps to the north. The initial attack was a success and considerable gains were made, but wet weather in August hampered the advance. Dryer weather in September allowed the advance to continue and by the beginning of October, the advance had nearly reached the Passchendaele Ridge which was the last natural barrier between the allies and the interior of Belgium. In ordinary terms, the Passchendaele Ridge was not much of an obstacle. Its highest point is only 60 yards above sea level and its average height is no more than 50 yards, but for the last three years the Germans had been laying thick belts of barbed wire, constructing hundreds of substantial concrete pill-boxes and digging complex trench systems with deep bunkers in anticipation of an allied advance.

October 1917

Monday 1 October was fine and sunny and the day was spent cleaning kit and skill at arms training. The 2nd was another fine day and training continued from 9am to 12.30pm. There was an officers' conference regarding impending operations, and the Adjutant, Major A.B. Clarkson MC, departed for a three-month senior officers' course at Aldershot. On 3 October 1917 at 7am, the battalion moved out of the billets and marched 13 miles to the town of Watou, 3 miles west of Poperinge, Belgium and were accommodated in billets at Tay Camp. Only two men fell out during the march. At 6.15am on the 4th, in the darkness and rain, the battalion marched 8 miles to Warrington Camp, near the town of Vlamertinge.

The 147 Brigade became the Corps reserve and orders were received that the battalion had to proceed 4 miles east to the area of Wieltje to relieve a brigade from the New Zealand Division. This news must have come as a bit of a surprise as there was a rush to issue ammunition and rations. A lot of the men would have been familiar with the area, as Wieltje is only a mile north-east of Ypres. At 12.05am on 5 October the battalion moved off in the pouring rain, marched 8 miles east, and crossed the Yser Canal on the northern outskirts of Ypres. Unpleasant memories from November and December 1915 must have been at the forefront of a lot of the men's thoughts.

They marched via Wieltje to Spree Farm at Fortuinhoek, just south of the village of St Julian. The accommodation for the wet and exhausted men consisted of water-filled shell holes. The battalion relieved the 1st Otago Regiment of the 1st New Zealand Brigade and fortunately the remainder of the night was quiet, probably due to the Germans withdrawing their artillery to prevent capture as the New Zealand Brigade advanced. At 6pm, the battalion moved up to the line. C and D Companies relieved the 2nd Auckland Battalion, with A and B relieving the 1st Wellington Battalion in support. Battalion HQ was at Kansas House.

As the relief was in progress, the SOS signal was sent up from the British lines and a heavy artillery barrage was launched against the enemy front. A retaliatory barrage landed and one man was wounded by shrapnel. On 6 October rain fell for most of the day making the shell hole accommodation even more unpleasant. Bombarded for three and a half years, the shell holes almost connected and whole villages were reduced to brick-coloured stains in the mud. Woodland areas were smashed stumps and roads obliterated, only passable using wooden trackways laid on top of bundles of brushwood. The naturally high water table, combined with destroyed drainage, made the ground a sea of mud. The surface was littered with unburied men and animals, destroyed tanks, smashed artillery guns and wagons.

Four men were killed by shell fire. Serjeant Arthur Smith (26) from Keighley, Private Herbert Newsholme from Bradford and Private William Moorhouse (21) from Skipton, all attached to 147 Machine Gun Company, and Corporal Fred Hall (26) from Shipley. Eight other men were also wounded.

Private William Moorhouse was a pre-war 'terrier' in the 1/6th DWR and was mobilised with the unit in August 1914. He transferred to the Machine Gun Corps on its formation in early 1916.

On 7 October rain fell and the German artillery was active. The benefit of the muddy ground meant that a lot of the German shells detonated deep in the mud, which absorbed the impact of the blast or failed to detonate due to a soft landing. Either way, many men were saved from death or injury. At 5.20pm, German troops were seen massing for an attack near a strongpoint called Peter Pan. The SOS signal was sent up and an artillery barrage was launched, as well as machine-gun and rifle fire. The enemy attack failed and many casualties were inflicted, which must have been a morale boost for the men. They were wet, exhausted,

Private William Moorhouse. (CPGW)

hungry, cold and filthy, but the sight of the enemy in open ground was enough to arouse the fighting spirit. That night, A and B Companies relieved C and D in the front line and one man was wounded by shell fire.

A major offensive had been planned for 8 October. The 49th Division was to attack on the extreme left of the Second Army, with the Fifth Army attacking to its left, and the 66th Division to its right. The 49th Division was to advance straight towards the spur of Belle Vue Ridge on a frontage of 1,500 yards and to capture and consolidate two objectives. In the 49th Divisional sector, 146 Brigade would attack on the left, 148 Brigade on the right and 147 Brigade would be the divisional reserve to exploit any gains and to mop up enemy positions. Heavy rain fell all night, causing the already soaked ground to become even worse. Units couldn't get to the jump-off points in time and artillery became bogged down in the mud. In the early hours of the 8th the attacking battalions formed up in the front line trenches and by 4.30am the 1/6th DWR moved to the rear at a position called Korek about 100 yards behind Calgary Grange. During the move, Private Harold Dyson from Golcar was killed by a shell and four other men were wounded.

At 5.20am the artillery barrage commenced and the first wave of attacking troops advanced towards the German trenches. Things began to go wrong almost at once. Two German machine guns at Wolf Farm, in well-protected concrete bunkers, had survived the barrage and were in full working order, as was one on Bellevue Spur. The second machine gun was positioned to enfilade or fire across the attacking troops. At 7.20am the battalion received a warning message that it should be ready to move and at 11.15am orders were received for two companies to report to support the 1/7th West Yorkshire Regiment. C and D Companies were sent and tasked with attacking the high ground between Yetta Houses and Wallemolen and to establish a strong post near the cemetery. A and B companies were to relocate to the area of Calgary Grange. At 11.40am the CO of the 1/7th West Yorks ordered C Company to return to Calgary Grange. During their movement across the battlefield, these two companies were under constant artillery and machine-gun fire, but owing to the soft ground and tactical awareness of the men, only one casualty was caused by a machine-gun bullet.

Meanwhile, D Company, commanded by Captain Barclay Godfrey Buxton MC, had pushed forward towards Peter Pan, but encountered heavy machine-gun fire coming from Wolf Farm. He and his men worked their way round the southern side of Peter Pan and prepared to conduct a flanking attack on Wolf Farm. Captain Buxton met up with Captain Fenton from the 1/4th DWR, who was in command of two companies of men which had also been sent forward to support the attack. He arranged for the 1/4th DWR to attack towards Wolf Copse to support his attack on Wolf Farm, but due to heavy machine-gun fire from the farm and Bellevue Spur, neither man could push the attack forward. Captain Buxton gathered the scattered men from the first attack wave of the 1/5th, 1/6th and 1/7th West Yorkshire Regiment and formed them into a hastily prepared strongpoint. This was the limit of 146 Brigade's advance that day. A, B and C Companies of the 1/6th DWR remained in reserve at Calgary Grange but at 7pm, orders were received to send A and B companies to reinforce the 1/7th and 1/8th West Yorkshire Regiment near Yetta Houses. They were to move at 11.30pm under the cover of an artillery barrage. A Company, under Lieutenant A. Smith, advanced his men to the position of the 1/7th West Yorks near Peter Pan and found this position strongly defended, so he and his men pushed forward about 400 yards but no enemy were to be found. They were then ordered to return to Calgary Grange.

B Company, under Captain T. Coulhurst, advanced and linked up with the CO of the 1/8th West Yorks and was informed that there were no Germans to mop up as the front line posts were still at the rear of Yetta Houses. Captain Coulhurst then withdrew to Kronprinz Farm in support of the 1/8th West Yorks.

The casualty figures for the 1/6th DWR on this day were extensive. Eight men were killed: Corporal Ernest Wakeling (33) from Keighley, Lance Corporal Sydney King (22) from Bingley and Lance Corporal Thomas H. Burnett from Worth, Private Thomas Shepherd (26) from Nelson, Private Charlie Clayton from Mossley, Lancs, Private David G. Womersley from Bradford, Private Thomas D. Hall from Mossley, Lancs and Private William G. Rampling from Skipton. Two men were also missing and forty-two others were wounded.

At daybreak on 10 October, A Company returned to Korek and B Company was attached to the 1/8th West Yorks, who were still positioned near Yetta Houses. B Company was tasked with finding out if Yetta Houses were still occupied by the enemy. This was purely for reconnaissance and two small patrols were sent. They saw that there was no sign of German occupation and on their return plans were made to capture the houses at dusk. At 7.15pm, half of A Company moved out and quietly surrounded the houses, which were found to be abandoned. Meanwhile, the other half of A Company was tasked with confirming if the road from Yetta Houses

Private T. Healey. (CPGW)

towards the cemetery was occupied by British troops, as reported by aircraft reconnaissance. A patrol of twenty men commanded by Lieutenant Spencer advanced from Yetta Houses at midnight on a compass bearing towards the cemetery. Not long after setting off, they encountered a patrol of twelve Germans who, on seeing the British, ran back towards their own lines. Lieutenant Spencer and his men were in hot pursuit, but encountered German rifle fire and grenades. They tried a flanking manoeuvre to the right of the Germans, but the defence was too strong and the patrol withdrew.

In the early hours of the 10th the battalion was relieved by the 3rd New Zealand Brigade, and marched 4 miles west to St Jean near the village of Wieltje, on the north-east outskirts of Ypres. During the relief, Private Thomas Healey (26) from Salterfirth near Barnoldswick, was killed by a shell and two other men were wounded by shrapnel.

Private William G. Rampling from Russel Street, Skipton was a pre-war 'terrier' who worked as a foreman at Belle View Mills and played football with Niffany Rovers. He is buried at Douchy Farm New British Cemetery.

Private Thomas Healey had worked at Albert Hartley & Co, Sheeting Works in Barnoldswick and was part of a Lewis gun team at the time of his death. He has no known grave and is commemorated on panel 82 at the Tyne Cot Memorial.

Private W.G. Rampling. (CPGW)

Private T. Healey is commemorated on panel 82 at Tyne Cot Cemetery.

On 11 October two officers and thirty-eight men reported sick with badly swollen feet from the onset of trench foot. The battalion was accommodated in tents and the weather was appalling, with wind and rain. The men were exhausted after seven days without real sleep and the weather on 12 October had not improved, with the men waking to cold wind, rain and mud. The day was spent cleaning weapons and equipment with a little drill thrown in to warm the men up. The bad weather continued on the 13th with heavy rain and hail followed by sunny spells. In the afternoon, 150 men acted as stretcher-bearers to bring wounded men from the front and at 8pm 110 men were sent on working parties, not returning until the early hours of the 14th.

The men acting as stretcher-bearers worked relentlessly evacuating the wounded men, mainly New Zealanders and the following letter was sent to the GOC of 147 Brigade by the New Zealand Division's commander, Major General A.W. Russell:

My dear General,
Please express to the officers and men of your brigade who came forward to assist in getting in the wounded, the very hearty thanks of myself, staff and the whole division. I have heard the warmest expressions of praise for the way in which your men volunteered to come forward to undertake what was certainly a very exhausting and maybe dangerous task.

I hope they did not suffer any casualties or, if so, that they were light. The New Zealand Division will not forget the debt they owe to the officers and men of the 147th Brigade.
A.W. Russell, Major-General, G.O.C. New Zealand Division

The sun reappeared on 14 October, but the fine weather meant the German aircraft were active and several bombs were dropped around the camp. A British observation balloon was attacked and brought down in flames, but both the observers were seen to descend safely by parachute. On this day, Private Percy Elliott (22) from Skipton died of wounds received in July 1916 at No.83 General Hospital in Boulogne. On 26 October, the *Craven Herald* newspaper reported his death:

Private Percy Elliott.
(CPGW)

Another Skiptonian who has given his life for the great cause is Private Percy Elliott, West Riding Regiment, who died from wounds in France on October 14th. His sister, Mrs. J.S. Mooney, 16 Back Water Street, Skipton received a letter from the matron of the 83rd General Hospital, France, stating that he had been dangerously wounded in the neck and face and that his condition was causing great anxiety; and this was followed by a second letter expressing regret that Pte. Elliott had died from wounds at 12-15 p.m. on the 14th inst., and stating that everything had been done to make his last hours as easy and peaceful as possible.

Pte. Elliott, who was 22 years of age, enlisted in January 1915, and went out to France the following Christmas Day. He was also wounded in the Big Push in July last. In civil life, he was an apprentice to looming and twisting at Firth Shed (Messrs. S. Farey & Son Ltd.), and was connected with the Congregational Church and Sunday School. His eldest brother, Pte. Frank Elliott, East [sic] Staffordshire Regiment, who has also been wounded, is at present serving in India, while his brother-in-law, Sergt. Mooney, is a prisoner of war in Germany.

A large working party of four officers and 237 men was provided on 15 October and on the 16th, the battalion relocated 3 miles west of Ypres to the town of Vlamertinge where they were accommodated in Nissen huts, named after its designer, Major Peter Norman Nissen. He was an officer in the Royal Engineers who designed the structure to be portable, sturdy and easy to construct.

The 17th was spent cleaning kit and the men saw a German aircraft being shot down in flames near to the camp. On 18 October a brigade parade was held and addressed by the outgoing divisional commander, Major General Perceval. He commended the work of the brigade during the time he had commanded it and during recent operations and was warmly cheered by the assembled men. The routine for the next five days was one of kit inspections, training, and baths.

On the 24th the battalion was transported 10 miles west by bus to the town of Winnezeele where they became the divisional reserve battalion. Two more days of parades and inspections were carried out before moving a mile south to the town of Steenvoorde. On 27 October, the new Divisional GOC, Major General N.J.G. Cameron inspected the battalion. The remainder of October 1917 was spent on training, route marches, shooting practice and gas drills.

On 31 October 1917 the strength of the battalion was 42 officers and 792 men.

CASUALTIES: During October 1917, the battalion had 13 men killed, 48 wounded and 2 missing. In addition, 40 men reported sick with trench foot.

November 1917
On 1 November the CO, Lieutenant Colonel Bateman, was placed in temporary command of 147 Brigade and Captain Hugh Dixon became the acting CO. The training routine continued up to 9 November when the battalion boarded buses and moved 7 miles east to the area of Dickebusch, 2 miles south-west of Ypres. The 10th was spent cleaning kit and performing a little close order drill. The stretcher-bearers and medical staff were particularly concerned with the condition of the men's feet and instructions were given to apply a foot rub of whale oil. Sunday 11 November was cold and damp. Church services were held in the huts and small work parties were despatched to provide Lewis gun anti-aircraft defence. The men were operating hand pumps at drinking water collection posts and collecting and detonating unexploded artillery shells.

Example of a water pumping post. (Big Push magazine)

On 12 November the battalion was on the move again. They marched 3 miles east to the area of Zillebeke, a mile south-east of Ypres. The accommodation consisted of small roughly built shelters which were rather spread out. The rest of the day was spent trying to improve the shelters using sandbags and other spare *materiel* to hand. The 13th continued dull and overcast and the day was spent training in the morning and improving the accommodation in the afternoon. Several selected officers and NCOs reconnoitred the route to support the battalion to the east. The weather improved on 14 November and training resumed with the men practising crossing rough ground in full kit and wearing SBRs. Training continued on the 15th and the next day a consignment of building supplies arrived courtesy of the Royal Engineers. As a result, the grids (wooden walkways) and shelters were greatly improved. A new battalion HQ was also built using large elephant frames (curved sheets of corrugated iron) that were bolted together to create a bunker.

Fine weather on 17 November saw a working party of 100 men sent to assist the Royal Engineers while Lewis gun training was conducted by the remainder of the companies. On the 18th work continued improving the camp and the surrounding area was searched for war salvage (fired shell cases, discarded rifles, steel helmets etc) which was gathered in a central point for recycling. Several officers and NCOs were sent to the front line to prepare for the relief. The next day was fine and the battalion scouts were sent to a reserve camp for specialist training. The remainder of the battalion relieved the 1/8th West Yorkshire Regiment in the Molenaarelsthoek sector just south

Example of an elephant-frame bunker at the Zonnebeke museum.

of Zonnebeke. The battalion area of responsibility was opposite Justice Wood in the south to Flinte Copse in the north, a front of about 1,300 yards. No casualties were sustained during the relief.

On 20 November work began to improve the front line. The men constructed defensive posts by connecting and fortifying shell holes and that night, a substantial trench was dug to connect the posts. The Germans shelled the front with gas and one man was wounded. The 21st was a fine day and work began digging communication trenches. Patrols were sent out at night, but no Germans were encountered.

On this day Private Harry Kilburn (27), a married man from Southowram near Halifax, was killed. At the time of his death he was attached to the 147th Trench Mortar Battery. On 22 November three men were wounded by shrapnel. In the early hours of 23 November, a heavy German bombardment landed on the British lines. Second Lieutenant Victor Rupert Atkinson (20) from Settle, Serjeant William McShee from Keighley, Lance Corporal Fred Barrett from Skipton, Private Herbert William White (28) from Ingrow and Private Horace Roff (19) from Keighley were killed by shrapnel. Ten other men were also wounded.

Second Lieutenant Victor Rupert Atkinson. (CPGW)

152

Serjeant William McShee, Private Herbert W. White and Private Horace Roff have no known grave and are commemorated at Tyne Cot Cemetery.

Lance Corporal Fred Barrett of Newmarket Street, Skipton was the youngest of three brothers who served in the Great War and is buried in Dochy Farm New British Cemetery, 5 miles north-east of Ypres. He enlisted in October 1914 and was deployed to France with the battalion in April 1915. Before the war he was employed at the Craven Lead Works and played cricket with the Skipton Church Institute Club and football for the Cononley Association Football Club. His elder brother, Private Arthur Barrett, serving in the Northumberland Fusiliers, lost his right arm in the early months of the war. His other brother, Corporal George Barrett, who also served in the ranks of the 1/6th DWR survived, and was transferred back to the reserves in early 1919.

Lance Corporal Fred Barrett. (CPGW)

He was the uncle of Lionel Barrett (19) of East Gate, Skipton who was killed on 8 October 1918 whilst serving in the 9th (Service) Battalion, the King's Own Yorkshire Light Infantry.

Second Lieutenant Victor Atkinson was the only son of Dr Francis and Mary Atkinson, of 'Bowerley', Langcliffe, near Settle. He was educated at Giggleswick Grammar School where he was in the OTC. On leaving he joined the Inns of Court OTC and had fifteen months training at the Cadet School at Berkhamsted. He was commissioned at the beginning of March, and after three weeks at Clipstone Camp, went to the front on April 5th. He is buried in Aeroplane Cemetery, 3 miles north-east of Ypres.

On the evening of 23 November, the battalion was relieved by the 1/4th DWR, and marched a mile south-west to reserve positions at Polygon Wood. On the 24th the weather was fine and battalion HQ was housed in a small concrete pillbox. Accommodation for the rest of the battalion was considerably worse as the companies were in shelters dug into the sides of impact craters but, despite the whole area being heavily shelled, no casualties were caused.

On this day Private Fred Chapman (30) from Victoria Terrace, Bradley near Keighley died from wounds received the previous day. He was wounded in the right arm and both legs and died at No.17 CCS. He enlisted in March 1916 and had been in France for eighteen months. He had just returned from home leave when he was wounded and is buried at Lijssenthoek Military Cemetery.

On 25 November, the battalion moved half a mile north to a position called Garter Point. Battalion HQ was in a larger pillbox with rest of the battalion in shell hole dug-outs again. On the 26th the men were kept busy on ration and water carrying parties and for the next four days, the men worked taking the same up to the 1/4th DWR at the front. On 27 November the battalion marched 3 miles west to Ypres and spent the night safely ensconced in the ramparts of the

Private Fred Chapman. (CPGW)

town. There was intermittent shelling of the tracks as the battalion marched to Ypres, but no casualties were sustained. On this day, Private Jeremiah Sullivan from Halifax died of wounds at No.10 CCS and is buried at Lijssenthoek Military Cemetery.

On 28 November the weather was fine and the battalion was relieved by the 1/5th West Yorkshire Regiment. The men then marched 6 miles south-west to Devonshire Camp, near Reninghelst, arriving just before dusk. They were accommodated in comfortable wooden huts and the detached units rejoined the battalion. The morning of the 29th was spent cleaning clothes, equipment and in kit inspections and in the afternoon an inter-company rugby competition was held, with a win for B Company. On 30 November all the men visited the baths and work was started on a miniature rifle range.

CASUALTIES: During November 1917, the battalion had 5 men killed and 4 wounded.

December 1917
The weather on 1 December 1917 was fine but very cold. Training was carried out around the camp and work continued in the construction of a miniature rifle range. In the afternoon, a rugby match was played against the Otago Battalion of the New Zealand Army, which the Kiwis won 11-3. A concert was held in the evening and on the 2nd divine service was held, and SBR drills practised. A large working party of three officers and 114 men left Devonshire Camp and were attached to the 9th Army Tramway Company (ATC) and were billeted at Vlamertinge. The ATC was a branch of the Royal Engineers that was responsible for the construction, maintenance and operation of the trench tramways system. The tracks were further forward than the light railways and were operated by the Director General of Transport.

On 3 December another large working party from A and D Companies was sent to assist the Royal Engineers at Anzac Post, just west of Garter Post. On the 4th those men remaining in camp continued with the construction of the rifle range. The weather on 5 December was still bitterly cold and work was carried out to improve the camp. Drains were cleared and sandbag walls were built around the huts. On the 6th the battalion moved to the Belgian Army infantry barracks on the Esplanade in Ypres where were joined by the working party from the tramway. During the move, three men were wounded by gas and shrapnel shells. In pre-war days, the barracks had been occupied by a regiment of the Belgian army and as such, it had been constructed with thick stone walls and vaulted cellars. Even after nearly three years of constant bombardment, parts if it were still habitable and several of the rooms were fitted with wire beds. On 7 December, the battalion, less the working party at Anzac Post, moved a mile east to Hussar Farm in Potijze.

The accommodation here was described as poor and the working party from Anzac arrived about 4.30pm. Once again, working parties were not without danger: Private Ernest Hardacre (21) from Old Lane Inn,

Private Hardacre's name on the Tyne Cot Memor

Halifax was killed by a shell, and two other men wounded whilst working on the tramway. He has no known grave and is commemorated on panel 83 at Tyne Cot cemetery.

On 8 December the battalion relieved the 2nd Argyll and Sutherland Highlanders in the Nieuwemolen sector, 200 yards south-east of Tyne Cot. B and C Companies were at the front, with A and D in reserve.

2016. A German bunker located in the south-west corner of Tyne Cot cemetery.

Sunday 9 December was fine and cold but there was very little enemy activity. In the evening, D Company was repositioned into five posts that had been occupied by B Company. D Company had been replaced in reserve by a company from the 1/6th West Yorkshire Regiment who were attached to the battalion. One man was wounded by shell fire. On the 10th thick fog had descended on the front making the sky safe from German planes. That evening, C Company relieved B at the front, which in turn, moved into the support line, whilst A remained in reserve. The transport section of battalion HQ had a tough time bringing up rations to the front when two men were wounded and two horses were killed by artillery at Daring Crossing. Two other men were wounded by shell fire.

On the 11th the battalion was relieved by the 1/7th DWR and moved to support positions north of Polygon Wood. Battalion HQ, A and C Companies were located at Anzac, B at Westhoek and D at Albania. The relief passed off without casualties, despite B and D Companies being heavily shelled en route to their positions. Overnight into the 12th December, C Company's post near Anzac was heavily shelled and three men who were sheltering in a dug-out were killed. Lance Corporal Joshua Booth (24) was one of the men. He was recruited at Guiseley and landed in France in April 1915.

In 1911 he was living at Esholt, where his father Fred was an inn keeper. He is buried at Dochy Farm New British Cemetery. The two other men were Serjeant Charles Peachy MM from Settle and Private Walter Robinson (24) from Thornton. Two other men were also wounded. Serjeant Peachy was one of the 'lucky thirteen' photographed at Riby in October 1914 and one of the men who participated in the cricket match at Fleurbaix on 17 June 1915.

He was a pre-war 'terrier' who deployed to France with the battalion in April 1915. Before the war he worked as a dresser (preparing threads for weaving) at King's Mill in Settle and played cricket with the Settle second eleven. He was also a member of the Settle Choral Society and had been home on leave a week before his death. He is buried at Dochy Farm New British Cemetery.

Serjeant Charles Peachy MM. (CPGW)

Private Walter Robinson from Ivy Mount, Thornton in Craven enlisted in September 1914 and had previously been wounded three times. Before the war he was employed as a weaver at Watson and Sons, Albion Shed, Earby. He has no known grave and is commemorated on panel 84 on the Tyne Cot Memorial.

On 13 and 14 December the weather was dry but cloudy and German aircraft were active over the line, but the German artillery was quiet. On the 15th the tracks around Anzac were shelled and German aircraft were active. That afternoon the battalion relieved the 1/7th DWR in the Niewemolen sector of the front line. The relief passed off without casualties, A and B Companies were in

Private Walter Robinson. (CPGW)

the front posts, with D in support and C in reserve. The weather on 16 December had turned much colder with a strong wind. The German artillery had shelled the line throughout the night but no casualties resulted. During the day the bombardment moved to the reserve area and yet again a dug-out occupied by C Company was hit. Lance Corporal Fred Longbottom (29) from

Private Walter Robinson and Private Horace Roff commemorated at Tyne Cot.

Brighouse and Lance Corporal Edward Browning (24) from Boyton Street, Edge Hill, Liverpool (but recruited at Halifax) were killed and three other men were wounded. Both men are buried at Dochy Farm New British Cemetery.

Monday 17 December was a dry, clear day and German aircraft were again active. The shelling had also increased but quietened down in the afternoon, which was fortunate as the battalion was relieved by the 1/5th DWR. The men then marched to billets at Hussar Farm in Potijze, where on arrival hot tea was served. The 18th was bitterly cold with a hard frost as the battalion marched 2 miles west to the reserve position at Vancouver Camp near Vlamertinge, arriving at midday. A working party of 100 men from A and D Companies was detached from the battalion and billeted with the 9th Army Tramway Company, Royal Engineers and an officer and nine men were attached to 57 Field Company, Royal Engineers. Two men were wounded by shrapnel.

The morning of the 19th was spent changing the canisters on the SBRs and treating the men's feet with camphor to prevent trench foot. In the afternoon an inter-company football competition was played. The next day was still cold and all men in Vancouver Camp visited the baths. The working party at the tramway company was rotated with men from B Company and nine men from C Company relieved the men with 57 Company, Royal Engineers.

The 22nd continued frosty and in the morning training was carried out near the camp. In the afternoon, a football match was played against the 1/4th DWR, who won 4-1. At 9.40am on 23 December, the battalion entrained at Vlamertinge and moved east on the light railway to relieve the 1/5th York and Lancashire Regiment at the front. The relief was completed by 6.15pm without casualties.

On Christmas Eve 1917 thick fog enabled wiring parties to strengthen the defences of the front line posts. Despite heavy shelling all day, no casualties were caused. Christmas Day 1917 was bright and clear and German aircraft were flying low over the British lines, probably on aerial photography missions. Visits and greetings were exchanged with the 1/4th DWR who were holding the line to the right and, apart from a little shelling, there was little activity on either side.

A stockpile of German barbed wire had been located by a patrol, so later that night it was used to strengthen the defences. The ground was covered in snow, so the men were issued with white camouflage overalls. One man was wounded by shell fire. On Boxing Day a little light snow fell. Serjeant Cecil Rhodes MM (21) from Ingrow near Keighley was killed by a shell. He is buried at Belgian Battery Corner Cemetery.

The SOS signal was sent up by a unit on the battalion's left, and was repeated by a Forward Observation Officer (FOO) in the trenches of the battalion. It was later discovered that it was a false alarm, but it was noticed that the German counter battery was noticeably weak. The 27th was cold and dull and, apart from a few enemy aircraft and a little shelling, the day passed off quietly. The 28th December was bright and clear, but the battalion to the left of the line reported a large German patrol working their way along the front. All the men stood to, but the anticipated attack never materialized. On the 29th December, the battalion was relieved by the 1/7th DWR and moved to billets at Dragoon Camp, near Potijze, to become the brigade reserve battalion. The men arrived at 7pm and received a hot meal. The next day, December 30th, a working party of 200 men was selected from all companies, with the remaining men spending the day cleaning kit and equipment.

Private Arthur Foster. (CPGW)

In the early hours of New Year's Eve 1917 eight shells landed in the camp and Private Arthur Foster from Addingham was severely wounded with two broken legs. He died later that day at a CCS. Working parties were found as per the previous day, plus an extra forty men for work on support strongpoints.

Private Arthur Foster (37) of Cockshott Fold, Addingham enlisted in August 1916 and was a carter for the Co-operative Society. He had recently been discharged from a base hospital after suffering from trench foot. He left a widow and two children and is buried at Lijssenthoek Military Cemetery.

For the remaining men, camphor foot treatment was administered and the SBRs inspected. Major Anthony Bairstow Clarkson returned from his senior officer's course in Aldershot and took over command of the battalion from the newly promoted Major Hugh Dixon, who in turn became the second-in-command. Two men were wounded by shell fire whilst on a working party for the 57th Field Company, Royal Engineers.

Major Hugh Dixon and Major Anthony Bairstow Clarkson MC (CPGW)

CASUALTIES: During December 1917, the battalion had 18 men killed and 8 wounded.

January 1918

New Year's Day 1918 was clear and sunny and the working parties continued. Those men remaining in camp spent the day recovering war salvage in the surrounding area and those not on working parties visited the baths at Ypres. On the 2nd and 3rd the working parties were rotated, giving the rest of the men the opportunity to visit the baths. On 4 January the battalion was relieved at Dragoon Camp by 1/6th West Yorks Regiment and 147 Brigade withdrew west to the Yser Canal area to become divisional reserve and where the men were comfortably billeted in Nissan huts

From 5 to 7 January every available man was engaged on working parties transporting rations and ammunition forward. On the 8th eight officers, including the CO and 225 men, boarded a light railway at 6.30am and travelled to Hellfire Junction, just south of Hellfire Corner. From there they made their way to Windhoek Post where they worked on strengthening the corps reserve posts. The day was very windy with heavy snow falling until midday. On this day Private Christopher James Newsholme (26) from Ingleton, who was serving on the Royal Army Pay Corps (RAPC), died from infection after an operation to remove his appendix at Woking Hospital. He had previously served in the ranks of the 1/6th DWR before transferring to the RAPC.

Private C.J. Newsholme. (CPGW)

Work on the strongpoints continued on 9 January, but on the 10th all the men remained in camp and had their feet treated with camphor and whale oil in an attempt to prevent trench foot. Hellfire Corner was so named due to the German gunners' ability to shell the area with uncanny accuracy. They had a commanding view of the junction and the co-ordinates were pre-registered on their guns, so it was easy to fire shells at targets of opportunity when they appeared. The junction was usually crossed at a full sprint if on foot, full gallop if on horseback or full speed if motorised. Canvas screens were erected to provide some cover from view, but shrapnel, high explosives and the weather frequently conspired to destroy this attempt at stealth.

On 11 January the battalion moved 6 miles south-west to the area of Reninghelst, south-east of Poperinge. The accommodation was described as good and the men were settled in by midday. On 13 January work restarted on the corps reserve line and at 5am the working party marched a mile north-east to Brandhoek and boarded a light railway to travel to Windhoek. The men returned to camp at 1.40pm. Heavy snow fell and the cold spell continued and those men not working travelled to Reninghelst to visit the baths. From 14 to 25 January work continued on the corps reserve line without incident. The only thing of note was on the 24th when Lieutenant Colonel Bateman rejoined the battalion from sick leave. On 26 January the battalion provided working parties in the morning and in the afternoon the men boarded the light railway and travelled 8 miles west to Hondeghem in France. They arrived at 6pm and, although somewhat scattered, the billets were described as comfortable.

The morning of 27 January was spent cleaning kit and visiting the mobile bath unit. In the evening, an officers' conference was held and Major Clarkson gave a lecture on the Playfair Code (a communications encryption cipher devised by Lord Playfair in 1854). Cleaning of kit and equipment continued on the 28th and those men who missed out on baths had the opportunity to visit. Football was played in the afternoon to practise for an inter-company competition. On 29 January, a draft of 8 officers and 195 men were posted to the battalion from the 1/5th DWR. This was the result of a reorganisation of the BEF as each infantry brigade was being reduced to three battalions. In 147 Infantry Brigade, the 1/5th DWR was disbanded and the men posted to the remaining battalions of the 1/4th, 1/6th and 1/7th DWR. Two weeks later, a further draft of 5 officers and 100 men arrived from the 8th DWR of the 11th Division, which also had been disbanded. These must have been a welcome addition to the battalion as most were battle experienced men from the same parent regiment.

The first round of the football competition was held. A v B Company ended with a resounding 5-0 victory for A and C v D Company finished 2-3. On 30 January the new arrivals were posted to the companies and because of the increase of men, the rifle companies were reorganised from three platoons to four. On the morning of 31 January, A and C Companies visited the rifle range whilst B and D practised skill at arms in the camp. The final of the inter-company football competition was held in the afternoon between B and D Companies. The B Company team won 9-2.

CASUALTIES: During January 1918, the battalion had no fatalities or casualties.

Chapter 14

The German Spring Offensive of 1918

February 1918

The first three days of February 1918 were spent training and shooting on a miniature firing range. On the 4th B Company played football against 147 Brigade HQ with B Company winning 3-2. On 5 February the battalion moved 11 miles west to the town of Moulle. First they marched 4 miles to the railhead at Ebblinghem, then boarded a train and travelled 9$^{1}/_{2}$ miles to the village of Watten where they detrained and marched the final 3$^{1}/_{2}$ miles to Moulle. There was some difficulty finding billets on arrival as the battalion billeting party, who had set off in advance of the main body, had taken a different route and were noticeable by their absence at the camp, but by 7pm billets were allocated and a hot meal provided for the men. On 6 February, all the companies conducted target practice on the rifle range, located about 2 miles from the camp, but this was cut short by bad weather.

On 8 February the bad weather continued, but it did not prevent the brigade inter-platoon shooting competition taking place. The winners were a platoon from the 1/4th DWR, but an objection was raised by the team from the 1/7th DWR and a re-shoot was ordered for the following day. The weather had improved on the 9th and the result of the re-shoot was a victory for the 1/7th DWR. On 10 February, at 10am the battalion marched 6$^{1}/_{2}$ miles east to the village of Broxeele, arriving at 1.30pm. They spent the night there and the next day marched 8$^{1}/_{2}$ miles south-east to the village of Hondeghem. On 12 February a brigade drill competition was held, so in the afternoon the companies paraded in front of the CO, who chose D Company to represent the battalion.

On 13 February, a 'flame projector' lecture and demonstration was to be presented to the men, but bad weather resulted in it being postponed. The weather had improved the following day so the lecture and demonstration went ahead. The device was the Livens Large Gallery Flame Projector, named after its designer Captain William H. Livens of the Royal Engineers, designer of the Livens projector. It was to be used from a tunnel dug under no man's land which housed the fuel tanks and pump. Just before an attack, a periscope-type nozzle would be pushed up though the earth and a jet of flammable liquid would be forced out under pressure and ignited towards the German lines. (In 2011, an episode of the television series *Time Team* excavated the site of a Livens flame projector at Mametz in France and a full size working replica was built and tested to prove the efficiency of the weapon.) The device was 56 feet long, weighed

An original flame projector being tested. In combat, the only part above ground would be the nozzle.

2.5 tons, and required a carrying party of 300 men to transport and assemble. It was operated by a crew of eight, had a range of up to 300ft and stored enough fuel for three ten-second bursts.

In the afternoon shooting practice was held and physical training conducted near the billets. On 15 February the battalion received notice of a forthcoming gas drill and rifle grenade competition which required all the companies to refresh their skills. D Company competed in the drill competition, but the 1/7th DWR were the eventual winners. On the 16th the battalion scouts, under the command of Lieutenant Spencer, took part in the brigade scouting competition and the companies continued with gas drill and rifle grenade practice. A and B Companies were selected for the gas drill competition and C Company was selected for the rifle grenade competition.

On 17 February divine service was held in the morning and C Company took part in the rifle grenade competition, taking first place. On the 18th all ranks had their SBRs tested in the gas chamber and the brigade gas drill competition was held. The next day the men had their feet treated with camphor, supervised by the medical officer. The CO and company commanders spent the day reconnoitring future positions at the front line. On 20 February the Corps commander decorated fifteen men with Military Medal ribbons and one man with a DCM ribbon. On the afternoon of the 20 February, the battalion departed Hondeghem and boarded a train heading east towards the front. At 5pm they arrived at a camp named Belgian Chateau, a mile south-west of Ypres and spent the night in huts.

On 22 February the battalion relieved the 2nd Canterbury Battalion of the New Zealand Army in the Centre Judge Sector, 4 miles east of Ypres. The relief was carried out without casualties, although the German machine guns were active at night. A and B Companies were at the front with C and D in support.

The 23rd was a quiet day, but in the evening the enemy carried out a raid on the West Yorkshire Regiment to the left of the line. A British artillery barrage was fired, but the German response was light although two men received shrapnel wounds. The following day the British artillery shelled the enemy-held village of Reutel, just to the south of Judge Copse. In reply the Germans shelled the area of the Butte, which was

161

a series of bunkers at the north-east tip of Polygon Wood, where battalion HQ was located, wounding one man.

Saturday 25 February was a quiet day with only a few incoming trench mortar rounds that wounded one man; another man was accidently wounded by a bayonet. On the 26th the companies were rotated with C and D Companies relieving A and B at the front and at 4am the British artillery launched a barrage towards Polderhoek where it was believed a German attack was massing. On the 27th the Germans launched a heavy artillery barrage on the Judge Sector front, possibly in response to the previous night's British bombardment and five men were killed. Lance Corporal James Briggs (26) from Bradford, Private Henry Parrington from Skipton, Private Albert Halliday (23) from Shipley, Private Horace Hallgate (19) from Doncaster and Private William Henry (Harry) Coupland (20) from Guiseley were all killed and seven other men were wounded.

Before the war, Private Coupland worked as a woollen spinner and lived at Granville Terrace with his parents, Watson and Hannah Coupland, two sisters and a brother. He joined up on the 12th December 1915 at Guiseley but was not mobilised until May 1916 and was posted to France on 25 December 1916. He is buried at Buttes New British Military Cemetery in Polygon Wood.

Private Henry Parrington of Rowland Street, Skipton enlisted in 1916 and was employed as a porter for the Midland Railway at Skipton station. He is buried in Polygon Wood Cemetery. He was the brother-in-law of Private Albert Taylor Smith (30) from Greenside, Skipton who was serving in the South Staffordshire Regiment when he was killed in action on 28 May 1918.

Private H. Parringt (CPGW)

At 3am on 28 February the British artillery fired a barrage on the enemy lines which prompted a retaliation during which three men were killed. Private Edgar Scott (36) from Keighley died immediately and Private Richard Dove Whittaker (32) from Skipton and Private John Shaw from Elland near Halifax both died soon after of shrapnel wounds. Just before the barrage fell, battalion HQ had relocated further back from the Butte into Polygon Wood. This simple tactical move meant the casualty list was considerably lower than it otherwise would have been. The German guns also fired on tracks and support trenches that had so far escaped shelling. The dead men are buried at Polygon Wood Cemetery.

Private Richard Dove Whittaker (28) of Devonshire Place, Skipton enlisted in 1916 and was working as a warpdresser at Firth & Moorhouse textile mill. He was one of three brothers who served in the Great War, only one of whom survived. His brother, Private James Whittaker also served in the 1/6th DWR and was killed in action on 3 May 1918. His other brother, Edgar Whittaker, served as a gunner in the Royal Field Artillery.

Private R.D. Whittaker. (CPGW)

<u>CASUALTIES</u>: In February 1918, the battalion had 8 men killed and 10 wounded.

March 1918

Friday, 1 March was a cold day and snow fell in the evening. There was hardly any German activity except for intermittent shelling, but one man was wounded in the back by machine-gun fire. On the afternoon of the 2nd the battalion was relieved by the 1/4th York and Lancaster Regiment and moved to the Belgian Infantry Barracks at Ypres. On 3 March A and B Companies provided an early morning working party for the Royal Engineers, whilst the remainder of the men took part in church parades, kit inspections and baths. On the 4th the companies rotated and training, working and bathing was the routine for the next five days. On 10 March the battalion relieved the 1/4th York and Lancaster Regiment in the Judge Sector of the line. The relief was completed at 7pm without casualties.

On 11 March the enemy fired gas shells at battalion HQ and C and D Companies in the support and reserve areas. Private Robert Ellis (23), a married man from Mossley, Lancs was killed. He is buried in Polygon Wood Cemetery. The 12 March was a milder day and only one man was wounded.

On the 13th at 7am the 1/4th DWR raided the enemy lines south of Judge Sector at Polderhoek which seems to have stirred the Germans up, as their artillery was active for most of the day. Private Herbert Barker (25) from Bradford was killed and eight other men were wounded. He is buried in Polygon Wood Cemetery.

One of the men from the 1/4th DWR, Lance Corporal Richard Arthur Hudson (25) from Yeadon, was awarded the DCM for his actions during the raid. His citation in the *London Gazette* reads:

> *For conspicuous gallantry and devotion to duty in a raid on the enemy's lines. He commanded a flanking section which rushed a trench and killed several of the enemy. His platoon captured thirty-seven prisoners and three machine guns and inflicted heavy casualties on the enemy. He showed splendid determination and initiative.*

He enlisted on 27 June 1916 at Halifax and survived the war. He was discharged in June 1919 and returned to his job as a dyer's labourer at Green Lane Dye Works, Rawdon. He was a member of Yeadon Brass Band and died at Yeadon in 1959, aged 64. As was often the case, he lost two family members during the war. His cousin, Private Harry Hudson (19) from Yeadon died on 18th October 1918 whilst serving in the 1/7th West Yorkshire Regiment and his brother-in-law, Tom Kirkbright, also from Yeadon, died on 2 January 1917 whilst serving in Kenya with the 2nd Loyal North Lancashires and is commemorated on the Nairobi British and Indian memorial.

Private (later Acting Serjeant) Richard A. Hudson.

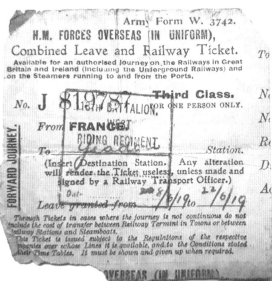

Private Richard A. Hudson, seated bareheaded on the second rank, fourth from the right.

Richard A. Hudson in later life.

His ticket home to Yeadon after transferring to the Z class reserve in June 1919.

Acting Serjeant Richard A. Hudson's DCM, War and Victory medals. (Photos courtesy of Mark Hudson)

The 14th March was a quieter day and the companies rotated the support, reserve and front line positions. The 15th was a fine, clear day and British aircraft were active, conducting numerous bombing missions on the German lines. The support and reserve lines were shelled but without casualties. On the 16th there was a little shelling of the front line but again without casualties.

In the early hours of 17 March the Germans conducted a large raid on the trenches of the Judge Sector. After a heavy bombardment, the enemy attempted to enter the trenches occupied by C Company, but were driven off by sustained rifle and Lewis gun fire with several casualties inflicted on the raiders. At daybreak three German rifles and a cap were found in front of the trench. The number of British casualties stands as a testament to the ferocity of the fight. Serjeant Robert Green, (31) from Bingley, Private William Barrett (21) from Huntington, Private Wilfrid Smith (39) from Golcar, and Private Charles Atha from Leeds were all killed and sixteen other men wounded. All the men, except Wilfred Smith who is buried in Polygon Wood Cemetery, have no known graves and are commemorated on the Tyne Cot Memorial.

Private J.S. Williamson. (CPGW)

On this day Private James Stanley Williamson (23) died of wounds at No.10 CCS and is buried at Lijssenthoek Military Cemetery. He landed in France in June 1915 and before the war he was employed as a weaver. He was born in Chelsea but was living in Albion Street, Earby near Barnoldswick when he enlisted at Skipton. Private Nathanial Smith (24) from Diamond Street, Hunslet, Leeds was also wounded and died at No.10 CCS and is also buried in Lijssenthoek Military Cemetery.

On 18 March the battalion was relieved by the 1/4th York and Lancaster Regiment and marched to Birr Cross Roads near Hellfire Corner and moved south-west to the rest camp by train. The relief was completed by 7.30pm without casualties. The next seven days consisted of the usual routine of working parties, inspections, kit maintenance and baths. The men constructed a grenade throwing range, an assault course and a 30-yard shooting range. Huts were also tarred and sandbag walls constructed and so, as usual, time in the rest area did not include much rest.

Meanwhile in Russia, the Bolsheviks had seized power and taken the country out of the war. Upwards of one million fresh German troops poured towards the Western Front and by March 1918, seventy-five German divisions were in position opposite thirty-seven British divisions which were holding the southern sector of the line from north of Arras down to St Quentin. General Ludendorff's plan was to attack and drive a wedge between the British and French armies. A German attack was anticipated as trench raids had been probing the British defences in growing numbers and intelligence from German prisoners indicated an attack was imminent. On 21 March 1918 the German assault – the *Kaiserschlacht* or Kaiser's Battle – began near Arras and St Quentin. All leave was cancelled and officers and men who were on leave were recalled.

On 26 March the battalion entrained on the light railway at Howe Sidings and were transported to Birr Cross Roads. They marched to the Judge Sector once again and relieved the 1/4th York and Lancaster Regiment, with one man being wounded during the relief. The 27th and 28th were remarkably quiet and, apart from some light shelling and heavy rain, there was not much to report. Patrols from A and B Companies were sent into no man's land, but no enemy were encountered. On 29 March, C and D Companies rotated with A and B in the front line trenches and one man was wounded. The 30th was a fine, sunny day and the enemy aircraft and artillery were quiet. A patrol from D Company was sent out during the night, but had nothing to report. The 31st was another sunny day and it was noticed that the Germans were firing at British aircraft with trench mortars, not an accurate anti-aircraft weapon, but more than capable of bringing down a plane.

A patrol from A Company was sent out during the night and passed off quietly. Serjeant John J. Brown DCM, originally from Jarrow but enlisted at Skipton, was hit in the head by a sniper's bullet and killed. Serjeant Brown (29) of East Gate, Skipton enlisted shortly after war was declared and landed in France with the battalion in April 1915. Before the war he was employed at Belle Vue Mills in the town. He is buried at Belgian Battery Corner Cemetery near Ypres. He was awarded the Distinguished Conduct Medal. The citation, which was published on 21 October 1918 and therefore after his death in the *London Gazette*, reads:

Serjeant John J.
Brown DCM. (CPC

For conspicuous gallantry and devotion to duty. Acting as Coy. Sgt.-Maj. he continually conducted ration and supply carrying parties to detached and isolated posts, over exposed areas swept by artillery and machine gun fire. He was wounded in the chest by a machine gun bullet, but declined to be evacuated, and remained at duty till the battalion was relieved.

CASUALTIES: During March 1918, the battalion had 7 men killed and 26 wounded.

April 1918

The first day of April was fine and, apart from a few trench mortars, the day passed quietly with only one man being wounded. In the early hours of the 2nd the enemy launched an artillery barrage on the right section of the Judge Sector, where C Company was located. A German raiding party then attacked the trench which was repelled with two casualties to the defenders, but at daybreak, a dead German soldier was found on the British wire. His unit, the 70th Regiment, 1st Company, was identified from marks found on his respirator. On 3 April the battalion was relieved by the 9th Norfolk Regiment and moved to Tor Top Tunnels in the Polderhoek reserve sector at the south-west end of Sanctuary Wood. The 4th was very wet and the day was spent cleaning kit and the billets which were found to be in a very dirty state.

On the morning of 5 April the battalion provided a working party of two officers and 200 men to work on the Corps reserve line and in the afternoon they moved to Otago Camp, between the Lille Gate at Ypres and Zillebeke. The 6th was spent cleaning

The preserved trench system at Sanctuary Wood in 2016.

kit, conducting inspections and visiting the baths. A and B Companies visited the rifle range at the Belgian army barracks at Ypres to practise rapid rifle firing and a draft of seventy-seven men joined the battalion. On 7 April those men who missed out on baths had the opportunity to visit and a working party of two officers and 200 men was provided. On 8 April training was carried out near the camp and instruction was given on the new type 36 rifle grenade. This replaced the type 23 rifle grenade with the attached rod as it was found to be damaging the rifling of the barrel when fired. The type 36 was fired, using a special blank round, from a cup-type device which was attached to the muzzle of the rifle. Instead of a rod, the grenade had a circular plate fixed to the base and, like its predecessor, it was launched with the rifle butt firmly placed on the ground.

Type 36 grenade and launcher.

Chapter 15

The Battle of the Lys

O n 9 April the battalion marched 4 miles west to a camp near Busseboom, a mile south-east of Poperinge. At 12.15am on the 10th the men were hurriedly awoken. Extra ammunition and rations were issued and by 2am the battalion and the rest of 147 Brigade had boarded buses and driven 9 miles south to the French village of La Crèche, located between Bailleul and Armentières, arriving at 5am. The brigade had been placed under the temporary command of 101 Infantry Brigade of the 34th Division, commanded by Brigadier General B.C. Gore. On 9 April the enemy had bombarded the Portuguese Division, who were holding the Neuve Chapelle/Fleurbaix front 8 miles to the south-west, and then attacked in strength, driving the Portuguese back. The Germans then crossed the River Lys at Bac-St-Maur, 3 miles south-west of Armentières, exposing the flank of 147 Brigade. Meanwhile 101 Brigade was holding the line south of the Bac-St-Maur to Armentières railway line with the 16th Royal Scots to the right and 11th Suffolk Regiment to the left. The Germans had penetrated the line where the two battalions met at the Rue Delpierre.

The 1/6th DWR hurriedly marched 3 miles south to a farm called La Veau where a halt was called. Along the road, civilians were fleeing their homes and flocking to the rear. This was a sight most men in the battalion had not seen before as, up to this time, the civilian population had been evacuated from the combat areas before the men of the 1/6th DWR had arrived. The civilians, mainly old people, women and young children, had loaded their possessions in handcarts to escape the German advance. The lack of military age men was testament to the sacrifice the men of France had made in the defence of their country. Fortunately, the enemy artillery was not shelling the road so the brigade was able to advance without too much hindrance.

Back packs were stacked, tea was brewed and orders for the next move issued. At 9am the battalion moved off and took up a position at L'Epinette crossroads, a mile to the south-east. A and B Companies were to the south side of the junction, with C and D to the north. Two companies of the 1/4th DWR proceeded to the town of Erquingham-Lys, crossing the River Lys by a wooden foot bridge, and held a position at the west side of the town. The remaining two companies of the 1/4th DWR and the entire 1/7th DWR took a position to the left of 1/6th DWR. From 10.30am onwards, Erquingham-Lys was heavily shelled by German artillery. Little was known of the situation; but from observations it appeared that the British forces were withdrawing to the north bank of the River Lys. On the outskirts of Erquingham-Lys, the men from the 1/4th DWR were on the receiving end of heavy German machine-gun and rifle fire from a farmhouse. Closer observation revealed that a large store of Mills bombs and Stokes mortar shells were in a shed next to the building. The Lewis gunners of the 1/4th DWR poured concentrated fire on the shed without any result until suddenly the stored munitions exploded, destroying the adjacent farmhouse and the occupying Germans.

The enemy persisted with the attack on Erquingham-Lys and it was here that Private Arthur Poulter of the 1/4th DWR won the Victoria Cross. He was born in East Witton near Middleham, North Yorkshire, but on enlistment lived in Leeds and was working as a drayman for the Timothy Taylor brewery in the city. He had originally attempted to join the Royal Navy but had been rejected due to his bad teeth and he eventually enlisted in the 1/4th DWR in March 1916. Whilst acting as a

Private Arthur Poulter VC. (Author)

stretcher-bearer, on at least ten occasions he carried badly wounded men on his back to safety through heavy machine-gun and artillery fire. Again, after being ordered back across the River Lys, in full view of the enemy, he rescued another man who had been left behind and provided first aid to at least forty men whilst under enemy fire. He was himself seriously wounded on 27 April near Kemmel when he was hit in the head by a bullet while attempting another rescue. He survived the war and died in 1956 aged 62. He buried in New Wortley Cemetery near Leeds. His VC was donated by his family to the Duke of Wellington's Regimental Museum at Halifax.

At 1pm orders were received for the 1/6th DWR to move east to the Nieppe Defence Line which consisted of well-prepared trenches with thick belts of barbed wire. D Company took a position on the left side near the Armentières Road, B and C were on the right near the railway embankment and A was in close support. During the day, withdrawing stragglers from the 22nd and 25th Northumberland Fusiliers and soldiers from the 15th and 16th Royal Scots, filled the trenches. One complete company of the 23rd Northumberland Fusiliers, which was in retreat, crowded into the trenches on the left of the line. All the stragglers were placed under the command of Lieutenant Colonel Charles M. Bateman.

Apart from some gas shelling of Nieppe, the night passed quietly but Private Harold Kilburn from Cleckheaton was killed and three other men were wounded.

The Divisional Commander, Major General N.G. Cameron issued the following message to all ranks:

In forwarding the attached copy of a Special Order of the Day by Field-Marshal Sir Douglas Haig, I wish to say at once that I have complete confidence that the 49th (West Riding) Division will acquit itself gloriously in whatever circumstances it may be placed.

Remember that other divisions elsewhere are at this moment holding up splendidly against the most strenuous efforts of the enemy to force a decision. Remember also that if we are called upon to fight here, we shall be fighting on the historic ground that the 'contemptible little British army' fought and defeated the enemy's first great effort to destroy it in 1914. In that year, we defeated him with the rifle. With the rifle, we can and will defeat him again – the more thoroughly this time, as we have our wire to give our rifles a better opportunity than they had in 1914. Go on improving your wire, look carefully to your rifles, machine guns and Lewis guns and ammunition and exercise vigilance every moment of the day to see that every yard of your front is watched and can be shot into. We can then best see off any attack.

So much for the defensive, we must be aggressive. Every front line company must send out at least one fighting patrol every night to look for opportunities to kill or capture enemy patrols or posts.

Identifications are of great importance but more important still is the object of making ourselves masters of no-man's-land and inducing the enemy to increase his strength against us on this portion of the front thus helping to reduce the pressure against our comrades further south.

N.G. Cameron, Major-General,
Commanding 49th (West Riding) Division

SPECIAL ORDER OF THE DAY By FIELD-MARSHAL SIR DOUGLAS HAIG K.T., G.C.B., G.C.V.O., K.C.I.E. Commander-in-Chief, British Armies in France.

To: ALL RANKS OF THE BRITISH ARMY IN FRANCE AND FLANDERS. Three weeks ago to-day the enemy began his terrific attacks against us on a fifty mile front. His objects are to separate us from the French, to take the Channel Ports and destroy the British Army.

In spite of throwing already 106 Divisions into the battle and enduring the most reckless sacrifice of human life, he has as yet made little progress towards his goals. We owe this to the determined fighting and self-sacrifice of our troops. Words fail me to express the admiration which I feel for the splendid resistance offered by all ranks of our Army under the most trying circumstances. Many amongst us now are tired. To those I would say that Victory will belong to the side which holds out the longest. The French Army is moving rapidly and in great force to our support.

There is no other course open to us but to fight it out. Every position must be held to the last man: there must be no retirement. With our backs to the wall and believing in the justice of our cause each one of us must fight on to the end. The safety of our homes and the freedom of mankind alike depend upon the conduct of each one of us at this critical moment.

(Signed) D. Haig F.M. Commander-in-Chief
General Headquarters British Armies in France
Tuesday, April 11th, 1918

The morning of 11 April was to be the costliest in lives the battalion had experienced to date. The ferocity of this engagement is evident from the casualty list and the individual acts of courage and selflessness are testament to the bravery of the men who served in the 1/6th DWR.

The Germans opened fire just before 11am with machine guns which they had covertly moved up to the outskirts of Nieppe. At 11am a trench mortar and artillery bombardment began and at 1pm the German infantry assault commenced.

They attacked B Company's position on the Rue d'Armentières, working their way along an abandoned trench. Some men from the Northumberland Fusiliers under the command of the 1/6th DWR surrendered with undue haste with hands raised, allowing the Germans to enter the British trench. Two platoons from C Company were despatched to assist, but with no hand grenades they were unable to dislodge the enemy. It was impossible to attack over the top of the trench due to heavy machine-gun fire raking the parapet and Second Lieutenant Charles Richard Shaw (29) from Greetland, near Elland was killed in the attempt. He has no known grave and is commemorated on panel 82 at the Tyne Cot Memorial.

A defensive obstacle was quickly built across the trench but the intensity of the trench mortar barrage increased and Second Lieutenant George Stewart (19) from Westbourne Avenue, Hull was killed. He is buried in Trois Arbres Cemetery near Steenwerck. About 4pm a supply of hand grenades was found and a plan was formulated by Captain Kenneth Ogston, C Company commander, to drive the Germans from the British lines. The Germans continued to push along the trench so, despite the machine-gun fire, the attack was made across the top of the trench towards the rear of the enemy, which finally succeeded in ejecting them from the trench. Captain Ogston, along with Second Lieutenant Whitehead and Second Lieutenant Baker led their men as they launched the attack. Twenty Germans were killed and one captured but Second Lieutenant Baker was seriously wounded

Serjeant G.W. Burrows. (CPGW)

and Serjeant George William Burrows (32) from Milton Street, Skipton was killed and is believed to be buried in Trois Arbres Cemetery. He enlisted in June 1915 and had been on active service for two years. Before enlisting he was a Police Constable in the West Riding Constabulary and served at Crosshills, Barnoldswick and Skipton. His wife received a letter from the CO about the manner in which her husband met his death:

He called some men around him and, jumping out of the trenches shouted, 'Come on, lads, follow me,' and they dashed across the open to help some men who had been surrounded by the enemy. Just as they reached their objective he was shot dead.

A machine gun team from 34 Machine Gun Company provided invaluable assistance to the battalion, in particular, Private James Womersley of another formation, who had previously served in the DWR, demonstrated great courage in keeping his gun firing despite a serious wound to his arm. He enlisted in November 1915 and was medically discharged on 11 November 1918.

The enemy continued to enter the trenches in B and C Companies' location. On seeing this, the CO, Lieutenant Colonel Bateman, rallied his men and led a successful counter-attack to eject them. At 7pm orders were received to withdraw 4 miles north-west towards Bailleul Crossroad. This was completed by 11.30pm and the battalion took up a position just south of crossroads.

Other fatalities on 11 April are as follows:

Serjeant Harry Smith from Shipley
Serjeant Arthur Stott from Skipton
Corporal Walter Nicholson from Sowerby Bridge
Lance Corporal Fred Metcalfe from Weeton (formerly East Yorkshire Regiment)
Lance Corporal Elijah Sayer from Durham
Private William E. Maycock from Burton-on-Trent,
Private Frederick Cox from Hackney, London (formerly of the Royal Fusiliers)
Private William Brittle from Birmingham,
Private William Thomson from Glasgow (formerly of the Argyll and Sutherland
  Highlanders)
Private Charles A. Emmott from Ilkley
Private Harrison Rawnsley from Brighouse,
Private William Horsman from Keighley
Private Harold Hill from Ingrow
Private William G. Briggs from Gargrave,
Private Harry Holland from Greetland near Halifax
Private George L.B. Harper from Edinburgh (formerly RAMC)
Private William Naylor from Huddersfield
Private John R. Parker (19) from Barnoldswick
Private John Adamthwaite from Low Bentham, Lancashire (formerly ASC)
Private Percy Howe from Bradford
Private Shaw Hardy from Brighouse
Private William F. Rowe from Stoke on Trent (formerly AOC)
Private Harry Gooding from Nelson, Lancashire
Private Bertie Steel from Sheffield,
Private George E. Holliday from South Shields
Private Percy Ingham from Huddersfield
Private Frederick Cartwright from York
Private Robert T. Lamb from Sunderland,
Private William Rushworth from Huddersfield
Private John Gaunt from Keighley
Private Fred Evans from Bradford.
Private Percy Taylor from East Morton died of wounds on 16 April 1918
Private Joseph Moore from Shipley was reported missing but died of wounds
  on 22 April.

Captain Kenneth Ogston. (CPGW)

Serjeant A. Stott. (CPGW)

Private J. Adamthwaite. (CPGW)

Private W.G. Briggs. (CPGW)

Lance Corporal Arthur Bamforth died of wounds on 8 March 1919 and is interred at Keighley (Morton) Cemetery.

Private Christopher Bennett from Oldham was captured and died as a prisoner of war on 4 July 1918.

Most of these men have no known grave and are commemorated on panels 83 to 85 at Tyne Cot and on a special memorial at Trois Arbres Cemetery. Seventy-five other men were wounded and twenty-four others reported as missing.

At 8am on 12 April, two field kitchens served breakfast to the men and the situation appeared to have quietened down. At 9.45am a patrol of fifteen men and an officer was sent out to check the area of Blanc Maison, a mile to the south-west, to verify the presence of the enemy at that location and to establish if any friendly forces were in the vicinity. They reported that various groups of British soldiers were withdrawing under the command of officers and the Germans could clearly be seen advancing. Orders were received to establish a defensive line along a stream called the Becque de la Flanche to the west of Bailleul. B Company remained in reserve, A was on the right, astride the Bailleul to Hazebrouck railway line about 300 yards west of Bailleul train station, C Company was in the centre and D Company to the left, adjoining the 16th Royal Scots.

A well-stocked YMCA canteen had been found in Bailleul and a guard was posted to prevent looting. The supplies were soon commandeered, divided up and issued to the men of the brigade to supplement their rations and prevent their capture by the Germans. The men dug in overnight, but during the afternoon of 12 April, the Germans launched a heavy artillery and mortar bombardment of the line. Machine guns added to the storm of fire and the C Company commander, Captain Kenneth Ogston was hit in the thigh by a bullet and died of his wounds. He has no known grave and is commemorated on the Tyne Cot Memorial. Before the war he lived at 8 Laurel Crescent, Keighley and was working as a designer in the cloth trade.

Serjeant Stott (22) was a pre-war 'terrier' and a prominent member of the Skipton bulldog scout troop. He has no known grave and is commemorated on panel 82 on the Tyne Cot Memorial.

On 26 April, the *West Yorkshire Pioneer* newspaper reported the death of Private William Gilbert Briggs:

> *Signaller Wm. Briggs, of the Duke of Wellington's West Riding Regiment, only son of Mr and Mrs Wm. Briggs, of 8, High Street, Skipton, was killed in action on April 12th. At the time, he was in a trench along with a Serjeant and corporal, when a bomb fell between them, killing him and the Serjeant. He was 22 years of age, and had been in France about three years. He was formerly employed as an electrical engineer at Eshton Hall. He was only recently home on leave.*

He has no known grave and is commemorated on panel 83 on the Tyne Cot Memorial.

Panel 83 at Tyne Cot Cemetery.

Before the war, Private John Adamthwaite (21) from Low Bentham worked as a cashier at the Royal Lancaster Infirmary and was a keen amateur photographer. In November 1916 he was conscripted into the Army Service Corps (ASC) but later transferred to the 1/6th DWR and was posted to France in August 1917. He has no known grave and is commemorated on panel 83 on the Tyne Cot Memorial.

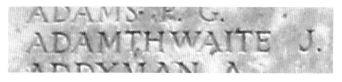

Panel 83 at Tyne Cot Cemetery.

Private John Robert Parker (19) from Queen Street, Barnoldswick had only been in France six months before he was killed. Before enlisting, he worked in the cloth trade and was employed by Mr T. Nutter at Calf Shed, Barnoldswick. He has no known grave and is commemorated on panel 84 on the Tyne Cot Memorial. He was the brother-in-law of Private William Lister (27) also from Barnoldswick, who was serving in the ranks of the 1/6th DWR when he was killed in action on 18 July 1915.

Private John R. Parker. (CPGW)

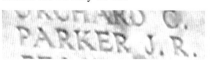

Panel 84 on the Tyne Cot Memorial.

The following fatalities also occurred on 12 April:

Second Lieutenant John W. Probyn, from Tanfield Road, Birkby near
  Huddersfield
Serjeant Claude Harding MM, from Skipton,
Corporal George Page MM, from Ingrow
Corporal William Severs from Newcastle (formerly of the Yorkshire Regiment)
Private Harold Briggs from Bradford
Private Norman F. Fletcher from Marsden
Private Charles Threadgale from Oldham
Private Tom Purshouse from Smethwick near Warwick
Private Albert V. Nicholls from Tipton in Staffordshire
Private Albert Lund from Keighley
Private Milford Brown from Oakworth,
Private Harold Loynds from Hyde in Lancashire
Private George Henry Smith (23) from Otley.
Private George Hill from Cudworth was seriously wounded and died on 24 April.

Forty other men were wounded and two reported missing. None of the men killed on 12 April has a known grave and all are commemorated on memorial panels 83 to 85 on the Tyne Cot Memorial.

Serjeant C. Harding MM. (CPGW)

Serjeant Claude Harding MM (23) of Bradley Street, Skipton was a pre-war 'terrier' who was formerly employed as an engineer at Keighley. He was one of three brothers who saw service in the Great War, only one of whom was to survive. Two of his brothers had emigrated to Canada and at the outbreak of war, both men enlisted in the Canadian Army. Private Fred Harding was serving in the 1st Canadian Mounted Rifles when he was killed on 9 April 1917 and is buried at Nine Elms Military Cemetery near Vimy. His other brother, Willie Harding was severely wounded in the leg which required amputation and he returned to Canada.

The early hours of 13 April were quiet and by 4.30am rations had been delivered to the companies. At 5am the CO and intelligence officer, Lieutenant Spencer, conducted an inspection of the defences and found them to be in good order. At 3pm the enemy began to shell the line and launched an infantry attack on the Royal Scots on the left flank. The Germans also began to attack A Company's position near the railway line, but were defeated with accurate rifle and Lewis gun fire. The Royal Scots on the left flank gave ground leaving D Company's flank exposed. The Germans worked their way round the flank, and although they were delayed by rifle and Lewis gun fire for a considerable time, they eventually worked their way round both flanks of D Company. To prevent encirclement, D Company was withdrawn, but it is certain that they accounted for a large number of German troops although they also suffered for their stand. Amongst the fallen of D Company was Serjeant James Bury DCM MM.

On 26 April, the *Craven Herald* newspaper reported his death:

A promising and honourable career has been cut short by the death of Serjeant James Bury, D.C.M., M.M., of the Duke of Wellington's Regiment, particulars of which have been received in the following letter to Mr. Jas. Bury, 6 East Parade, Barnoldswick, from Captain B. Godfrey Buxton, O.C., 'D' Company:

Serjeant J. Bury. (CPGW)

'Dear Mr. Bury,
No words can express my grief in having to inform you that your son, Serjeant James Bury, was killed in action whilst commanding his platoon in defence against a great German attack. At the time they were fairly surrounded, and he had just completed his orders for them to fight their way through when he was hit through the chest and killed. The platoon carried out his orders with the greatest courage.

There are, indeed, few fathers who have more reason to be prouder of their sons than you. He was a leader born, and he died leading. Earlier in the day, in a warm corner, his next platoon commander asked, when the enemy were attacking and no one was on their flanks: "Are we to go back or forward?" "Forward!" said Serjeant Bury, and they met the enemy successfully with the bayonet.

I have often, perhaps six months in all, had him Acting Company Serjeant-Major and found, when going around with him during bombardment, or in the attack at Passchendale last time, he proved himself a brave and inspired comrade, and one whose advice was always worth listening to with care. He was the next N.C.O. in the battalion for C.S.M., and had already refused the post of C.Q.M.S. because he said he knew he could lead the men and get more out of them than most. There was none in the Division who knew more about bombs and explosives, or who taught men in action better how to use them. He usually made a poor soldier a good one by his enthusiasm, but perhaps the best proof of his excellence is the fact that the first bombers he trained are now my senior, and best N.C.O.s.

Please accept from us all in 'D' Company, as well as all his friends in the Battalion and Brigade, our very real sympathy in the loss of so gallant a son. Yours sincerely, B. Godfrey Buxton, Capt.'

Serjeant Bury was 32 years of age and unmarried. He had previously served in South Africa, whither he went at the age of 16 years, and stayed just over two years. He rejoined the Colours immediately after the outbreak of war, and went to France on April 14th 1915. The. D.C.M. was conferred upon him in June 1916, and the M.M. in April last year.

Before the war he lived on Victoria Road, Barnoldswick and was employed as cotton weaver. In Late December 1916 he was fortunate to be granted leave and he was the guest of honour at the Barnoldswick Methodist Sunday School Christmas gathering where he was presented with a wrist watch with a luminous dial in recognition of winning the DCM. His pre-war employers, Messrs Dugdale & Dewhurst of Wellhouse Mill, also presented him with an inscribed marble mantle clock. He has no known grave and is commemorated on the Ploegsteert Memorial to the Missing.

B Company was called up from reserve and, despite heavy machine-gun fire, they moved up to a forward position and managed to stop the German advance. At 9.45pm, orders were received to withdraw to the southern outskirts of Bailleul where a new defensive line was established.

The other fatalities on 13 April were as follows:

Corporal John W. Tillottson from Benthorpe
Corporal Norman A. Rymer from Cleckheaton,
Private Arthur Wood from Huddersfield,
Private Robert V. Casson (31) from Clapham, Lancashire
Private Ernest Hawksby
Private Frank Haywood (42) from Bradford died of wounds on 14 April
Private Harry O'Melia (21) from Holmfirth died of wounds on 23 April.

Thirty other men were wounded and six men reported missing. The missing men presumed dead were:

Private William Stephenson (19) from Sunderland
Private Henry E. Bennett (23) from Sheffield
Private James Magson Smith (23) from Bradford
Private Henry A. Maddeys (22) from Great Yarmouth
Private Charles Connell from Huddersfield (but born in West Ham)
Private Arthur Griffin from Paisley, Scotland was captured and died as a prisoner
of war in Germany.

Private William (Willie) Watson (30) was severely wounded during this action and evacuated to the UK. He was the son of Walter Watson from Guiseley and had originally served in the 3rd Volunteer Battalion of the West Riding Regiment and was a pre-war 'terrier'. In 1911 he was living with his married sister Florence at 3 James Street, Rawdon and was working as a scourer at a woollen mill. He was treated at a war hospital at Stoke-on-Trent, but died of his wounds on 14 June 1918 and is buried in the graveyard of St Oswald's Church at Guiseley.

Private W. Watson's headstone.

Private Robert Victor Casson originally enlisted under Lord Derby's recruitment scheme in December 1915. At that time, he was working on his father's farm at Hammond Head, Clapham. He was conscripted in March 1916 and posted to France in June 1916. He was invalided back to the UK in October 1916 with serious septic infection but returned to the battalion in March 1917. He is buried at Le Grand Beaumart British Cemetery, Steenwerck. He was the brother of Gunner Thomas Casson who was serving in D Battery of 79 Brigade Royal Field Artillery when he was killed on 14 April 1917.

Private R.V. Casson (CPGW)

The morning of 14 April was quiet, but despite their fatigue, the men were in high spirits. By midday the German trench mortar and artillery fire had increased and about 3.30pm, German troops were seen massing for an attack about 300 yards from battalion HQ. They were engaged by the HQ orderlies, runners, signallers and officers' batmen as well as by Lieutenant Colonel Bateman, Lieutenant Stewart, signals officer, and Regimental Serjeant Major Richardson. Rapid fire was poured on to the enemy who withdrew in confusion. Their actions undoubtedly stopped a German flanking manoeuvre as well as inflicting many casualties on the attackers. One platoon from C Company was sent to assist, which allowed the HQ contingent to withdraw to a safer location. For his gallantry and devotion to duty, Regimental Serjeant Major Richardson was awarded the DCM.

The following men were killed on that day:

Serjeant Albert Taylor from Skipton
Corporal Thomas Howard from Holmfirth
Private Wilfred Charlesworth from Holmfirth
Private George Lamb from Bradford
Private Wilfred G. Smith from Shipley
Private Walter W. Cooper from Mirfield
Private John W. Hilton from Langcliffe
Private John Lockwood from Springhead, Lancashire
Private Joseph Taylor from Normanton
Private Hubert Wails from Cleckheaton
Private Oliver Stenton from Conisborough.

Private John William Hilton. (CPGW)

Forty-two men were wounded and two reported missing.

Serjeant John Willie Russell, one of the wounded, was evacuated to the UK but died of his injuries on 7 May 1918 in a military hospital at Farnham. He is buried at Waltonwrays Cemetery, Skipton. He had a brother and cousin who also served in the 1/6th DWR and who were both killed. Private David Russell died of wounds on 14 October 1916

Serjeant John Willie Russell. (CPGW)

178

and is buried at Étaples and his cousin, also called David Russell, was killed on 16 December 1915 near the Yser Canal. John Willie had previously served in the 3rd (Volunteer) DWR and transferred to the 1/6th DWR in 1908. He left the TF in 1910 having completed ten years' service. Before the war he worked as a packer at the English Sewing Cotton Company at Skipton.

At 4am on 15 April the battalion was relieved by two companies of the 5th North Staffordshire Regiment from 176 Brigade and withdrew 3 miles north to a farm near Saint-Jans-Cappel. On arrival, breakfast was served and weapons cleaned. At 6am orders were received that in the event of an emergency, the battalion would hold an as yet un-dug reserve line to the south of Saint-Jans-Cappel where they were to become IX Corps' reserve. Around 5pm it became evident that the reserve line needed digging with all speed as the Germans were reported to be advancing from the south-east. Entrenching tools were sent for and local farm implements commandeered to speed up the construction of the trenches. A line of defences approximately half a mile long was prepared and the 1/4th DWR, who were to

Serjeant John Willie Russell's headstone.

the right, had dug a defensive line of a similar distance. The new trenches were ready and occupied by 7.45pm, not a moment too soon as the troops from 176 Brigade, who had relieved the battalion the previous day, were retreating in confusion and crowding into the newly dug trenches. At 11pm orders were received to send the men from 176 Brigade to the rear and work continued improving the reserve line. It was clear that Bailleul, which the battalion had bravely defended for three days, had fallen to the Germans.

The battalion scouts were sent forward to provide intelligence and warning of enemy movements. On that day Private Tom Ramsden (23) from Ovendon near Halifax, was killed and one other man was wounded. During the morning of the 16th the Germans fired a barrage of mortar bombs and field guns on to the newly dug reserve line and had also moved their machine guns up which were pouring bullets on to the line. The British artillery provided the battalion with a supporting barrage when the Germans were seen massing for an attack, but at 4pm, a heavy German artillery barrage landed on the line.

The enemy launched an attack on A Company's trenches but it was repulsed with the help of the 147th Trench Mortar (Stokes) Battery and a counter-attack was mounted by A Company, led by Major Tanner and Company Serjeant Major Owen McDermott from Skipton, who captured sixteen prisoners and two light machine guns. The attacking Germans did not get within 300 yards of the British line before they were stopped. Company Serjeant Major McDermott was awarded the DCM for his devotion to duty and gallantry during this action and his consistent good work since 1915. His citation reads:

For marked gallantry and devotion to duty during the period 25th February to 16th September 1918, especially between 10th and 21st April, when the battalion was fighting near Nieppe and Bailleul. He displayed good leadership, and showed great initiative in taking out a patrol immediately after an attack had been repulsed, capturing several prisoners and two light machine guns. He has done consistent good work since 1915.

Unfortunately, he was killed in action six months later.

The remainder of the day and night passed quietly and barbed wire was fixed in front of the line. Private Arthur J. Haigh from Milnsbridge, Huddersfield and Lance Corporal John Maurice Stamford from Brightside, Sheffield were both killed and eleven other men wounded. Private Arthur Aldridge (27) from Victoria Road, Earby was also killed. He was attached to the 147th (Stokes) Trench Mortar Battery and had previously served in the 8th DWR during the Gallipoli campaign, taking part in the Suvla Bay landing. After a brief stay in Egypt, he was posted to the Western Front in October 1916. He is buried at Mont Noir Military Cemetery, Saint-Jans-Cappel.

Private A. Aldridge. (CPGW)

One of the wounded men, Private Joseph M. Buckley (31) from Clayton in Bradford, died of his wounds on 9 May 1918. This was the furthest advance the Germans made in this sector. The trenches the men of 147 Brigade had dug with hand tools and farm implements on 15 April had now become the new British front line.

Private Thomas Whitney Smith (24) from Rose Cottage, Lothersdale died at No.36 CCS of wounds received the previous day. He enlisted at the outbreak of war and is buried at Haringe Military Cemetery, Belgium. He was the brother of Private William Robert Smith who was killed on 7 July 1916 while was serving in the 9th (Service) Battalion of the DWR. William has no known grave and is commemorated on the Thiepval Memorial.

Private T.W. Smith. (CPGW)

On 17 April the town of Saint-Jans-Cappel was heavily shelled, but more barbed wire was laid in front of the battalion's position. Congratulatory messages were received from the corps and divisional GOCs regarding the battalion's gallant efforts. Second Lieutenant Joseph M. Hick from Undercliffe Lane, Bradford and Private David W. Cole from Great Yarmouth (formerly of the Norfolk Regiment) were both killed and eleven other men wounded. Private Leonard Parker (21) from Guycroft, Otley died of wounds received the previous day and is buried at Mendinghem Military Cemetery, about 15 miles north-west of Ypres.

Private L. Parker. (Michael and Betty Hutchinson)

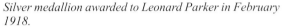

Silver medallion awarded to Leonard Parker in February 1918.

Leonard Parker's memorial plaque.

In the early 1920s pilgrimages were arranged by the YMCA for bereaved families to visit the war graves of their loved ones. Mrs Mary Parker, mother of Leonard, obtained a passport and travelled to Belgium as part of an organised trip to visit his grave. Any near relatives, two in each family, could be taken out to visit the grave entirely free of charge if they could not afford to contribute towards the expense.

On 16 June 1922, the *Wharfedale Observer* newspaper reported the visit of the group from Otley to the Western Front:

Mary Parker's photo from her passport.

Sir,
May we be allowed through your paper to say how thankful we are to the Y.M.C.A. for giving us the privilege of visiting the graves in France and Belgium –
28ᵗʰ May to June 2ⁿᵈ. We stayed two nights at the hostel in Euston Sq, London and would like to thank them for their kindness. There were six of us who went to France and we were treated with every kindness and consideration by the Y.M.C.A.

Seven of us went to Belgium and we were fortunate enough to find Mr Tarr (who had recently lectured in Otley) at Ypres. He took us to Menin and through a lot of battlefields and made our visit something long to be remembered. The hostel at Ypres is a 'home from home'.

We would like to thank all those who have done so much to make our visit to the continent so great a success, particularly we are indebted to Miss Wilson and Mr Tarr for the interest and kindness they have shown towards us.

We cannot say a big enough thank you to the Y.M.C.A. and all the workers and guides connected with it.

We are, yours sincerely,
The Otley Party, June 21ˢᵗ 1922.

The Memorial Plaque was issued after the First World War to the next of kin of all British and Empire service personnel who were killed as a result of the war. The plaques were cast in bronze and became popularly known as the Dead Man's Penny, because of the similarity in appearance to the smaller penny coin. In all 1,355,000 plaques were issued and continued to be issued into the 1930s. The name of the deceased is cast in raised letters as opposed to engraved.

There was sporadic shelling on 18 and 19 April and in the early hours of the 20th, the battalion was relieved by the 18th King's Liverpool Regiment, 99 Brigade of the 30th Division. They then withdrew a mile north-east to an area just west of Mont Noir where the remainder of the day was spent resting and cleaning weapons.

At 4am on 21 April the battalion moved 4 miles north-west to the New Zealand army camp at Abeele on the French/Belgian border where breakfast was served. At 4pm that afternoon the battalion marched 3 miles north-east to Poperinge, arriving at 6pm and settled into billets. The 22nd April was spent cleaning kit and the men had the opportunity to visit the baths. The same routine was continued on the 23rd and training was carried out near the billets. A small working party was used for laying electric cables. Whilst conducting this duty, Private Francis John Kay (25) from Skipton was accidently electrocuted. He is buried in Poperinge New Military Cemetery. He was the cousin of Gunner Harry Kay (37) from Barnoldswick who was serving in the Royal Garrison Artillery when he was killed in action on 5 October 1918.

Private F.J. Kay. (CPGW)

Overnight into 24 April German aircraft and artillery bombed and shelled the town with mustard gas shells and aerial bombs. One of the gas bombs landed on the quartermaster's store, causing several casualties. At 9am on the 25th a shell landed on the stable where the transport section horses were located. Private Arthur Dinsdale from Ingrow and Private Fred Wardman from Bingley were killed and six other men seriously wounded. Two horses were also badly wounded and had to be destroyed.

At 10.15am the battalion received orders to move 3 miles south-east to the town of Ouderdom. The men boarded buses and arrived at 12.15 p.m. Further orders were received to set up a defensive line with the 1/7th DWR, between the French army's flank at Millekruisse cross roads, extending south along a road named Milky Way to Beaver Corner, a line of some 1,300 yards. The situation was again confusing as it was believed that the enemy had captured Mount Kemmel (also known as Kemmel Hill) to the south, but nothing was known for sure. The battalion began to dig in with A and B Companies at the front, C in support and D in reserve. At 6pm further orders were received to take over a line a few hundred yards west of Milky Way which was being held by the units of the 4th Royal Scots and 8th Black Watch from 26 Brigade. A and B Companies moved to these positions whilst C and D Companies remained in their original positions. At 8.40pm information was received via the Royal Air Force that French troops had been seen on Mount Kemmel, 2 miles to the south. Lieutenant Spencer was detailed to contact the French army HQ at La Clytte, 200 yards to the west, but the French could not confirm the report. The area of Mount Kemmel was in the line of the German advance and was believed to be under their control.

At 3am on 26 April the British 25th Division, assisted by the 1/4th DWR and elements of the French army, launched an attack on Mount Kemmel. The 25th Division successfully advanced towards their objective, but owing to a heavy artillery barrage, the French struggled to gain ground and failed to advance. As a result the British were withdrawn back to their start point. The only positive result was that numerous enemy troops were captured. The remainder of the day passed quietly and barbed wire was placed out overnight. Private Charles Gerald Ingram (19) from Hull was killed and nine men were wounded.

In the early hours of 27 April Second Lieutenant George Swaby, from Market Rasen, was in charge of a resupply party returning to the front line. In the darkness, he inadvertently led the party past the British line in to no man's land. In an attempt to ascertain his location, he and his orderly, Private Harry Stansfield from Keighley, went forward and several shots were heard. Both men were reported missing and, despite patrols being sent to look for them, neither man was found. Private Stansfield was killed that night and Second Lieutenant Swaby was captured and spent the remainder of the war in a German prisoner of war camp. He was eventually repatriated on 18 December 1918.

Private (Jonathan) Clifford Dove. (Aireborough Historical Society)

The German artillery continued to bombard the British lines for the remainder of the day, Serjeant Robert J. Durkin (37) from Beverley (formerly of the Yorkshire Regiment), Corporal Edgar Hird (22) from Bingley, Private Robert Welsh from Huddersfield and Private Stanley Rhodes (30) from Bradford were killed and eight other men were wounded.

The 28th was a quiet day until 7.30pm when the line was heavily bombarded from La Clytte to 4 miles north-east to Ypres. This lasted for two hours but there was no follow up infantry attack. Private Albert Wilson from Bradford, Private Myers Thompson from Barnoldswick, Private Jess Lawson MM (25) from Tosside, near Long Preston and Private (Jonathan) Clifford Dove (24) from Guiseley were killed. Before the war, (Jonathan) Clifford Dove worked as a boot maker and lived at 19 Park Row Guiseley. He enlisted at Skipton after 1915 (as his medal record shows he was not entitled to the 1914-15 star) and as he has no known grave, he is commemorated on panel 83 at the Tyne Cot Memorial.

Panel 83 at Tyne Cot Memorial, Belgium.

On 17 May the *Craven Herald* newspaper reported the death of Private Myers Thompson:

Pte. Myers Thompson Duke of Wellington's Regiment, was killed in action on April 28th, three weeks after returning to France. He was formerly the occupier of Carr House Farm, Barnoldswick, and went abroad in March last year. He returned home in December to undertake ploughing work under the War Agricultural Committee's scheme. He followed this occupation until disabled in February by an accident to his knee, which necessitated a stay of several weeks in hospital at Halifax, and had barely recovered when owing to the German onslaught he was again drafted to the fighting line. A native of Foulridge, Pte. Thompson was 29 years of age, and leaves a wife but no family. One of his brothers is in Salonika (wounded) and another a prisoner in Germany.

War Agricultural Executive Committees were government-backed organisations tasked with increasing agricultural production in each county of the UK during the First World War. German submarines were severely restricting the amount of imported food arriving in the UK, a problem compounded by the fact the Royal Navy was slow to adopt convoy practices. Enlistment in the armed forces and work in munitions factories had depleted the rural labour supply and although the Military Service Act contained a provision that exempted skilled agriculturalists, such as bailiffs, horsemen and tractor mechanics from military service, general labourers under the age of 25 remained unprotected. Exemptions only applied to skilled men who were in their position before 15 August 1916. Even with these regulations in place, there were still not enough men available to sow the crops or bring in the harvest. The Food Production Department, under Regulation 2L of the Defence of the Realm

Private Myers Thompson. (CPGW)

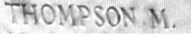

Panel 84 at Tyne Cot Cemetery.

Act (DORA), was granted permission to seize unoccupied land for agricultural use and could negotiate with the military authorities to secure the necessary labour by the temporary release of men from the armed forces. As a ploughman, Myers Thompson appears to have benefited from the provisions of the scheme, albeit on a temporary basis. He has no known grave and is commemorated on panel 84 on the Tyne Cot Memorial.

Before the war, Private Jess Lawson MM from the village of Tosside, 4 miles west of Long Preston, was working as a farmhand on the family farm. He was the cousin of Gunner Sam Lawson (23) of Halton, Lancashire who was serving in the Royal Garrison Artillery when he died of wounds on 26 September 1918.

Private Jess Lawson MM. (CPGW)

On 14 February 1919, the *Craven Herald* newspaper reported the posthumous award of the Military Medal to Private Lawson:

Mr. and Mrs. Wm. Lawson of Crow Trees Farm, Tosside, have received a letter from Lieut. C.H.E. Lowther, stating that their late son, Private Jess Lawson has

been awarded the Military Medal for conspicuous gallantry and devotion to duty. Lieut. Lowther adds:

'He was recommended for this before his death in action, and it is sad to think that he never lived to enjoy the fruits of his good work. I am sure this news will be some little consolation to you in your great grief at the death of your son. You will receive the medal your son would have won, and I know how proud of it you will be, just as 'A' Company will always be proud of your son.' Mr. and Mrs. Lawson have since received the medal.

At 3am on 29 April, the Germans launched a heavy artillery bombardment with high explosive and gas shells on the front and rear lines that lasted until 7am. At that time a mass German infantry attack was launched against the 21st, 25th and 49th Divisions. The line was held and the Germans were caught in a British artillery barrage. The men of the 1/6th DWR fired Lewis guns and rifles into the advancing Germans, stopping the attack, but the bombardment of the rear areas with gas and high explosive shells continued until 10am. The commander of D Company, Captain Barclay Godfrey Buxton MC, was severely wounded in both legs.

The following men were killed on that day:

Corporal Edward Joynes MM from Darnall
Corporal Charles Horner (23) from Halton Gill
Corporal Charles H. Brown (RAMC) from East Ham, London
Private Leonard Gallon from Bradford
Private George Procter from Keighley (born in Scotland)
Private John Butterworth from Skipton
Private Robert Riddell from Beamish, Co Durham
Private Herbert Jackson (19) from Otley.

Before the war, Herbert Jackson was employed as a carter and lived at 14 Craven Terrace, Otley. He was conscripted in February 1917, enlisted at Halifax and went to France in October of that year. He is buried in Lijssenthoek Military Cemetery, between Poperinge and Ypres.

Twenty-seven other men were wounded, including the signals officer, Lieutenant John N.W.A. Procter MC from Rylstone. This battle heralded the collapse of the German Spring Offensive against the British and for the second time in less than three weeks, the men of 147 Brigade had brought the German advance to a standstill and created a new front line. On this day Corporal William Reynolds Armstrong (24) of George Street, Skipton died of wounds at No.10 CCS. He enlisted in September 1914 and is buried in Arneke British Cemetery in France.

At 2.45am on 30 April the French 39th Division launched an attack from their line at La Clytte (Klijte) towards Pompier Farm, assisted by the British 75 Brigade. A track named Kim Road, to the south-east

Corporal W.R. Armstrong. (CPGW)

185

of Pompier Farm was captured by the British, but they had to withdraw as the French troops again failed to advance.

At 7pm orders were received for an attack on the front line just north of Pompier Farm across to Milky Way. The attack would be made by a French division and 7 Brigade. C and Support Companies from the 1/6th DWR were detailed to assist the attack. Zero hour was 8pm which left only an hour to plan, so hurried arrangements had to be made. A British artillery barrage was launched at 7.50pm, and the attack commenced at zero hour. The British objectives were taken, but as the French troops again failed to advance, 7 Brigade, including the two companies from the 1/6th DWR had to withdraw back to the start line. During this attack, the following men were killed:

Serjeant Edwin Stead from Cleckheaton
Corporal Harry Shaw from Huddersfield
Corporal Walter D. Gibson DCM from Skipton
Corporal Walter J. Lewis from Edmonton, London
Private James Tuddenham (21), from Earby, near Barnoldswick (born in Gretna, Scotland)
Private Walter Haigh from Keighley
Private Edgar T. Grisdale from Newcastle
Private Thomas Hackston (29) from Sutton-in-Craven
Private Harry Pickles from Buttershaw. Fifteen other men were wounded.

Pictured during training at Strensall Camp in 1915, twin brothers Thomas and William Hackston are kneeling first and second from the left. Thomas is on the right. (CPGW)

Private J. Tuddenham. Private Thomas
(CPGW)   Hackston. (CPGW)

Private (later Corporal)
W.D. Gibson DCM (CPGW)

On 3 October 1918, Corporal Walter Davis Gibson was posthumously awarded the DCM. His citation in the *London Gazette* reads:

> *For conspicuous gallantry and devotion to duty whilst in charge of patrols. This NCO's patrol attacked a machine gun located in a farmhouse, drove the enemy away, inflicted casualties, obtained identifications, and prevented the line from being harassed by enemy fire. The next two days he took out patrols and brought back highly useful information about the enemy's positions. Throughout he showed a total disregard of danger, and set a splendid example to all.*

He has no known grave and is commemorated on panel 82 to 85 on the Tyne Cot Memorial. He was also the half-brother of Private Frank Myers (19) from Skipton who was serving in the 2nd DWR when he was killed on 30 May 1918.

CASUALTIES: In April 1918, the battalion had 107 men killed, 290 wounded and 34 missing.

May 1918

The first day of May 1918 passed quietly, but German troop movement was seen on the lower slopes of Kemmel Hill. It was suspected they were massing for an attack, so an artillery barrage was ordered that effectively scattered them. One man from the 1/6th DWR was wounded by shrapnel. On this day, Private William Johnson (34) from Yeadon, died of wounds. He was a pre-war 'terrier' and before the war he lived at 4 Booth's Yard, Yeadon. He is buried in Arneke British Cemetery, 40 miles south-east of Calais.

On 2 May the battalion was relieved by the 146th Composite Battalion (made up of the remnants of 146 Infantry Brigade and the 19th Lancashire Fusiliers) and deployed as follows: A Company was placed in support of the 1/4th DWR, B Company was placed in support of the 146th Composite Battalion and C, D and HQ Companies withdrew to Millekruisse. Advance parties from the French 1st and 3rd Battalions of the 80th Regiment arrived to prepare for the relief. One man from the 1/6th DWR was wounded by shrapnel.

Lieutenant John N.W.A. Procter. (CPGW)

On this day Lieutenant John Norman William Atkinson Procter MC (23) of The Manor House, Rylstone, died at No.3 Australian CCS of wounds received during the fighting of 27 April. He is buried in Esquelbecq Military Cemetery, 18 miles south of Dunkirk. He enlisted in November 1914 and was commissioned in the 1/6th DWR. He was the signals officer for the battalion and had been mentioned in despatches and awarded the Military Cross.

The citation for his Military Cross reads:

For gallantry and most consistent devotion to duty as signalling officer throughout the period 26/2/17 – 20/9/17, especially when in the trenches near Hulloch (Hulluch) in June 1917. When the lines to companies were constantly cut by hostile shell and trench mortar fire he laid a new set of lines at great personal risk and maintained communication to companies under very trying and difficult conditions and also, when in trenches near Nieuport in August 1917, he established visual communication to companies and was constantly out working on the line to Brigade, which was often cut by hostile shelling. He maintained this line across the Yser canal to the Nieuport side. It is entirely owing to this officer's energy and diligence since he took over the duties of signaling officer in August 1915, that the battalion signallers have attained their present high standard of efficiency.

On 3 May final orders were received regarding the relief by French forces and the day passed quietly. At 8.30pm, before the relief could take place, a heavy German artillery barrage landed on the front and support lines. The SOS signal was sent up and reports were received that the Germans were attacking but this was found to be a false alarm. During the barrage, Private Thomas Skinner (21) and Private Wilfred Shires, both from Barnoldswick, Private James Willie Whittaker from Skipton and Private

James Fulton from Marsden were all killed. Corporal Ernest Foster from Settle died of wounds the following day. Seven other men were wounded. The battalion was eventually relieved by the French 3rd Battalion of the 80th Regiment on the morning of 4 May and marched 5 miles north to Road Camp at Sint-Jan-ter-Biezen.

Private James Willie Whittaker was the brother of Private Richard Dove Whittaker, who was killed on 28 February 1918.

Private Thomas Skinner enlisted in September 1914 and was previously wounded near the Yser Canal during the gas attack on 19 December 1915.

Private J.W. Whittaker. (CPGW)

Corporal Ernest Foster (29) was a pre-war 'terrier' who worked as a miner at Ingleton Colliery. He was also the cousin of Private Leonard Foster (26) of Long Preston who was serving in the 74th Battalion, Machine Gun Corps when he was killed on 1 November 1918.

Private Wilfred Shires (20) of Lower North Avenue, Barnoldswick was another pre-war 'terrier', who was sent to France in April 1915 when he was 17. His brother, Private Herbert Shires, served in the 2/5th DWR and was killed in action on 27 November 1917. He has no known grave and is commemorated on the Cambrai Memorial at Louveral, France.

Corporal E. Foster. (CPGW)

The actions of 147 Brigade had not gone unnoticed by the BEF command. The Commander-in-Chief, Field Marshal Sir Douglas Haig sent the following message:

> *I desire to express my appreciation of the very valuable and gallant services performed by troops of the 49th (West Riding) Division since the since the entry of the 147th Brigade into the Battle of Armentieres. The courage and determination showed by this division has played no small part in checking the enemy's advance and I wish to convey to General Cameron and all the officers and men under his command my thanks for all they have done.*

Private W. Shires. (CPGW)

The commander of the French 2nd Cavalry Corps, General Robillot, also offered his congratulations:

> *G.O.C. 2nd Cavalry Corps warmly congratulates the brave British troops who have heroically assisted in the defence of the chain of hills and, who [with] admirable resistance, have broken down the enemy's effort and barred the way to Dunkerque. Shelterless, under a bombardment of the heaviest description, surrounded by*

Private T. Skinner. (CPGW)

189

poisonous gasses of various descriptions, stubbornly disputing every foot of ground, they have held their own against repeated attacks by greatly superior numbers and, though at first overwhelmed by weight of numbers, they were obliged to give ground, they have inflicted such heavy losses on the enemy that his forces have been exhausted. Once more the Germans have seen their hopes dashed to the ground. France will remember that!
Robillot.

Major General N.G. Cameron, 49th Divisional commander was clearly proud of what 147 Brigade achieved, but knew that the war was far from over. The Germans were far from defeated and there was a lot more fighting to be done. He wrote:

The reputation which you have won for courage, determination and efficiency during recent operations has its very joyous aspect and is deeply precious to us all. It also has a serious aspect for us. It lays on each of us a responsibility – a personal responsibility for doing what he can to ensure that the next time the division is engaged it will perform an even better service than it has in the past.
We shall shortly, we hope, be filling up with new men. Let every old hand put his shoulder to the wheel in instilling into our new blood the spirit of courage, determination and efficiency which has carried you through your recent trial so successfully.
Never fail to impress on all new hands what the rifle and bayonet can do in the hands of a determined British soldier who knows how to look after and use them.

The GOC of the 34th Division, Major-General C.L. Nicholson, also communicated his thanks:

The G.O.C. 34th Division wishes to place on record his great appreciation of the services rendered by 147 Brigade during the period it has been attached to the division under my command. The action of one battalion south of the River Lys on the 10th April, the skilful rearguard fighting under cover of which the division withdrew from the Nieppe position, the stubborn defence of the right of the division at Steam Mill and the complete defeat of an entire German regiment on the 16th April are exploits of which the whole brigade may well be proud of. Throughout the period, the steadiness, gallantry and endurance of all ranks has been worthy of the highest traditions of the British infantry and the GOC of the 34th Division is proud to have such troops under his command.

The GOC of 147 Brigade, Brigadier General L.G. Lewis, wrote:

The Brigadier-General commanding wishes to add his personal thanks to all ranks for their splendid work during the past ten days. The Brigade can congratulate itself on not having evacuated ground without orders from a superior authority and which was rendered necessary by events outside the brigade area. All ranks can be proud that they have shown that with rifle and bayonet the Bosche can be defeated. The spirit shown by all units throughout was admirable: each battalion vying with one another to prove its superiority. Battalion esprit de corps is everything, nothing else matters.

Private P. Coulson. (CPGW)

On 4 May Private Preston Coulson (26) died of wounds at No.3 (Australian) CCS at Esquelbecq. Born in Longtown, near Carlisle, he was working as a porter for the Midland Railway Co. at Ingleton. He was a pre-war 'terrier' who had been wounded twice.

Corporal Percy Barton (24) also died of wounds at No.10 CCS. Before the war he was a grocery assistant at the Skipton Co-operative Society and enlisted in September 1914. He was posted to France in April 1915 and trained as a Lewis gunner. He must have shown a great deal of aptitude with the weapon as he spent time as an instructor at the gunnery training school in France as an acting serjeant. In January 1919, he was posthumously awarded the Military Medal, which was presented to his parents. The citation reads:

Corporal P. Barton.(CPGW)

He, along with Private Maude, were the only two left of the platoon Lewis gun team on the night of 11th and 12th April 1918, at Nieppe. On the withdrawal of their company to a new position, they remained behind and gave covering fire until the whole company had safely withdrawn. They have repeatedly used their Lewis gun with good effect during the recent fighting, often at great personal risk, and have gained the admiration of their platoon.

Private (later Lance Corporal) George Maude from Guiseley was also awarded the Military Medal for this action, but just over six months later he was killed in action.

At Road Camp the battalion was accommodated in Nissan huts but some of the older hands would have recognised the area. Their current accommodation was located about 400 yards from a wooded area where the battalion was billeted in tents during July 1915. Sunday 5 May was spent cleaning kit and re-equipping and on the 6th Corporal Albert Midgley of D Company was awarded the French *Croix de Guerre*. Unfortunately, Corporal (later promoted to Serjeant) Midgley would not live to see the Armistice.

On 7 and 8 May skill at arms and Lewis gun training was carried out and for the next five days, the routine was training, baths and parades.

On 14 May the battalion boarded motor buses and were transported 30 miles west to the village of Saint-Martin-au-Laërt, near Saint-Omer. The men then marched along the Cormette Road to a tented camp. The battalion was to spend the next seven days on the rifle and Lewis gun range with the added benefit of fine weather. On 15 May Lance Serjeant John Gregson (28), born in Wellington, Shropshire, died of wounds at Lichfield Hospital.

Serjeant John Gregson. (CPGW)

On 22 May the men carried out training near the camp and at 5.15pm, they marched 3 miles north to new camps in the village of Proven. HQ and A Companies were billeted in Peterboro Camp, and B, C and D Companies were billeted at Pekin Camp. The weather was very hot, hence the late departure in the cool of the evening. For the next four days, the battalion provided working parties to improve the Poperinge to Elverdinghe light railway and Poperinge to Vlamertinge road. On the afternoon of 26 May the battalion marched back to Road Camp at Sint-Jans-Biezen. The morning of the 27th was spent cleaning uniforms, with physical exercise and close order drill in the afternoon. For the next two days, training and shooting practice resumed, although occasionally training was cancelled due to German shells falling on the training area.

A demonstration of the message carrying rocket or MCR was given by the brigade signal officer. The MCR was invented by Lieutenant William H.G. Geake, an engineer in the Australian army. He was appointed to the Board of Inventions and devised the MCR in 1917. It was made of steel, 3 feet in length, with a range of up to $1^1/2$ miles. It was a simple idea which eventually proved ineffective in the confusion of battle. In theory, messages could be quickly sent from the front to rear areas. It included a propellant, a whistle at the tip and a two-piece tube that carried a smoke and flare composition to make it easier to find, and a receptacle for carrying messages.

Thursday 30 May was devoted to a brigade sports competition and the prizes were presented by the GOC II Corps, Lieutenant General Sir Claude William Jacob.

On 31 May training for the Lewis gunners, scouts and signallers continued, whilst the remainder of the men conducted bayonet fighting, physical exercise and drill near the camp.

The strength of the battalion on 31 May 1918 was 43 officers and 781 men. A draft of 199 men had arrived, and 46 returned from hospital.

CASUALTIES: In May 1918, the battalion had 6 men killed and 8 wounded.

Chapter 16

Return to Ypres

June 1918

The morning of 1 June 1918 was spent training and an advance party of men comprising the CO, adjutant, signal officer and one officer per company proceeded by lorry to Ypres to reconnoitre the trenches to the east of the town, astride the Menin Road near Hellfire Corner as the battalion was to relieve the 12th East Surrey Regiment of 122 Brigade, 41st Division. The next day was very hot and a church parade was held. A draft of seventy-seven men arrived during the morning, most of whom were A4 classification, that is aged between 18½ to 19.

On 3 June the early part of the day was spent testing the Lewis guns and rifles on the range and inspecting SBRs. At 4.30pm the battalion marched a mile north to the railway sidings at Proven and boarded the light railway. They then travelled 10 miles east to Vlamertinge Chateau where they were met by the guides from the 12th East Surrey Regiment. They were guided towards Ypres via Rome Farm, Salvation Corner, Dead End, Ramparts and the trenches outside the Menin Gate. The relief must have been observed by the Germans because as the men moved through Ypres, a heavy mixed barrage of mustard and phosgene gas shells landed and SBRs had to be worn. Two men were wounded during the relief, which was completed at 1.30am on 4 June. The disposition of the companies was as follows: D Company was in the front line, A was in support, C was at the school (Ecole) and B at the Ypres ramparts. The rest of the day passed quietly with a few gas shells landing in Ypres in the evening.

Both the divisional and brigade GOCs visited the front line during the night and one man from the battalion was wounded. The 5th was another hot sunny day which again passed quietly apart from a few gas shells fired into Ypres. On the 6th, a party of three officers, Lieutenants F.A. Sam, S.W. Dickens and Harris, with five NCOs from the American 129th Infantry Regiment, were attached to the battalion for instruction and one man was wounded by mustard gas. The United States Congress had declared war on Germany on 6 April 1917 and Austria-Hungary on 7 December.

Friday 7 June was another quiet day with only sporadic German machine-gun fire at night. On the 8th the companies were rotated. A Company moved to the Ypres Ramparts, C moved to the front line on the Menin Road, D moved to the Ecole defences and B went in support. There was a little sneezing gas about, otherwise it was quiet. (Sneezing gas or Diphenylchloroarsine was intended to penetrate the SBR filter, causing respiratory irritation which would cause the wearer to remove the mask.)

The next day was quiet with a few shells landing on the school (Ecole) and Ypres during which one man was wounded in the back and leg by shrapnel. That night, the British artillery launched a barrage against the German support lines. The weather changed on the 10th as rain began to fall and continued most of the day. The American officers and NCOs were replaced by a new batch from the same 199th Infantry Regiment. A patrol was sent out from C Company along the Menin Road (Meenseweg) towards Hellfire Corner led by Lieutenant Huffam. They encountered a large enemy patrol and an intense fire fight took place during which three men were wounded and one reported missing. On 11 June several men fell ill with flu-type symptoms and twelve had to be hospitalised. A patrol was sent out to look for the missing man from the previous day, but no trace of him could be found. The 12th was a quiet day apart from a few shells into Ypres in the morning. The position in the school (Ecole) was bombarded and 150 shells landed near an observation post but no casualties were reported.

The 13th was a relatively quiet day, but in the early hours of the 14th the Germans holding the line to the right of the battalion at Zillebeke Lake sent up the SOS signal. French troops had launched an attack and captured the area but a German counter-attack pushed the French back to their original position. The American troops rotated and two officers and eighteen men from the 119th and 120th Regiments arrived for instruction. The next day passed quietly; patrols were sent out as usual and German aircraft were active. On 16 June information reached the battalion via the intelligence branch, that the Germans were planning a mass attack on the following morning. At midnight, the men climbed out of the front line trenches and crawled into no man's land and waited for the attack to commence. This tactic was used to avoid the expected bombardment of the front line but the anticipated attack never materialised and the men returned to their trenches. The rest of the day passed off quietly, but more men began to suffer with flu symptoms.

The 18th was quiet and two more American officers and some NCOs arrived for instruction. The next day was also quiet but the 1/4th DWR to the right of the 1/6th DWR conducted a successful trench raid and captured eleven prisoners. On the morning of 20 June two men were wounded by shrapnel as well as an NCO from the American forces.

In the late evening of the 20th the battalion was relieved by the 1/4th KOYLI of 148 Brigade. Rain fell all night and the relief was completed in the early hours of 21 June. The men then marched 6 miles west via the Menin gate, Salvation Corner and Rome Farm track to Orilla Camp near Vlamertinge Chateau. The camp was reached at dawn and the rest of the day was spent cleaning kit, bathing and resting. At 5.30am on the 22nd a party of 415 men was provided to work on the Vlamertinge to Elverdinghe light railway. The men worked for six hours and were back in camp by midday. A working party was provided for the railway on 23 June and the remainder of the battalion spent the day constructing barbed wire defences around Vlamertinge Chateau.

A list of honours and awards was also received for gallantry in the field between 10 May and 3 April 1918. Lieutenant Colonel Bateman received a bar to his

Distinguished Service Order and other awards included three Military Crosses, six Distinguished Conduct Medals, a bar to the Military Medal, twenty-seven Military Medals, one Meritorious Service Medal and three Mentions in Despatches.

On 24 June work continued on the Chateau defences and the CO addressed the officers and NCOs. The next day there was shooting practice on a 30-yard range and the SBRs were inspected. A lecture was given by the divisional gas officer on the effects of mustard gas. Training continued on the 26th and 27th and the men practised counter-attacking from the trenches, but the expected relief by 146 Brigade on the 28th was postponed for twenty-four hours. Instead the men provided working parties to improve the chateau defences. The morning of 29 June was spent inspecting rifles, SBRs and preparing to return to the front line.

At 10pm the battalion departed Orilla Camp and proceeded to the Ypres area, where they were to be the reserve for 147 Brigade, and proceeded to relieve the 1/6th West Yorkshire Regiment in Ypres. The relief was completed in the early hours of the 30th. A Company was in the Ypres defence area near the Menin Gate, D was in the Kaaie defences at the northern edge of the town, C was in support at the western edge of the town near Salvation Corner and B took up a position in reserve at nearby Suicide Corner. During the relief, Lance Corporal Francis Golden (22) from Bingley was killed by a shell and two other men were wounded. Lance Corporal Golden was a former Keighley Boys Grammar School pupil and enlisted in October 1914. Before the war he worked in an office at the wool mill of E.H. Gates. He is buried at Gwalia Cemetery, 8 miles west of Ypres.

Lance Corporal F. Golden's original grave marker. (Keighley News)

The strength of the battalion on 30 June 1918 was 40 officers and 694 men.

CASUALTIES: In June 1918, 1 man was killed, 8 wounded and 1 missing.

July 1918

Monday, 1 July passed quietly and work was carried out improving the defences in the Kaaie area, including constructing barbed wire entanglements. The 2nd was a hot day that was spent salvaging equipment and stores, as well as improving the Kaaie defences during which one man was wounded by shrapnel. The 3rd was another hot day and B Company relocated from Suicide Corner to an old gun position near Salvation Corner. The fine weather continued and the 4th, 5th and 6th were spent working on the defences of Kaaie sector. On 7 July the battalion relieved the 1/7th

The Menin Gate in 2016. Carved on its walls are the names of 54,395 men of the British and Dominion forces whose mortal remains have never been identified or found.

DWR on the front line at Potijze. The relief started at 10pm and was completed at midnight. This was the second visit by the battalion to the Potijze area and those men who were serving in the battalion on 6 December 1917 would probably be familiar with the area. The battalion front extended from Potijze Chateau in the north to a position due south for one mile, with the Belgian Army holding the line to the north of the chateau.

The Germans shelled the line on 8 July, with battalion HQ taking a few hits, but no casualties were caused. American troops from the 118th Infantry Regiment arrived for instruction in the trenches and on the 9th a reconnaissance patrol comprising Lieutenant Lowther and seven men proceeded to Mill Cot in no man's land to observe the German trenches near Crump Farm. A similar patrol was also sent out to observe the German defences on Cambridge Road. The object of these patrols was to gather intelligence that was to be used in planning trench raids. The CO of the battalion had always held the opinion that the control of no man's land was important to keep the Germans fearful of attack, especially at night, to disrupt German attempts at constructing wire defences and gave the men familiarity with the ground in front of the line and which prevented them from becoming complaisant. The rest of the day passed quietly except for a few shells on battalion HQ. More patrols were sent out on the 10th but, apart from heavy

The Potijze front showing the Chateau, Mill Cot and Cambridge Road.

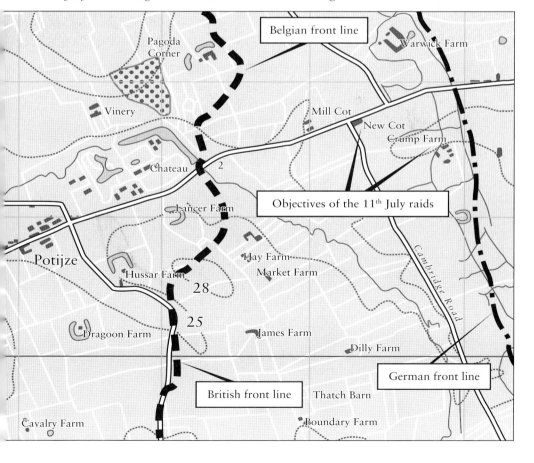

thunderstorms, the day passed quietly. One man was also wounded by machine-gun fire.

At 1.45am.on 11 July Lieutenant C.H. Lowther and Second Lieutenant H. Farrar from A Company led a trench raid against two German posts located between New Cot and Crump Farm. Each raiding party consisted of an officer, two NCOs and nine men. Both patrols moved off heading 600 yards east into no man's land and by 4.45am they were in position about 50 yards from the German trenches. By this time it was light, and at 5.05am Lieutenant Lowther gave the signal for both patrols to rush the enemy positions. The Germans were taken by complete surprise with only one man found to be awake when they entered the trench who, on seeing the patrol, ran off and hid in a nearby dug-out. Lieutenant Lowther's patrol found the Germans hiding in a sandbagged Nissan hut and a dug-out. The men in the Nissan hut refused to surrender, so a grenade was thrown at the back of the hut which successfully encouraged them. Second Lieutenant Farrar's patrol found six Germans in a dug-out shelter who also refused to surrender. They could not be persuaded, so hand grenades were thrown in and they were all killed. Eighty rifles and pistols were discovered which were either destroyed or captured.

At 5.50am both raiding parties then withdrew the 600 yards back to the British lines with four prisoners. No casualties were sustained and strangely, no hostile fire, which was remarkable as the Germans held the high ground and had excellent observation from Westhoek Ridge. The four prisoners belonged to the 11th Company, 3rd Battalion of the 33rd Landwehr Regiment which included two serjeants and a platoon commander. They appeared to be older men and gave valuable information when interrogated.

The men of the raiding parties were wet through so they were taken to battalion HQ where their uniforms were dried and each man had a bath. It was decided to exploit the success of the raids by re-occupying the two posts attacked earlier in the day. At 8.15pm two further patrols from D Company moved out from the British lines and headed across no man's land. One patrol was led by Second Lieutenant Reginald Oughton with thirteen men, the other by Company Serjeant Major Wiseman with eleven men. The party led by Second Lieutenant Oughton occupied the first post without opposition but it was evident the Germans had been back as the dead had been removed. They remained in the post until 11pm as it appeared the Germans had noticed their presence as machine-gun bullets began to land around the post.

The other patrol, under the command of Company Serjeant Major Wiseman, occupied the second post at 9.45pm, also without opposition. At 10.15pm, a patrol of twenty Germans was seen approaching the post and allowed to get within 15 yards when they were challenged and ordered to surrender. Several of the men put their hands up, but the officer in charge drew his pistol and was immediately shot dead by Company Serjeant Major Wiseman. Several of the Germans at the rear of the patrol threw stick grenades so the British patrol opened fire with rifle and Lewis guns. The Germans fled, but only two were seen to make good their escape. Company Serjeant Major Wiseman and his patrol stayed in the post until 11pm, when they withdrew as the enemy were seen to be trying to outflank the post.

Private Allen Stocks from Oldham was severely wounded by a machine-gun bullet in the stomach and died in the British line. One other man was lightly wounded. Company Serjeant Major Wiseman was awarded the DCM for his exceptional leadership during the patrol.

Heavy showers fell on the morning of 12 July. The prisoners captured the previous day had given details of the layout of the German lines opposite including the locations of machine guns, so later that evening, a Stokes mortar barrage was launched on the identified areas. Overnight, the British artillery kept up a constant bombardment of the German lines, with only token German response. The 13th was a quiet day, but on the morning of the 14th, a heavy British bombardment took place to the south of the battalion. This was for an attack by the British 6th Division on the German line at Ridge Wood. Probably because of this attack, the German artillery was active in the battalion's sector and two men were wounded. At midnight and in the early hours of 15 July the British artillery fired a barrage at the German support lines opposite the battalion as a troop relief was suspected to be taking place. In the late evening of the 15th the battalion was relieved by the 1/5th York and Lancaster Regiment of 148 Brigade, which was completed in the early hours of 16th. The men then marched, via

The front line in the Zillebeke sector that the battalion held in July 1918.

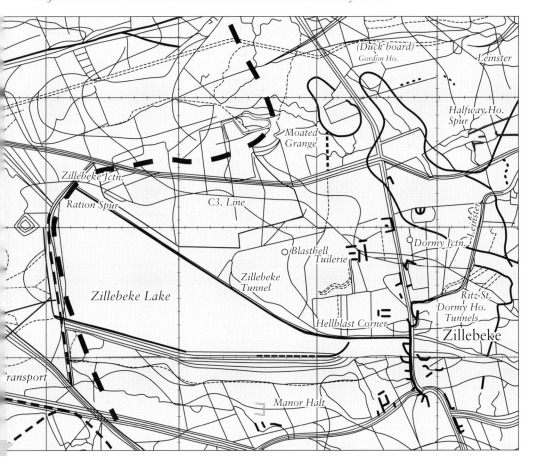

Rome Farm track, to Orilla Camp at Vlamertinge Chateau and occupied the same billets as before.

Two companies from the American 117th Infantry Regiment of the 30th Division were attached to the battalion. Working parties were provided for the next four days. On the night of 18 July, a large German air raid took place near the Chateau, but fortunately no bombs fell in the camp.

The 21st and 22nd were spent training, but on the 23rd preparations were made to return to the front line. At 10pm the battalion moved to the Zillebeke Lake sector, south-east of Ypres and relieved the 1/7th West Yorks. In the early hours of 24 July, as the relief was in progress, gas was successfully discharged along the whole brigade front towards the German lines. The relief was completed at 1.15am and Americans from A Company, 2nd Battalion of the 117th Regiment was attached to the battalion.

The battalion held the line from the railway on the southern side of Zillebeke Lake, round the west side of the lake, across to the Moated Grange and ended just above the 'Y' shaped junction at Pioneer Track, just below Hellfire Corner. A, B and C Companies were in the front line, with D in support. Rations and ammunition were delivered to Lille Gate at Ypres for collection. Thursday 25 July passed quietly, but in the evening a heavy German artillery bombardment landed in the centre of the line on B and D Companies. Private William R. Parker from Keighley, Private Arthur Smith and Private John O. Pearson, both from Bradford were killed by shell fire. Eight other men were wounded.

The 26th passed quietly but heavy rain fell in the evening and a few large calibre shells landed near to battalion HQ at the Lille Gate. In the late evening, H Company of the American 2nd Battalion, 117th Regiment relieved B Company in the front line and two American soldiers were wounded by machine-gun fire.

The wet weather on 27 July continued and the American companies rotated. On the 28th patrols were sent out to gather intelligence on the German positions to the north and south of Zillebeke Lake. All the patrols encountered enemy posts which were engaged with hand grenades. Identification of the German unit at Rifle Farm near Hellfire Corner showed it to be the 1st Landwehr Division, which was being relieved by the 6th Cavalry Division. This intelligence was confirmed by prisoners captured by the Belgian Army. German aircraft were active during the 28th July and their artillery bombarded the area of Lille Gate with about fifty large calibre high explosive shells and that night, a barrage of sneezing gas shells landed.

The weather on 30 July had improved and the German artillery fired shrapnel shells after dark. That evening the battalion was relieved by the American 2nd Battalion, 117th Infantry Regiment, 59 Brigade of the 30th Division. Several officers from the 1/6th DWR remained with the American unit for forty-eight hours in an advisory capacity. Overnight into the 31st July, the rest of the battalion moved to the south-west of Ypres to a position in the support line.

The strength of the battalion on 31 July 1918 was 41 officers and 848 men.

CASUALTIES: During July 4 were men killed and 11 wounded.

August 1918

The first day of August was a quiet day with fine weather. In the late evening, the battalion moved into the support line and relieved the 1/4th DWR. The relief was completed in the early hours of 2 August. The companies were positioned as follows: Battalion HQ was at Bobstay Castle, D Company was between Dolls House and Lille Gate, B was near the Kruisstraat/Ypres-Comines canal, with A and C astride the Ypres to Vlamertinge Road. The 3rd was a wet day, but working parties were provided to reinforce the support line trenches. Rain fell again on the afternoon of the 4th and a party of fourteen men was sent 20 miles west to the town of Tatinghem in France for a parade and church service to commemorate the fourth anniversary of the start of the war. Working parties were provided on the 5th, but on the 6th, one officer and sixteen men travelled 11 miles west to the Chateau La Lovie, a mile north of Poperinge, for the visit of HM King George V to the 49th Division. The men attended as representatives of the battalion and had the honour of lining the main entrance driveway to the chateau as the king drove past. If nothing else, this was a nice break from the line for the lucky few.

The 7th was a hot, sunny day but back at the front the Germans shelled D Company's position in the afternoon and two men were wounded. On 8 August the battalion was relieved by the 1/4th York and Lancaster Regiment and moved back to Orillia Camp near Vlamertinge Chateau. The next day was spent cleaning kit and bathing. A few shells fell in the camp overnight but no injuries were caused. On the 10th training was carried out and in the afternoon the battalion was reorganized. The strength of the companies was increased to four platoons instead of three as several new drafts had recently arrived. The 11th was another fine day and practice in ground support took place with aircraft from No.7 Squadron of the RAF. The morning of 12 August was spent conducting skill at arms and in the afternoon, the area to the west of the Chateau was reconnoitred for trench construction. On the 13th at 4.30am working parties from all the companies marched from camp to an area between Machine Gun Siding on the light railway and Plank Road to construct a new set of defences called the Brielen Line. Each company had a task of digging 175 yards of trench, including 'A' framing, revetting and sandbagging the same. An 'A' frame, so called as it resembles an inverted letter A, is a wooden construction which runs along the length of the trench. It provided drainage and a platform to walk on. Revetting is wooden planks or corrugated metal sheets fastened to the side walls of the trench to prevent collapse.

On 14 August work continued on the Brielen Line and by 11am A and C Companies had completed their task. B Company finished at 11.30am and D shortly afterwards. The whole task should have taken three days but was completed by midday of the second day. As a reward for finishing the task early, the men were given the next day off, with only a rifle inspection and a visit to the baths. The 16th was a hot, sunny day and was spent in preparing to return to the front. At 7.45pm that evening, the battalion relieved the 1/5th West Yorkshire Regiment in the front line to the east of Ypres between Cork Cot and the British/Belgian line at Potijze. The 17th was a wet day with steady rain falling in the afternoon and evening.

Example of an 'A' framed, revetted and sandbagged trench at the Zonnebeke Museum near Ypres.

On 18 August at 8am three escaped Italian prisoners of war approached the British trenches. After they were safely recovered, the men were debriefed and stated they had been on the run for seven days. One of them was wounded so they were provided with medical care, given a hot meal and sent to the rear for a full intelligence debrief. Although a member of the Triple-Alliance with Germany and Austria-Hungary, Italy declined to enter the war. The alliance with those two empires dated back to 1882 and had been renewed periodically. Essentially, it was a secret pact to promise mutual support if the other was attacked by another power. Despite this, in the years leading up to the Great War, Italy had improved its diplomatic relations with Great Britain and France and, on 3 May 1915, Italy officially revoked the Triple Alliance. On 23 May Italy declared war on the empire of Austria-Hungary followed by declarations of war against the Ottoman Empire on 21 August 1915, Bulgaria on 19 October 1915 and the German Empire on 28 August 1916. Italian troops fought mostly against Austro-Hungarian troops along the northern alpine border but also saw action in the Balkans during the defence of Albania, the Salonika Front in Greece, the Palestine Campaign and the Western Front, most noticeably during the Second Battle of the Marne in July and August 1918.

The 19th was a quiet day and advance parties from the 5th King's Own Scottish

Border Regiment (KOSB) arrived to prepare for a relief. The 20th was another quiet day and the battalion was relieved by 5th KOSB. The battalion then marched 6 miles east to Border Camp, a mile north-east of Vlamertinge Chateau, arriving in the early hours of the 21st. There was fine weather for the rest of the day which was spent cleaning equipment and taking baths. The 22nd was a very hot day and preparations were made for an expected move. The battalion transport, with the exception of the field kitchens and water cart, moved off at 8am and headed west to the area of the French village of Louches, a distance of some 30 miles.

On 23 August at 6.15am the battalion departed Border Camp and marched to a light railway and boarded trains. They were joined by the 1/4th DWR and 147 Brigade HQ. At 7pm they arrived at the railhead in Audruicq and marched 5 miles south-east to Louches where the men were settled in the billets by 10pm and tea was served. The field kitchens and water cart arrived at 11pm and the remainder of the battalion transport arrived the next day, which was spent rearranging the camp and cleaning kit and equipment.

Sunday 25 August was another hot day and the only parade was a church service held in the morning. The 26th started with heavy rain and platoon training was held in the morning but at 11am, a warning order was received to prepare for a move at short notice, so all equipment and baggage was packed and the men placed on standby. At 4.30pm orders were received for the battalion transport to immediately move 14 miles south-west to the village of Helfaut. At 5.30pm orders were received for the battalion to entrain the next morning at the Nortkerque railhead, 5 miles to the north-east, and proceed to Helfaut. However, at 6.45 am on the 27th the battalion arrived at the railhead, only to find the train delayed. Tents were pitched and tea was brewed. It appears that by this stage of the war the battalion was experienced in travelling on military trains and the expectation was that they never ran on time and contingency arrangements seem to have been well in hand. The train eventually arrived at 1pm, the men boarded and departed an hour later. They travelled 45 miles south to the railhead at Wavrans-sur-Ternoise, arriving at 11pm. They then marched a mile to billets in the village of Pierremont, near Saint-Pol-sur-Ternoise. The 28th and 29th were spent settling in and improving the billets.

The next day the battalion watched a demonstration of an infantry attack with tank support. C Company from the 1/6th DWR, one company each from the 1/4th and 1/7th DWR and one from the 147th Trench Mortar Battalion, took part as the attacking troops. A little rain fell on the morning of the 31st but cleared up after breakfast. Training was carried out near the billets and the CO inspected A Company, but this was cut short as orders were received for the entire 49th Division to be prepared to move at short notice. Surplus stores were taken to a storage area and the men put on standby. Late in the day a message was received that the division would not move until the following day. The strength of the battalion on 31 August 1918 was 43 officers and 949 men.

CASUALTIES: During August 1918, the battalion had 2 men wounded.

Chapter 17

Naves and Famars

September 1918

At 1.45pm on 1 September 1918, orders were received for 147 Brigade to board motor buses and move 20 miles east to the area of Estrée-Cauchy, 10 miles north-west of Arras. They arrived at 11.30pm and were allocated billets. On the 2nd several extra Lewis guns were distributed to the companies and in the afternoon, a battalion parade was held for the outgoing Brigade GOC, Brigadier General Lewes, who was leaving to take up a command in England. He expressed his regrets at leaving and was given three hearty cheers by the men. He was replaced by Brigadier General Hubert H.S. Morant DSO, formerly of the Durham Light Infantry.

The next eleven days were spent training, including shooting and tactical exercises as well as aircraft and tank close support attacks. Rifle grenade practice was also conducted and the statutory church parades were held. On the afternoon of 13 September the battalion departed Estrée-Cauchy and marched 10 miles south-west to Duff Camp, near the village of Roclincourt, a mile north of Arras. They arrived in the early evening and were billeted in Nissan huts with tea and a hot meal provided on arrival. Training continued on the 14th, including a lecture from a tank corps officer. The next day church parade was held and the CO, adjutant and company commanders reconnoitred the front line positions. The 16th was spent on a training exercise involving tanks and on the 17th and 18th the men were given instruction on how to use German heavy and light machine guns, including live firing of the weapons.

Tactical training and attack exercises continued, but just because the men were well behind the front line, it was not a guarantee of safety. On 22 September, whilst conducting an exercise, a German shell landed and killed Private John Willie Firth from Baildon and Private Edgar C. White from Bedminster, Gloucestershire (formerly ASC). Neither man has a known grave and they are commemorated on panel 6 of the Vis-en-Artois Memorial, 8 miles south-east of Arras. Private Robert George Whitehead (22) from Leicester (formerly ASC) died of wounds seven days later and two other men were wounded.

On 23 September the battalion marched 3 miles south to the village of Tilloy-les-Mofflaines, a mile south-west of Arras. The billets here consisted of tents and training continued until the end of the month.

The strength of the battalion on 30 September 1918 was 42 officers and 1,038 men.

CASUALTIES: During September the battalion had 3 men killed and 2 wounded.

October 1918

The first week of October 1918 was spent training, with brigade practice attacks around Blangy and Athies, suburbs to the east of Arras. On 6 October at 5.30pm the men boarded motor buses and moved 14 miles south-east to the village of Buissy where they were accommodated in tents on a part of the old German front line called The Switch. On the 7th the weather was quite warm for the time of year and a large amount of salvage was collected to improve the camp area. The next day was also fine and the CO reconnoitred the line near Blécourt, a mile north of Cambrai, but on the 9th information was received that Cambrai had been captured by the 2nd and 3rd Canadian Divisions and so new orders were received to march 3 miles south-east to the village of Sailly-lez-Cambrai where the men spent an uncomfortable night in the open. On 10 October, the men marched 6 miles west to Escaudoeuvres where they took up a position in the grounds of a chateau. Tea and a hot meal was served and full-scale ammunition was issued. This was usually 150 rounds of .303 rifle ammunition in the equipment pouches, a cloth bandolier containing 100 extra rounds per man and as many hand and rifle grenades that could be carried.

The plan was for the 49th Division to attack the German lines near the village of Naves then head north towards Valenciennes to cut off the German forces in the town

The position by the railway in Naves is to the left and the sunken road to the right.

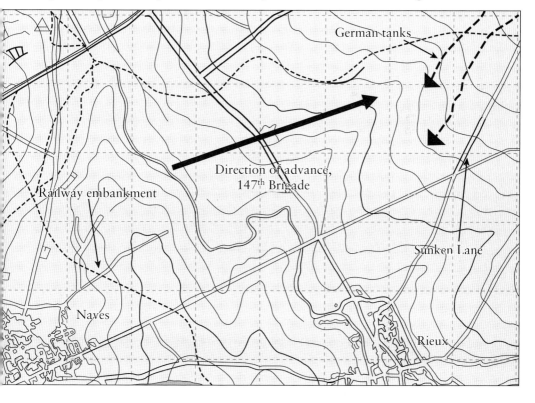

of Douai. Here 146 Brigade (West Yorkshire Regiment) would attack on the left and 147 Brigade on the right. The 1/4th and 1/5th DWR would lead the attack for 147 Brigade with the 1/6th in support. The Germans held an area of high ground to the north of Roeux and on the night of 10 October, the Canadian 2nd Division would attack the German positions and, if successful, 147 Brigade would advance through the Canadian position. The 49th Division's commander ordered that the high ground must be taken at all costs.

At 12.15am on 11 October the battalion moved off and marched a mile east to the village of Naves, which had been the target of a heavy German mustard gas attack. The men took up a position on the line of the railway to the east of the village and waited for orders whilst under constant German artillery fire. The Canadian night attack was unsuccessful, so 147 Brigade was ordered to attack. An artillery barrage was to commence at 8.30am on the 11th and which was to last for half an hour. At 9am the attack would commence with the help of a creeping barrage, that is an artillery barrage which would creep or move in front of the attacking troops at a rate of 100 yards every three minutes.

The attack was launched at zero hour with the Canadian 2nd Division to the left, the 49th Division in the centre and the 24th Division to the right. The 49th Division's plan of attack was to have 147 and 146 Brigade at the front, with 148 Brigade in reserve. The 1/6th DWR was positioned as the reserve of 147 Brigade. Initially the attack was a success, the high ground was taken and about 200 prisoners captured. The battalion followed up at the rear of the attack and reached a sunken lane to the north-east of Roeux.

At 10.15am the enemy launched a strong counter-attack from the village of Avesnes-le-Sec, about a mile to the north-east. The Germans attacked with infantry and eight AV7 tanks causing the leading British troops to withdraw to the line of the sunken lane that the 1/6th DWR were holding. Four of the German tanks headed in the direction of the sunken lane so Lieutenant Hopwood, Corporal Ames and the D Company Lewis gunners opened up with concentrated fire on the leading tank. The battalion held its ground with the other mixed units as the lead tank began to withdraw. The following tank was engaged in a similar manner until all the tanks either retreated or were disabled. The men fired at the vision openings of the tank, and a strike from a .303 round on the armour plate would cause metal splinters to fly off inside the vehicle. The Lewis gun was an excellent infantry weapon and had a rate of fire of 500 – 600 rounds per minute. Later in the day, British guns were manhandled up to the sunken lane and the barrels lowered so that they could directly engage the German tanks should they return.

For his conspicuous gallantry and devotion to duty during the action, Serjeant E. Rosenthal from Bingley was awarded the DCM His citation reads:

Whilst leading a platoon during the counter-attack, he kept the platoon firing on the advancing enemy in spite of heavy shelling and machine gun fire, finally withdrawing his men in good order.

The sunken lane on the D114 Naves to Villers-en-Cauchies road, scene of heavy fighting on 11 October 1918.

The view further up the sunken lane.

Serjeant Timothy Green from Keighley was also awarded the DCM. His citation reads:

> *For conspicuous gallantry and devotion to duty on the 11th October whilst in command of a platoon and later a company. Throughout the action, he displayed splendid spirit when the enemy counter-attacked with tanks when his fine courage and powers of leadership steadied his men and was instrumental in causing the enemy severe casualties.*

The area at the top of the sunken lane over which the German tanks attacked.

The only surviving, original German AV7 tank at the Queensland Museum, Brisbane, Australia. (Australian War Memorial)

Abandoned German AV7 tank north of Roeux, 11 October 1918.

Another DCM was awarded to Serjeant G.E. Calvert from Cullingworth. His citation reads:

For conspicuous gallantry and devotion to duty near Naves on the 11ᵗʰ October 1918. Owing to officer casualties, his responsibilities as acting Company Serjeant Major were heavy, but he displayed fine powers of leadership and great courage in the performance of his duties.

The high ground was secured and that evening the battalion held the line in the sunken road. The battalion paid a heavy price for their stand on 11 October. The following men were killed:

Captain Temple Coulthurst (B Company commander) from Ealing, London
Second Lieutenant Reginald Oughton and Second Lieutenant Robert Rycroft from Laisterdyke, Bradford.
Company Serjeant Major Owen McDermott DCM, *Croix de Guerre* from Skipton
Serjeant George E. Godwin MM from Skipton
Serjeant Albert Midgley from Keighley
Corporal James W. Scarff MM from Halifax
Corporal Harry Crossley from Earby
Lance Corporal Harry Stanley from Smethwick, Warwick
Lance Corporal Herbert E. Haw from Kirkburton
Lance Corporal James E. Simpson from Burnley (formerly RAMC
Lance Corporal Luther Hartley from Holmfirth.
Private Ernest H. Jackson from Gateshead (formerly West Yorks Regiment)
Private George W. Fogg from Shoreditch, London
Private Harold Waddington from Keighley
Private Bertie Tyler from Hatfield, Herts (formerly Suffolk Regiment)
Private George Carter from Nottingham (formerly Leicester Regiment)
Private Arthur C. Jones from South Emsall
Private Albert E. Jones from Manchester
Private George E.T. Carpenter from Fulham
Private Arthur Matthews from Huddersfield
Private John Mummery from North Shields
Private Arthur W. Pegg from Shardlow, Derby
Private Sam Swallow from Halifax
Private John T. Walker from Durham (formerly DLI)
Private Henry Whitehouse from Willenhall, Staffs
Private Bert Bailey from Cloddian, Wales (formerly Royal Welsh Fusiliers)
Private Willie Smith from Skipton
Private William Rawling from Silsden.

Seventy-four other men were wounded by gas and two men were missing.

Company Serjeant Major O. McDermott DCM. (CPGW)

Serjeant G.E. Godwin MM. (CPGW)

Corporal H. Crossley. (CPGW)

Private W. Smith. (CPGW)

Company Serjeant Major Owen McDermott DCM (29) of Hill Street, Skipton was a pre-war 'terrier' who had been fighting in France since April 1915. Before the war he was working as a labourer at Belle Vue Mill in the town. He had been awarded the French *Croix de Guerre* for gallantry in the field.

Serjeant George E. Godwin MM (29), also from Hill Street, Skipton was also a pre-war 'terrier' who worked for the Leeds and Liverpool Canal Co. He had 'time-expired' in 1916 but re-enlisted and stayed with the battalion. Both men are buried in Wellington Cemetery, Rieux-en-Cambrésis.

Before the war, Corporal Harry Crossley (22) from Lynden Terrace, Earby was an employee of the Midland Railway Co. as a plate-layer. He had served for three years in France before he was killed.

One of the wounded men was Private Charles Young from Proctor Terrace, Dudley Hill, Bradford. He was 37 and married with six children when he was enlisted in

Charles and Mary Elizabeth Young with their six children. (Family pictures courtesy of David Whithorn)

Charles Young in training, taken at Clipstone Camp near Matlock, Derbyshire.

Charles Young in the centre.

August 1916. He was initially posted to the 7th DWR but was transferred to the 1/6th DWR at the end of that month.

He was sent to France on 25 December 1916 and posted to the battalion on the 27th of that month. On 11 October 1918 he was wounded in the shoulder by a bullet and evacuated to Naves. As the German artillery shelled the area with mustard gas, a medical orderly placed an SBR on him which saved his life. He was evacuated to the UK and eventually discharged at the end of March 1919. He died in 1960 aged 81.

On the morning of 12 October the battalion was still on the line in the sunken lane with the 1/4th DWR to their left and the 1/7th DWR in reserve. At 10am

Charles Young in later life (left).

reconnaissance patrols went forward and reported that the Germans were withdrawing. At 10.30am the battalion advanced a mile east to the village of Villers-en-Cauchies. A and B Companies took the lead with C and D in support. At 11.15am the village was entered without opposition, except for the machine guns of German aircraft, and the men dug in on the railway line to the east of the village. Patrols were sent out a mile east towards Saulzoir and at 4.30pm the battalion began to advance. On the western approach to Saulzoir, the advance patrols encountered sporadic German resistance, which was driven back towards the town, but the patrols reported the Germans were holding the west side of Saulzoir in strength.

The battalion halted and the men dug in as best they could but five men were killed during the advance:

Lance Corporal George Bowman MM (25) from Charles Street, Otley, Lance Corporal Claude Greenwood from Oxenhope, Private Alfred Ambler from Thornton, Private Joseph Satoria from Whitehaven (formerly Lincolnshire Regiment) and Private James Thomson from Bishop Auckland (formerly DLI) were all killed and nine other men were wounded. Private John Leslie Stacey from Pimlico, London was wounded and died later at No.33 CCS.

At 9am on 13 October 147 Brigade, reinforced by the 19th Lancashire Fusiliers, launched an attack on Saulzoir. The plan was to advance and cross the River Selle which ran through the town whilst the 51st (Highland) Division simultaneously attacked to the north and the 24th Division to the south. A British artillery barrage was fired at the east bank of the River Selle, but strong German opposition was encountered and little progress was made by any of the attacking divisions. The battalion did have some success when No.16 Platoon of D Company managed to advance and establish a defensive position at the western side of the town. They captured two prisoners and a machine gun, but the post was heavily shelled that night and the men had to withdraw. Serjeant Arthur Sykes from Moldgreen, Huddersfield (formerly 1/5th DWR) was awarded the DCM for his bravery and initiative during this action and for conspicuous gallantry and devotion to duty during the action near Naves on 11 October.

The casualties for 13 October 1918 were as follows:

Corporal Thomas Thompson from Hebden Bridge was seriously wounded and died on 18 October and Private William Watson died of wounds on 30 October. Three other men were wounded. Private Friend Sharp (19) from Colne Bridge, Huddersfield died at No.33 CCS from gunshot wounds to his face and head received on 11 October. He enlisted at Halifax in September 1917 and was working as a cloth finisher. He was initially posted to No.53 Young Soldiers Battalion at Rugeley Camp, Stafford and was posted to Étaples on 21 May 1918. He joined the 1/6th DWR on the 21 May 1918 and is buried at Bucquoy Road Cemetery, Ficheux.

The following congratulatory messages were received:

To General Cameron, 49th Division:
Please accept for yourself and convey to Generals Rennie and Morant and all ranks of the 146th and 147th Brigades and to General Forman and your artillery my heartiest congratulations on the gallant and successful attacks made by the Division yesterday and today.
General Godley, commanding XXII Corps, 12th October 1918.

To 147th Brigade:
It is with feelings of great pride and pleasure that I forward you the attached copy of a message received from the XXII Corps commander.
Evidence accumulates to show that your attack on the 11th October was a very real success. It cost the enemy heavily and dealt him a severe and much-needed blow. It entirely turned the enemies position at Iwuy, the possession of which was necessary to further the advance of the right wing of the First Army in the required direction.
My heartiest congratulations to you all.
N.G. Cameron, Major-General,
Commanding 49th (WR) Division. 13th October 1918.

The Brigadier wishes to heartily endorse the remarks of the Corps and Divisional commanders and to express his admiration of the gallantry and endurance displayed by all ranks of the 147th Brigade group during the severe fighting of the last few days.
The way in which officers, NCO's and men have cheerfully and promptly responded to repeated calls to undertake difficult operations in the face of considerable opposition could not have been surpassed by any troops.
He congratulates officers commanding units on the splendid spirit and soldierly conduct displayed by their officers NCO's and men.
L.C. Arnold (Captain)
Brigade Major, 147th Brigade. 13th October 1918,

On 14 October the German artillery bombarded the area to the west of Saulzoir with high explosive and mustard gas shells and their machine guns were constantly active, but the battalion held its position. Private Ernest Brown from Stepney, London, died on 16 October from wounds he received on that day, two men were wounded and seven other men suffered the effects of mustard gas.

That night D Company advanced forward to the River Selle and established three bridgeheads on the east bank. The River Selle was only about 5 yards wide in the town and was crossed using beams of wood as bridges. As the men advanced into the town, they encountered sixty French civilians sheltering in cellars of houses. These people were evacuated to the rear area, but even though some of them were suffering from the effects of mustard gas, the townsfolk insisted on providing the men with coffee to show their appreciation. That same evening the battalion was relieved by the 1/6th West Yorkshire Regiment and withdrew to a reserve position to the west of the sunken lane.

The 15th was spent cleaning kit and reorganising after the recent heavy fighting and they were accommodated in improvised trench shelters. The weather on 16 October started off fine, but rain began to fall in the afternoon and continued into the evening. That night 147 Brigade relieved the 146 Brigade at the front. The battalion relieved the 1/6th West Yorkshire Regiment in the same sector as before. The German artillery shelled the area as they were moving towards the front, wounding four men. The bridgeheads across the River Selle were still in place, but the town itself had not been taken. A and D Companies were positioned at the bridgeheads with C and D in support.

On this day Private Ernest Brown, from Knott Street, Stepney, London died at No.33 CCS from gunshot wounds to his back and legs. He enlisted at Stepney in February 1917 aged 17 and was working as a horse shoeing smith. He was initially posted to the 100th Training Reserve Battalion at Aldershot for basic training and landed in France on 24 April 1918 when he was sent to No.40 Infantry Base Depot at Étaples and joined the 1/6th DWR on 30 April 1918. He is buried at Bucquoy Road Cemetery, Ficheux.

On 17 October the German artillery and machine guns were active and that night, patrols were sent further in to Saulzoir. More civilians were found hiding in cellars who again welcomed the men with hot coffee. Late in the evening, the Germans launched a massive mustard gas barrage and one shell landed in a cellar occupied by battalion HQ. The CO, Lieutenant Colonel Bateman DSO, the Adjutant, Captain Smith, the signals officer Lieutenant Stewart, the intelligence officer Second Lieutenant Thackray and Regimental Serjeant Major Richardson were all wounded by the effects of the gas. As a temporary measure, Lieutenant Colonel Mowat MC of the 1/4th DWR took over command of the battalion. Twenty-seven other men were also incapacitated by mustard gas.

On the 18th the German artillery continued to bombard the British lines with mustard gas and high explosive shells. Major A.B. Clarkson MC assumed command of the battalion and Private John Preston from Willington, Durham (born in Skipton) was killed.

At 9.45 p.m., the 49th Division was relieved by the 4th Division and in turn the battalion was relieved by the 2nd DWR, of 10 Brigade. The relief was completed at 11pm without casualties and the men withdrew to billets at Naves. The 19th, a wet day, was spent cleaning kit and reorganising the battalion. On 20 October heavy rain fell all day and the men visited the baths and were issued with clean uniforms. The 51st, 4th and 19th Divisions continued with the attack on Saulzoir which resulted in the Germans withdrawing to the east side of the River Selle. On the morning of the 20th the battalion departed Naves and marched 5 miles north to become the divisional

Private John (Jack) Preston. (CPGW)

214

reserve in Hordain, by the junction of the Canal de l'Escaut and the Canal de la Sensée. The men had to march cross-country as the roads and tracks were congested with men and equipment heading east towards the front. The billets the men occupied were of a good standard, but the previous German occupants had left them in a very dirty state, no doubt due to their quick departure. The men arrived around midday and spent the afternoon cleaning the billets and settling in.

On this day Private John Henry Lunt (34) from Sheffield died at No.33 CCS from a gunshot wound to his abdomen. He enlisted at Halifax on 6 September 1916 and landed in France on 12 January 1917. He was born in Hanley, Staffordshire but had been working as a coal miner in Sheffield before enlisting. He is buried in Bucquoy Road Cemetery, Ficheux. His military record shows that on the 10 August 1917 he received seven days Field Punishment No.2, also known as FP No.2 or No.2, for being absent from a medical parade and using 'improper and obscene language'. This differed from Field Punishment No.1, as the prisoner was not attached to a fixed object. He would still be placed in handcuffs or fetters for several hours a day and both punishments required the offender to conduct hard labour tasks under the supervision of the Regimental Police. These men were not military police, but part of the battalion responsible for discipline and order in the battalion and were not selected for their compassionate nature. Relatively minor infractions of discipline were dealt with by the commanding officer, but more serious cases were sent for court martial.

Rain fell for most of the day on 21 October, so the morning was spent training near the billets and cleaning the accommodation in the afternoon. The 23rd and 24th were spent training, but due to the heavy casualties in the recent fighting, the strength of the battalion numbered only 700 men which was lower than it had been for some time. Most of the men also managed to visit the baths that had been set up in the village. Training, baths and cleaning continued up to the 25th and during the day, two elderly occupants of the village gave the men an account of the German occupation. Unfortunately, no record exists of their story, but undoubtedly their experience with the German occupiers would not have been a happy one.

The 26th was a fine, mild day. C and D Companies spent the morning conducting a tactical exercise, attacking the nearby village of Lieu-Saint-Amand whilst A and B Companies conducted training near the billets. The afternoon was spent tidying up and improving the billets. On the morning of 27 October, the battalion marched 6 miles north-east to the town of Douchy, arriving at midday. It was also noticed that the French civilians had also begun to return to their homes. Early on the 28th orders were received that 147 Brigade was to relieve the Seaforth Highlanders from the 51st Division and The King's Own Royal (Lancaster) Regiment from the 4th Division at the front, south-east of the hamlet of Famars. The CO, temporarily promoted Lieutenant Colonel A.B. Clarkson MC DSO, and the company commanders departed to reconnoitre the line. At midday the battalion moved off by light railway and travelled 3 miles east to Thiant, where tea was provided.

The men waited until 4.30pm and then marched 4 miles east to Famars to take over the line. Three men were wounded as the battalion took up a position in a sunken lane, south-east of Famars. The 1/7th DWR was in support and the 1/4th DWR in reserve. Battalion HQ was in the cellar of a house near a railway bridge on the Famars to Quérénaing road and the night passed off quietly. In the early hours of the 29th the signals officer, Lieutenant Claridge, and a small party of men departed from battalion HQ to make contact with the front line companies. Unfortunately, they were unsure of their location and in the darkness, they passed through the British front and into no man's land. They were engaged by a German machine gun and Private John Bailey from Sticker Lane, Bradford was killed. Lieutenant Claridge and another man were wounded.

During the afternoon, battalion HQ was heavily shelled with high explosive and mustard gas, so they relocated slightly north to Caumont Farm on the Famars Road. That evening the CO held a meeting of company commanders as a brigade attack had been ordered for dawn the following day, but late in the evening, orders were received to delay the attack by twenty-four hours.

The 30th passed quietly, but German artillery fired mustard gas shells that wounded two men. The attack was postponed again and rescheduled for 1 November and another planning conference was held by the CO. On this day Serjeant Robert Hartley Milne (26) from Earby was accidently killed at Boulogne. On 22nd November, the *Craven Herald* reported his death:

Serjeant Robert H. Milne. (CPGW)

News has been received by Mr. and Mrs. Robert Milne, 40, Aspen Lane, Earby, of the death of their son, Sergt. Robert Hartley Milne, Duke of Wellington's Regiment, which took place on the 29th at Boulogne, as the result of an accident. It appears that Sergt. Milne slipped in attempting to board a train, and fell with both legs under the wheels. He was 26 years of age, and had spent 3½ years on the Western Front, going out with the first sixth in April 1915.

He is buried in Faubourg D'Amiens Cemetery, Arras.

The weather on 31 October began to change and rain set in. The day passed quietly, but the German artillery continued to cause casualties, as three men were wounded. Later that evening, a party of eight men and an NCO from the 19th Lancashire Fusiliers arrived, carrying six small wooden bridges. These were to be used to cross the La Rhonelle River and the carrying party would then follow the attacking troops.

The battalion had been selected to lead 147 Brigade's attack, with the 1/7th DWR in support and the 1/4th DWR in reserve; 146 Brigade (West Yorks Regiment) was to the left and 11 Brigade (1st Hampshire Regiment) of the 4th Division to the right.

The Famars area was no stranger to large scale battles. On 23 May 1793, during the War of the First Coalition, an allied Austrian, Hanoverian and British army defeated the French Army of the North. The Coalition was an unsuccessful attempt by the monarchies of Europe to defeat revolutionary France. The British/Hanoverian army

The La Rhonelle River. A Company of the 1/6th DWR advanced up the ridge in the distance.

was commanded by Frederick, Duke of York, the second son of King George III (The same Duke of York in the children's nursery rhyme). The descendant regiment of the DWR, the Yorkshire Regiment, has as its regimental march, the tune '*Ca Ira*', which was originally a French revolutionary song. This was appropriated by the band of the 14th Regiment of Foot as they attacked the French army and the colonel of the regiment commented that they would '*beat the French to their own damned tune*'. The 14th of Foot, which become part of the West Yorkshire Regiment, was awarded the tune as a battle honour and through regimental amalgamations, it became the current regimental march of The Yorkshire Regiment.

The attack on 1 November would be launched with A Company on the left and B on the right with the axis of advance towards the town of Saultain. Their task was to surprise the German forces west of the River Rhonelle, force a crossing and then advance up the opposite ridge to seize a lane called the Rue de Presau. C and D Companies were then to push through for 800 yards and seize the Presau to Marly Road, with the direction of attack towards Saultain. The supporting artillery barrage was planned by Lieutenant Colonel Kenneth Duncan from Otley, CO of the 4th (West

Looking north-east across A Company's line of advance showing the Rue de Presau in the distance by the line of trees (1st objective).

217

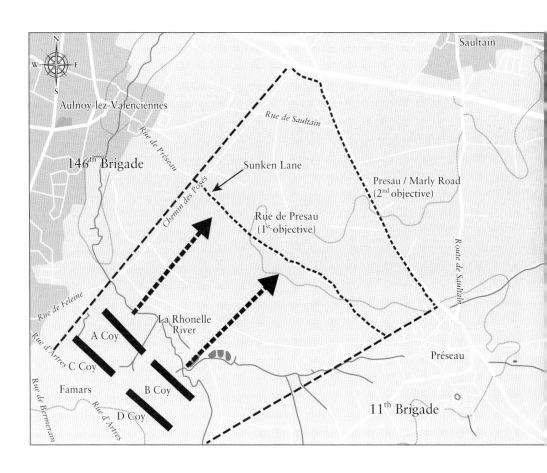

The view looking south-west from the German position towards A Company's line of advance.

The sunken lane end of the Rue de Presau (1st objective). This road was found to be full of surrendering German soldiers and a pack-horse supply column when it was captured.

Riding) Howitzer Brigade, Royal Field Artillery, who had provided one 18-pounder gun for every 12 yards of front line. This figure did not include the heavier guns to the rear that were also available.

The strength of the battalion on 31 October 1918 was 34 officers and 667 men.

<u>CASUALTIES</u>: In October 1918, the battalion had 44 men killed and 134 wounded.

November 1918
Zero hour on 1 November 1918 was 5.15am. The creeping barrage was intense and accurate and the bridges were carried forward and put in place. A Company on the left, commanded by Captain Farrar MC, crossed the river and attacked several machine-

Looking south-east along the Rue de Presau showing the field over which B Company advanced.

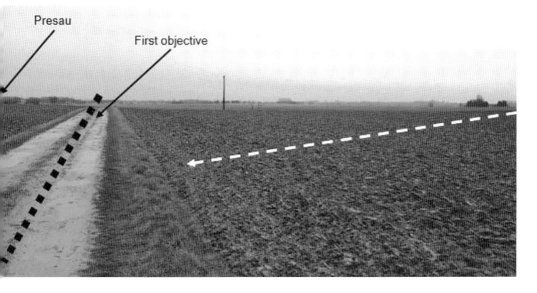

gun posts, killing dozens of Germans and capturing around 100 others. Despite increasing casualties, they advanced to the first objective, the Rue de Présau, which was found to be full of surrendering Germans including a packhorse supply column. B Company on the right found the going harder. All their officers had been killed or wounded within five minutes of the start as the German machine guns had opened fire on the advancing troops from the direction of Présau. Company Serjeant Major Thomas W. Limmer DCM, from Bramley, took command of the company and led the men to the first objective, winning a Military Cross for his efforts (the only such decoration awarded to an NCO in the battalion).

There was a ten minutes pause at the first objective whilst the British artillery moved the barrage to the second objective. C Company on the left, under the command of Lieutenant Walter Spratt MC, (as the company commander, Captain Herman J.L. Willink, had been wounded in the leg by a machine-gun bullet) pushed through and advanced towards the second objective and, despite heavy German resistance, managed to take it.

D Company, under the command of Acting Captain J. Hart MC, advanced on the right but soon began to suffer casualties. The attack on the village of Presau by 11 Brigade had begun to falter. After successfully taking the town, 11 Brigade was pushed back by a German counter-attack, which exposed the right flank of the 1/6th DWR to the German machine guns. Captain Hart and nearly all his company HQ were killed by machine-gun fire and the remainder of D Company was forced to dig in a few hundred yards short of the second objective. To compound the difficulties, 146 Brigade (West Yorkshire Regiment) to the left of the battalion also encountered stiff German resistance and were unable to take their objective. This left Lieutenant Spratt (who had been commissioned from the ranks of the battalion in July 1917) and the rest of C Company in a very vulnerable position, with both flanks exposed. They held the line as best as they could but sustained heavy casualties from German machine guns, including Lance Corporal George Maud MM from Guiseley and Serjeant Jim Upton from Skipton.

The CO, Lieutenant Colonel A.B. Clarkson MC, much to his credit, visited the front line and ordered Lieutenant Spratt to withdraw back to the first objective which A Company was holding. The battalion was reinforced in the afternoon by two companies from the 1/7th DWR, which was fortunate as in the early evening the enemy launched a counter-attack. The SOS signal was sent up and a heavy British artillery barrage landed on the advancing Germans. Sustained rifle and Lewis gun fire drove the attackers back towards the area of the Présau/Marly Road. Later that evening the battalion was relieved by the 1/7th DWR and moved into the reserve position near the start line at Famars.

Corporal Luke Jones from Bridlington was the recipient of a DCM for his conduct in this action. His citation reads:

For gallantry and good work during the period 17th September to 31st December 1918, particularly between the 11th October and 3rd November. On the 1st

November 1918 near Famars he inflicted heavy casualties on the enemy by his skilful handling of his Lewis Gun section and was largely responsible for success gained by his platoon.

The fatalities for 1 November 1918 were high:

Acting Captain James Hart MC from Myroe, Londonderry
Captain Herman J. L. Willink from Cumbria (Died of wounds at No.30 CCS, 5 November 1918)
Second Lieutenant Ernest Cartwright from Kirkby-in-Furness, Cumbria
Serjeant Jim Upton from Skipton
Corporal Harry Drake from Windhill, Shipley
Lance Corporal George A. Turner from Derby
Lance Corporal George Henry Maude MM (23) from Guiseley
Private William A. Northey from West Croydon
Private Thomas Atkinson from Middlesbrough (formerly Dragoons)
Private Albert Wilson from Bradford
Private George Hardy from Bulwell, Notts
Private Sydney J. Rumsby from Ruddington, Notts
Private Walter Stevenson from Irchester, Northants
Private William Roley from Gateshead
Private Alfred Banks from Barnoldswick
Private David Franks from Stratford
Private Ernest Smith from Hetten-Le-Hole, Durham (formerly DLI)
Private James W. Wright from Ilkley
Private Randolph V. Taylor from Bradford
Private Harry Wilkinson from Aylesby, Lincs
Private John A. Wilkinson from Bradford
Private Joseph Rae from Whitehaven (formerly RAVC)
Private Herbert E. Gorrill from Wimbledon
Private George Rewcastle from West Auckland, Durham
Private James Thornton MM from Bradford
Private Willie Fryer from Bradford
Private John A. Leach from Keighley
Private Matthew Ord from Wingate, Durham (formerly DLI)
Private Horace Robinson from Saltaire
Private John Attley from Ferryhill, Co Durham
Private Frederick Burroughs from Finsbury, London
Private Edwin Place from Houghton, Durham (formerly DLI),
Private George H. Stell from Nottingham

Lance Corporal G. Maude MM.

Private S.J. Rumsby.

Private D. Scott.   Private J. Cavanagh. Private F.H. White. Private C.B. Bicknell. Private S. Widdop

Private David Scott from Forfar, Scotland (formerly Royal Scots Fusiliers)
Private Arthur F. Dixon from Peckham, London (formerly West Surrey Regiment)
Private Fred H. Walker from Castleford
Private John Cavanagh from Glasgow (formerly The Royal Scots)
Private Frederick H. White from Smethwick, Staffs
Private Charles B. Bicknell from Islington, London
Private Squire Widdop (31) from Bingley.

There were 138 men wounded, one of whom was Lance Corporal Joseph William Nelson MM from Sutton-in-Craven. He received a gunshot wound to his stomach and eventually died of his wounds in 1922 at Beckett's Park Military Hospital in Leeds. Squire Widdop, from Marion Street, Bingley was a joiner in civilian life. He enlisted in December 1915 and mobilised in March 1916. He is buried in Saultain Communal Cemetery with six of his comrades who were also killed on 1 November.

Captain Herman James Lindale Willink of Endmoor, Kendal, Westmorland, was the youngest son of the late Rev. Arthur Willink. His wife Maye was the eldest daughter of Colonel J.W. Weston, MP for South Westmorland. At the time of his death he had two sons, Christopher Alfred, born in 1913 and Peter John, born in 1915. He had studied at Caius College, Cambridge and at the outbreak of war he enlisted in the 16th (Public Schools) Service Battalion of the Duke of Cambridge's Own Middlesex Regiment at Kempton Park. On

Captain H.J.L. Willink. (CPGW)

18 January 1915, he received a commission in the 1/6th DWR and was promoted to temporary captain in September 1915. He was engaged in training recruits in England for nearly two years, but in January 1917, he was posted to the 9th (Service) DWR in France as acting captain. On 30 April 1917 he transferred back to the 1/6th DWR and on 20 July 1917, he was promoted to full lieutenant and became acting captain on 24

222

October 1917 and was appointed C Company commander on 27 April 1918. After his death, Lieutenant Colonel Clarkson wrote to his widow:

Your husband was leading his Company forward in the most gallant manner when he was hit and it was largely owing to his excellent leadership that his Company did so very well and that our attack was such a success.

Private Alfred Banks's death was reported in the *Craven Herald* on 29 November:

Private Alfred Banks. (CPGW)

Private Alfred Banks, Duke of Wellington's, news of whose death came to hand last weekend, was killed in action on the 1st inst. He went out with the 1/6th Battalion in April 1915, and had been wounded twice previously. He was 23 years of age and married, his wife residing at 15 Arthur Street, Sough Bridge, Earby. Before enlisting he worked for the East End Manufacturing Co., Sough Bridge. He was the eldest son of Mr. and Mrs. J. W. Banks, 20 Louvain Street, Barnoldswick.

For his actions on 1 November, Lieutenant Colonel Clarkson was awarded the Distinguished Service Order; his citation reads:

For conspicuous gallantry and devotion to duty in command of his battalion near Valenciennes on Nov 1st, the attack over bare open slopes, was partially held up but due to his personal example in visiting every part of his front line, exposed to intense fire, he was largely responsible for its successful accomplishment.

The following day, 2 November, the 1/7th DWR attacked towards the second objective, the Marly/Présau Road, with the 1/4th DWR in support. It was taken and around 100 Germans were captured. Around 1.30pm a report was received from an RAF reconnaissance aircraft stating that the Germans were massing and advancing west on the Mons to Valenciennes Road. A counter-attack was expected as such a manoeuvre was standard German army practice, but it never materialised. The road was crowded with columns of German troops but the RAF spotter had mistaken their direction. They were heading east in full retreat.

Congratulatory messages from the corps, division and brigade commanders arrived at battalion HQ:

Message from XXII Corps Commander, General Godley, 2nd November 1918:
I wish to heartily congratulate you and your Division on the successful capture of all your objectives and the heavy loss inflicted on the enemy as the result of

your two days hard and gallant fighting. All three Infantry Brigades, your Artillery and Engineers have added another page to the distinguished record of the Division.

I send you herewith a copy of the message from the XXII Corps Commander. My hearty congratulations go with it.

Apart from the actual fighting, you have all had many serious difficulties and so much hard work to contend with, especially with the rapid changes in plan brought about by frequent changes in the situation. I admire the initiative and enthusiasm with which Infantry, Artillery and Engineers alike have met and overcome those difficulties and I congratulate you all most warmly on the well-earned success which has crowned your effort.

You have indeed added an honourable page to the history of the 49th (West Riding) Division.

N.G. Cameron, Major-General,
Commanding 49th (W.R.) Division.

I desire again to endorse the eulogistic remarks of the higher commanders of the performance of units of this Brigade in recent operations.

I need hardly say how proud I feel to be in command of officers and men who have so gallantly maintained the reputation of the Duke of Wellington's Regiment in the face of hardships and difficulties which I fully appreciate.

H.H.S. Morant, Brigadier-General,
Commanding 147th Infantry Brigade.

Chapter 18

Armistice and Demobilisation

The battalion spent 2 November reorganising and collecting the bodies of their fallen comrades for burial. In the evening, the 49th Division was relieved by troops of the 56th Division, with the 1/6th DWR relieved by the 5th London Regiment. The relief was completed by 7.15pm and the men proceeded 3 miles west to billets in town of Thiant. As they marched west, none of the men of the 1/6th DWR knew that they had just fought their last combat action of the Great War. The Germans continued to withdraw east and when the 56th Division launched an offensive to capture Saultain the following day, it was an unchallenged advance to take it.

The weather on 3 November was fine and the men rested until midday. After dinner, they marched a mile west to the town of Douchy where good billets awaited them. At 1.30pm on the 4th they boarded motor buses and were transported 10 miles north-west to the mining town of Auby, travelling via Douai. They arrived after dark and were allocated billets. The 5th was spent cleaning kit and settling into the new billets. Rain fell all day on the 6th and baths were provided for the men. In the afternoon the CO held a parade and congratulated the men for their performance in the recent operation. The weather on 7 November was fine, the CO inspected the men in the morning and cleaning of the billets was carried out in the afternoon. On the 8th Brigadier General Hubert H.S. Morant DSO, GOC 147 Brigade, inspected the battalion and congratulated the men on their excellent performance during the 1 November attack. He also congratulated Lieutenant Colonel A.B Clarkson on the excellent planning that contributed greatly to the success of the operation.

The fine weather continued into 9 November, the men continued with training and the CO and company commanders attended a conference at divisional HQ. On the 10th a brigade church service was held in a large shed near a pit-head in the town.

On 11 November 1918, in the early morning, a succession of telegrams arrived at battalion HQ regarding the impending armistice with Germany. It was known that a decision was to be made by 11am as wireless messages from Germany had been intercepted, which instructed the delegation to sign and official news was received that hostilities were to end at 11am. The brigade commander ordered a holiday to be given to the men, but a high state of alert was to be maintained.

The signing of the Armistice did not come as a surprise to many. At the end of September 1918, the German High Command had informed Kaiser Wilhelm II that the military situation was unwinnable and Quartermaster General Erich Ludendorff, head of the army, stated he could not guarantee the German line would hold and recommended that negotiations be opened with US President Woodrow Wilson. In January of 1918, the US president had made a speech containing 14 points the Germans must agree to, including the demand for the Kaiser to abdicate. Other points included an immediate ceasefire on land, sea and air and withdrawal from occupied lands. The politicians of the Reich did not look favourably on the demand for the abdication, and in late October, Ludendorff had a change of heart, declared the armistice demands unacceptable and ordered that the German army should fight on.

On the night of 29 October 1918, the German navy revolted at their base in Wilhelmshaven, which eventually spread across the whole country. On 5 November, Ludendorff was replaced by Wilhelm Groener and the Armistice negations resumed, which now included new demands from the allies for reparation payments, German demilitarisation and the allied occupation of the Rhineland. On 8 November a German delegation crossed the front line in a fleet of cars, boarded Marshall Foch's private train and were taken to a railway siding in the forest of Compiègne, 37 miles north of Paris. The Kaiser abdicated on 9 November and the delegation received a message from the Chief of the General Staff, Paul von Hindenburg, to sign without further negotiation. At 5am on 11 November, the German delegation agreed on the armistice terms. They were not able to bargain as the allied naval blockade had reduced most of the German population to starvation, the morale of the armed forces had collapsed, the country was in the midst of a revolution and the Kaiser had abdicated. At 5.12am the document was signed and was to come into effect at 11am that day. The time delay was to enable the message to be forwarded to the front line units, a delay which cost men their lives on the last morning of the Great War.

The end of the war was a sober occasion for the 1/6th DWR. The men were still on a war footing as there was no guarantee all the German troops would adhere to the Armistice and in any case, there was hardly any beer or wine for celebrating. Despite this, a smoking concert was held and the supply of SOS rockets was used for a more enjoyable purpose.

The weather on the 12th was fine and sunny. The morning was spent cleaning the billets and in the afternoon D and C Companies played in the inter-company brigade football competition. The morning of the 13th was again spent cleaning, with more football in the afternoon and that evening a divisional concert was held in a large hall in the village. On 14 November the men bathed in various water butts found in the village and mess rooms were found for them.

The next day all the equipment was cleaned and the men's caps were made stiff again using wire. The service or forage cap was given rigidity around the top rim using a wire band. An army general order in 1915 caused the wire to be removed, probably to make the head a smaller target for enemy snipers as this was prior to steel helmets being issued. The next ten days were spent setting up a shooting range, conducting route marches and training. Educational classes were held covering shorthand and book keeping, skills which could be of advantage on discharge. Work was started in turning a chateau in the town into an officer's mess. The roof was made watertight as the

Germans had stripped away all the lead and the shell holes were repaired. The final of the brigade football competition was also played, with C Company making it into the final but losing to brigade HQ.

On 22 November, Private Vincent Slinger from Ingleton died of pneumonia and was buried in Terlincthun British Military Cemetery at Wimille on the northern outskirts of Boulogne. Before the war he worked as a coachman at the Ingleton Hotel

Private V. Slinger. (CPGW)

and had seen service in the 3rd (Volunteer) DWR. He had been a pre-war 'terrier', serving for five years from April 1909 to April 1914, but re-enlisted at the outbreak of war. He landed in France on 14 April 1915 and served throughout the war with the battalion. His brother, Sinnet Slinger had also been a pre-war 'terrier' with the 1/6th DWR and had also landed in France in April 1914 but he was wounded and 'time expired' in

Headstone of Private V. Slinger. (CPGW)

January 1916 whilst in a military hospital. He died in 1963, aged 77. Vincent was also the uncle of Cyril (Syril) Tomlinson, who was killed on 17 December 1915.

On 25 November, the men spent the day collecting war salvage near the town of Courcelles, 2 miles to the north-west. This was the routine for the remainder of the month and on 28 November a draft of 120 men arrived. Ceremonial drill also made reappearance and on the evening of the 29th Captain Farrar, the commander of A Company, gave a lecture on the importance of sea power on British history.

The strength of the battalion on 30 November 1918 was 45 officers and 723 men.

CASUALTIES: During November 1918, the battalion had 36 men killed and 138 wounded.

December 1918

On 1 December a brigade church service was held in the morning and the CO inspected the new draft of men. Baths were also provided in the afternoon. A brigade ceremonial parade was held on the 2nd and on the 3rd, a battalion parade was held and the CO announced the award of Military Medals to a number of men for bravery during the 1 November attack. The remainder of the day was spent collecting salvage. The 4th was spent strengthening an embankment near the canal to prevent flooding in the town. Salvage work continued on 5 December, with Royal Artillery personnel accompanying the men to assess the safety of unexploded shells. An inter-battalion football competition was held in the afternoon and the 1/6th DWR lost 2-0 to the 1/1st West Riding Field Ambulance. Educational classes in French began in the evening. The remainder of the month was spent collecting salvage, ceremonial parades, educational classes and creating flood defences for Auby. A draft of seventy-two men arrived on 7 December, and on the 11th a party of officers travelled by lorry to visit the battlefield at Famars.

On the 13th December the battalion colours arrived from England and were carried on a parade. Four pigs were procured, at some expense, for Christmas Day dinner, which was accompanied by plum pudding and a healthy ration of local beer.

On 27 December, forty men received their demobilisation papers for transfer to the class Z reserve. This was a reserve of discharged men who were available for immediate recall to active service due to anticipated German violations of the Armistice agreement. Until the signing of the Versailles treaty on 28 June 1919, there was only an Armistice which certainly was not surrender. The German army had withdrawn to their national frontier and had only been partially disarmed. The original demobilisation scheme, drawn up in 1917 by the then War Secretary Lord Derby, proposed that the first men to be released from service should be those who held key jobs in certain branches of industry, including farm workers and coal miners. As these men were invariably those who had been called up in the latter stages of the war, it meant that men with the longest service were generally the last to be demobilised. Derby's Scheme, as shown in 1918 by the small-scale mutinies at British army camps in Calais, Clipstone and Folkestone and a demonstration of 3,000 soldiers in central London, was potentially a serious source of unrest.

One of Winston Churchill's first acts as the new War Secretary was to introduce a more equitable demobilisation scheme based on age, length of service and the number of times a man had been wounded in battle. This ensured that the longest serving soldiers were generally demobilised first and defused an explosive situation. The War Office had not wanted men to be discharged from the army until the peace treaty had been signed as there was always the suspicion the Germans would reform and launch another attack, but the political will of the German state and the demoralisation of the German army made this scenario very unlikely.

The strength of the battalion on 31 December 1918 was 47 officers and 793 men.

January 1919 consisted of salvage recovery and educational classes. The demobilisation process continued with six officers and 133 men receiving their discharges. A number of men had also returned from hospital and courses. The strength of the battalion on 31st January 1919 was 40 officers and 657 men. The first week of February 1919 was spent on educational classes and cleaning kit and equipment.

On 8 February, 8 officers and 212 men bade farewell to their comrades in the 1/6th DWR and were transferred to the 13th DWR, 178 Brigade of the 59th Division based at Dunkirk. These men were to form part of the Army of Occupation of the Rhineland, later known as the British Army of the Rhine (BAOR, not to be confused with its post Second World War successor). Just over 13,000 men formed the BAOR, which remained on German soil until 1929.

On 15 February all small arms ammunition was handed in. This must have been the moment when the men finally realised that the war was over. Up until this point, all the men had carried combat scale ammunition, even when in reserve. Apart from providing a small detail at Douai train station guarding rations, captured German arms and artillery, the men spent most of their time on education, physical exercise, baths and interior economy i.e. cleaning personal kit. The church services continued every Sunday and lectures were given on various subjects such as The British Empire, Bolshevism and women's part in the war. On 25 February, a further draft of three officers and thirty-three men transferred to the 13th DWR at Dunkirk. The rest of the month was spent on salvage recovery and interior economy.

As well as the men transferring to the 13th DWR, a further 8 officers and 172 men were disembodied. Amongst these officers was Major Alfred Bairstow Clarkson MC DSO, whose excellent plan ensured success at the battle of Famars on 1 November 1918, and undoubtedly saved the lives of many of the men under his command.

The strength of the battalion on 28th February 1919 was 21 officers and 235 men.

March 1919 comprised mainly salvage work, guards at Douai Station and interior economy. Two officers and 119 men were disembodied and nine men transferred to the 13th DWR at Dunkirk. A small number of men transferred to other units and some were placed on the sick list. The strength of the battalion on 31 March 1919 was sixteen officers and ninety-six men.

April 1919 was spent providing guard details at Douai Station and interior economy. Five officers and twenty-eight men transferred to the 15th DWR and a further five officers and five men were disembodied. Amongst these officers was Lieutenant Walter Spratt MC, who led C Company during the 1 November attack on Famars. The strength of the battalion on 30 April 1919 was eight officers and fifty-seven men.

In May 1919, nine men transferred to the 13th DWR and five officers and twenty-five men were demobilised. The remaining men packed their kit and prepared the equipment for a move to the French coast. The strength of the battalion on 31 May 1919 was three officers and twenty-three men.

On 7 June 1919, the remaining officers and men boarded a train and travelled to Dunkirk where they were billeted in the camp of the 13th DWR. On the 16th the CO, Lieutenant Colonel Bateman DSO, the Quartermaster, Captain John Churchman DCM, and the Adjutant, Captain F.V. Mellor, along with twenty-three men and the battalion colours, boarded the ship SS *St George* and sailed out of Dunkirk, heading for Southampton. They travelled to Ripon where they were dispersed to their homes. The battalion colours, carried by Quartermaster Captain John Churchman DCM, were deposited at Holy Trinity Church in Skipton and on 19 June the CO and a few selected men were given a civic reception by Skipton town council.

Captain and QM John Churchman DCM. (CPGW)

Quartermaster Captain John Churchman was a career soldier, born in Highgate, London. He had served in the ranks of the West Riding Regiment since 1885. He won his DCM in 1901 during the Second Boer War and was posted to Skipton Drill Hall as a serjeant

"FOR KING AND COUNTRY."

IN
LOVING MEMORY OF
CPL. JOHN CHURCHMAN,

1/6TH D. OF W. REGT. DIED NOV. 25. 1918,
FROM WOUNDS RECEIVED IN ACTION NEAR NAVES,
OCT. 11. 1918, AGED 24 YEARS.

Captain John Churchman's grave in Waltonwrays Cemetery, Skipton. This is also the grave of his son, Corporal John Churchman

instructor in 1905. He was also a former regimental serjeant major of the 1/6th DWR. His son, Corporal John Churchman Junior, also served in the 1/6th DWR and was wounded at Naves by shrapnel. He was evacuated to the UK but died of his wounds in the Military Hospital, London on 26 November 1918. Before the war he was employed as a cabinet maker. At the age of 47, Captain Churchman was the oldest officer to depart for France in April 1915. He retired from the army in 1924 and died in 1935. He is buried with his son and wife in Waltonwrays Cemetery, Skipton.

Corporal John Churchman. (CPGW)

The 1/6th Battalion, The Duke of Wellington's (West Riding) Regiment spent four years and thirty-four days on the Western Front and fought in some of the hardest battles of the Great War. In all the combat actions in which the battalion fought, they never retreated and the only ground given was done so under orders from a higher command or tactical withdrawals at company level. As the war progressed, replacement men from the training depot were allocated to units as and when they were required so that the

The colours of the 1/6th Battalion are displayed alongside the single colour (right) of the 2/6th Battalion. The King's Colour of the 1/6th Battalion (centre) is represented by the union flag with battle honours embroidered thereon. The Regimental colour (left) is represented by the cross of St George also with battle honours.

original recruiting ethos of 'local men for local regiments' was no longer feasible. If a regiment suffered casualties, men from any part of the country were posted to that regiment, so that a man from London could be sent to a Scottish Regiment and vice versa and the later war fatalities of the 1/6th DWR show that some of the men were recruited from places such as Wales, London, Durham and Nottingham.

For at least a decade after the war the Guiseley branch of the Royal British Legion held 'Estaminet nights' at the Drill Hall on Victoria Road. This was a social event for former soldiers and the main room was decorated to look like a French estaminet, with the addition of sand-bags and camouflage netting. Numerous 'mademoiselles' served 'vin-blonk', 'pommes-frites et oeuf' and 'bully beef' as well as 'encore biere'. The event was always well attended with several hundred ex-servicemen from across the district paying a 'bob' entrance fee. After the two minutes silence to remember fallen comrades, there would be rousing choruses of war time songs such as 'Tipperary',

'Mademoiselle from Armentieres', 'Pack up your troubles' and 'Serjeant Brown', which was a 1917 music hall hit by forces sweetheart Jenny Hartley.

Fred Exley served with the 1/6th DWR during the war and for twenty-five years he was the caretaker and armoury serjeant at the Guiseley Drill Hall. He also served in the Guiseley Home Guard during the Second World War and in his later years, he and his wife became one of the first residents of the newly built retirement homes in Towngate, Guiseley. The homes were funded by the Frank Parkinson Yorkshire Trust by the benefactor of the same name. Frank Parkinson was born in Guiseley in 1887 and became a major manufacturer of electrical components. He owned several large factories across the country and donated the money to construct the entrance hall and tower of Leeds University that still bears his name.

For us today, the Great War is almost ancient history and the battlefields of Belgium and France are once again farm land but the legacy of the war remains with the people of those two nations to this day. At the end of the war, the French and Belgian governments were forced to create exclusion areas known as Zone Rouge or Red Zones, in which over 160 square miles of former battlefield were isolated from human occupation due to chemical contamination, unexploded ordinance, as well as human and animal remains. The size of the original area has been greatly reduced over the years but there are still areas around Verdun and Ypres where housing and farming are forbidden due to soil contamination. Higher than average levels of chlorine, mercury, arsenic and lead can still be found in certain areas. Farmers who work the land on the former battlefields regularly produce what has become known as the 'iron harvest' of unexploded shells and grenades. These are usually placed at collection points at the side of the fields for a disposal unit to collect and some of these can be as dangerous now as they were 100 years ago, especially the shells containing chemicals.

I hope you have enjoyed reading this book as much as I did writing it and if you happen to find yourself in the towns of Barnoldswick, Bingley, Guiseley, Haworth, Keighley, Settle, Skipton or any other of the towns mentioned in this book, please take

2016. A British unexploded 18lb shell at the side of a field near Tyne Cot Cemetery.

a few minutes of your time to find the local war memorial and look for the names of men from the 1/6th Duke of Wellington's (West Riding) Regiment who gave their lives in the Great War.

Menin Gate, Ypres, 27 March 2016. The author laying a wreath in memory of the men who served in the 1/6th Duke of Wellington's (West Riding) Regiment who lost their lives in the Great War.

Bibliography

On-line sources
Kelly's Almanack 1912
Commonwealth War Graves Commission
Ancestry.co.uk – war diary of the 1/6th Duke of Wellington's Regiment
British Newspaper Archive
Cravens part in the Great War
Aireborough Historical Society
Duke of Wellington's Regiment
Imperial War Museum sound archives – Interview with Captain Godfrey Barclay
Buxton 1974

Bibliography
The History of the 1/4th Battalion Duke of Wellington's Regiment 1914 – 1919,
    Captain P.G. Bales CBE, 1920
Craven's part in the Great War, John T. Clayton, 1919
Drill and Rifle Instruction for the Corps of Rifle Volunteers, published by authority, 1859
West Yorkshire Rifle Volunteers 1859-1887, Dixon Pickup
Records of the 3rd Battalion, the Duke of Wellington's (West Riding) Regiment,
    Captain N.H. Moore 1920
The Big Push magazine, 1916
Modern Warfare (How our soldiers fight), Ubique, 1903

Newspapers
Leeds Mercury
Craven Herald
West Yorkshire Pioneer
Airedale and Wharfedale Observer
Yorkshire Post
Shipley Times

Other sources
Duke of Wellington's Regimental Museum, Banksfield Museum, Halifax
Jane and Mark Hudson
Michael and Betty Hutchison
Andy McGoldrick
Richard and Charles Smithson (Weegmanns pork butchers)
St Oswald's Church, Guiseley
St Michael's Church, Long Preston
Holy Trinity Church, Skipton
St Michael the Archangel Church, Kirkby Malham
Skipton Library

Index

237